THE BISHOPS
AND
NUCLEAR WEAPONS

THE BISHOPS
AND
NUCLEAR WEAPONS

The Catholic Pastoral Letter on War and Peace

James E. Dougherty

*Published in Association with the
Institute for Foreign Policy Analysis
Cambridge, Massachusetts*

ARCHON BOOKS
1984

Composition by The Publishing Nexus Incorporated,
1200 Boston Post Road, Guilford, Connecticut 06437
Printed in the United States of America

*The paper in this book meets the guidelines for permanence
and durability of the Committee on Production guidelines
for Book Longevity of the Council on Library Resources.*

Library of Congress Cataloging in Publication Data

Dougherty, James E.
The bishops and nuclear weapons.

"Published in association with the Institute for
Foreign Policy Analysis, Cambridge, Massachusetts."
Bibliography: p.
Includes index.
1. Catholic Church. National Conference of Catholic
Bishops. Challenge of peace. 2. Peace—Religious aspects—
Catholic Church. 3. Atomic warfare—Religious aspects—
Catholic Church. 4. Catholic Church—Doctrines.
I. Institute for Foreign Policy Analysis. II. Title.
BX1795.A85D68   1984   261.8'73'08822   84-2994
ISBN 0-208-02051-9

48,850

To my wife Maria
for bearing with it all

* * * * *

and to bishops and strategists everywhere
with a hope that the dialogue
recently begun will
continue

CONTENTS

PREFACE

Everyone who writes a book likes to think that it will have some enduring validity, without presuming it to be a work for the ages. An author who has the temerity to deal with the complex problems of war and peace in the nuclear age, problems that keep developing rapidly along with a dynamically changing military technology, can hardly escape the feeling that he is writing on water. If there is anything of enduring value in the present work, it is because of the subject matter which constitutes the central focus—the American Catholic bishops' pastoral letter of 1983, *The Challenge of Peace: God's Promise and Our Response.* In that document, the bishops present their analysis of the dangers and dilemmas posed by nuclear weapons, as well as the strategic policies that have been formulated to govern the management of those weapons through deterrence and, in the ultimate tragedy, their use in war. The bishops speak out of an intellectual tradition nourished by the Catholic Church for nearly two thousand years. The author shares the universal moral principles embodied in that tradition, even though he may disagree with some of the specific formulations by which the bishops apply those principles to contemporary political-strategic reality, according to their prudential judgment concerning the empirical data. The human mind cannot but be expanded as a result of exposure to the questions which the bishops raise and the answers which they offer.

Over the course of more than three decades of teaching, researching, writing, conferencing, and conversing about the issues of war and peace the author has become deeply indebted to many who have provided ideas and inspiration. He wishes especially to acknowledge the late John Courtney Murray, S.J., of Woodstock Theological College; the late Thomas E. Murray, former member of the U.S. Atomic Energy Commission; the late Thomas Corbishley, S.J., of Farm Street, London; William V. O'Brien, of Georgetown University; Ambassador Edward Rowny, Chief U.S. Negotiator in the Strategic Arms Reduction Talks; Paul Ramsey, of Princeton University; George Weigel, of the World without War Council; Michael Novak, of the American Enterprise Institute; and colleagues too numerous to mention by name at Saint Joseph's University and the Institute for Foreign Policy Analysis who have provided encouragement, insights and assistance. Mention should also be made of the wise advice gleaned for more than twenty years from His Eminence John Cardinal Krol, and in recent years from Bishop Francis B. Schulte, Bishop (now Archbishop) John J. O'Connor, Monsignor (now Archbishop) John P. Foley and other prelates and clergymen who must accept some responsibility for the evolution of my thinking over the long term, despite the fact that we may occasionally find ourselves diverging on the finer points.

A special word of thanks is in order to Stephanie Manganella, of the Institute for Foreign Policy Analysis, who typed and retyped the manuscript until she will probably remember its contents longer that the perpetrator of the deed. Finally, both the author and Robert L. Pfaltzgraff, Jr., Director of the Institute for Foreign Policy Analysis, wish to express their gratitude to the John M. Olin Foundation, Inc., whose grant of financial support made the study possible.

James E. Dougherty
Professor of Political Science
Saint Joseph's University
Philadelphia, Pennsylvania, and
Vice President
Institute for Foreign Policy Analysis, Inc.

1

THE CATHOLIC DEBATE

OVER

NUCLEAR WEAPONS

In the twentieth century, the number of Christians, Jews, other religious believers, and secular humanists, concerned over the nature of modern total war and the morality of modern weapons technology has grown steadily from small and scarcely noticed beginnings. Before the end of World War II, Pope Pius XII wrote: "War as an apt and appropriate means of solving international conflicts is now out of date . . . . The Christian and religious mentality [should] reject modern war with its monstrous means of conducting hostilities."[1]

Concern over the problem of war became more intense after the dawn of the nuclear age. The First Assembly of the World Council of Churches, meeting at Amsterdam in 1948, concluded that "the churches must continue to hold within their full fellowship" not only both traditional pacifists opposed to all war and those who believe that war, particularly defensive war, can be an instrument of justice, but also "those who hold that, even though entering a war may be a Christian's duty in particular circumstances, modern warfare, with its mass destruction, can never be an act of justice."[2] In 1954, Pope Pius XII warned that when atomic, biological, and chemical (ABC) warfare "essentially escapes from the control of man" and involves "the pure and simple annihilation of human life within the radius of action," it must be rejected as immoral and cannot be permitted for any reason whatsoever.[3] But the pope did not condemn nuclear weapons as immoral or evil in themselves (*mala in se*), nor would he label every use of them under all circumstances illicit.

Members of the Protestant Churches moved more quickly than individual Catholics (but not the Catholic Church itself) toward a position of nuclear pacifism, although several British Catholics espoused that view before the end of the 1950s. An international commission of the World Council produced a study document in 1958 which said in part:

> We are agreed on one point, this is that Christians should openly declare that the all-out use of these weapons should never be resorted to. Moreover, that Christians must oppose all policies which give evidence of leading to all-out war. Finally, if an all-out war should occur, Christians should urge a cease fire, if necessary, on the enemy's terms, and resort to non-violent resistance.[4]

Within the United States, starting with the Federal Council of Churches in 1950 and the National Council of the Churches of Christ in 1951, Protestant denominations issued a series of statements and pronouncements on the role of force in international relations and the problems of war and modern armaments, usually in simple pietistic terms, as Ralph B. Potter of the Harvard Divinity School noted.

> It cannot be said that any of these materials made a fresh contribution to ethical reflection upon the dilemmas surrounding the use of violence. They seldom exhibit a profound appreciation or even awareness of the ethical tradition of the Christian churches.[5]

Nevertheless, the late 1950s and early 1960s witnessed a burgeoning debate about nuclear weapons, the just war, and pacifism among U.S. Protestant and Catholic theologians and political thinkers, with the former tending to assume a leading role in probing new analytic approaches and the latter reacting by refining the traditional Catholic just war theory.

The principal Protestant figures included Reinhold Niebuhr, John C. Bennett, and Paul Ramsey among others; the two leading Catholic exponents of the just war tradition, both of whom were stimulated by Ramsey's interpretation of that doctrine, were John

Courtney Murray, S.J., and William V. O'Brien. All of these, and several colleagues who joined them in a series of symposia and conferences organized by The Church Peace Union (later known as The Council on Religion and International Affairs), The Catholic Association for International Peace and Georgetown University, were conversant with Christian and Catholic theological and philosophical thought on the state and international politics and with the problems of formulating adequate deterrence and defense strategies in the nuclear era.[6] From England came the views of F. H. Drinkwater, E. I.Watkin, and Walter Stein, spokesmen for a Catholic nuclear pacifist position based on the application of the criteria for a just war to the contemporary military situation. They were joined in this country by Justus George Lawler.[7] A rather novel addition to the Catholic scene in the United States was a tiny band of absolute pacifists who rejected the just war theory outright. They were led by Dorothy Day of the Catholic Worker movement, Thomas Merton of the Trappist order, James W. Douglass, and Gordon C. Zahn.[8] The last named had been scandalized as the result of research indicating that the Catholic Church in Germany had apparently supported the Nazi war effort or at least condoned it.

We can see, then, that the intellectual ferment over the dilemmas posed by nuclear weapons to the consciences of American Catholics is not entirely new. It certainly did not begin with the drafting of the National Conference of Catholic Bishops (NCCB) Pastoral Letter on the subject in the early 1980s. Thoughtful Catholics, like thoughtful Protestants and Jews, have been pondering these dilemmas for more than three decades.

What is new on the Catholic side is the democratization and, to a considerable extent, the emotionalization of a doctrinal discussion in a Church known throughout much of its history, and especially in recent centuries, for a rigid hierarchical structure, for the issuance of authoritative pronouncements on matters of faith and morals from the pope, and the treatment of doctrinal subjects pertaining to social ethics within a Scholastic intellectual framework, which combined a theology based on Scripture and Tradition with a political theory derived from the philosophy of the ages, the *philosophia perennis* rooted in classical wisdom. Aspects of the Church's teaching which had long appeared immutable have undergone substantial changes in recent years, not only in regard to war, but also to other important matters of Catholic belief and moral practice. "One suddenly has the feeling," writes James V. Schall, a Jesuit professor of government at Georgetown University, "that metaphysical and political realism has disappeared from great sections of the Christian community, especially from the Catholic segment."[9]

In some respects, the Catholic Church in the United States has felt the tensions of continuity and change more keenly than the European Catholic Church which has had vaster experience in living through religious and political turbulence, a longer immersion in Catholic culture, and a deeper intuitive understanding, derived from realism rather than idealism, of how the Catholic ought to approach the more or less intractable problems of this world.

A remarkable transformation of Catholic episcopal thinking is embodied in the bishops' pastoral letter—a document which, long before its final issuance, received more attention from the media than all the combined previous statements of the U.S. Catholic hierarchy received after promulgation. The letter went through three drafts before being presented to the bishops for consideration and a final vote at their Chicago meeting on May 2–3, 1983.[10] The three drafts were reported and speculated upon in the press against the background of an antinuclear protest movement in Western Europe (in which the churches were furnishing middle-class strength to the radical countercultural cadres of peace activists) and a rising national debate over the nuclear freeze, which more than half of the three hundred U.S. Catholic bishops were reported to favor. The debate was peppered by reports that the Archbishop of Seattle, Raymond Hunthausen, an avowed pacifist and advocate of unilateral disarmament, who called the Trident submarine based nearby "the Auschwitz of Puget Sound," refused to pay half his income taxes to protest the Reagan Administration's defense buildup,[11] and that Bishop Leroy T. Matthieson of Amarillo, the diocese in which the Pantex Corporation assembles warheads for the Lance missile, called President Reagan's decision to produce the neutron warhead "the latest in a series of tragic anti-life positions taken by our government."[12]

The first draft of the pastoral letter was initially handled somewhat confidentially and circulated only among bishops, and thus received a limited amount of attention from the secular media. The second draft generated a great deal of public interest and controversy in the fall of 1982.[13] Many newspaper headlines, editorials, and feature columns complimented the bishops for sounding a welcome note of reason amidst shrill talk about war, for producing a statement probably "destined to become the most important public document in more than a decade," and for "touching deeper parts of the American mind," while *Time* gave the letter a cover story.[14] There were serious criticisms from some Catholics and others that the bishops lacked competence in nuclear policy matters and thus should confine themselves to preaching broad moral principles and avoid the realms of politics and strategy. Michael Novak pointed out that it was dangerous for the bishops to invoke a sacred authority for positions on complex political and strategic questions to which Catholics and others of long-established expertise had strong and reasoned objections.[15] Two dozen former government officials, scientists, and scholars (only a few of whom were Catholic), defended the bishops' right to speak out on nuclear arms, rejected the view that "bishops don't know about nuclear weapons and should leave the matter to military and civilian experts," and declared: "If nuclear war were to come, present silence on their part would be unforgivable."[16]

Secretary of the Navy John F. Lehman, Jr., praised the bishops for stating so well the moral paradox of deterrence, but said that many of their specific policy recommendations were neither well-informed nor logical and could, if adopted, "lead directly to immoral consequences."[17] Archbishop Joseph Bernardin, Chairman of the *ad hoc* Committee on War and Peace, received a letter from former National Security Adviser William P. Clark clarifying and justifying U.S. nuclear deterrent policy.[18] He also heard from twenty-four Catholic members of the House of Representatives who, while recognizing the spiritual duty and political right of the bishops to express their convictions, urged them to be fair to the U.S. government, to judge its policy *in toto* in view of the totalitarian threat it confronts, and to reconsider specific recommendations which would, if adopted, weaken the effectiveness of the U.S. deterrent. "We would hope," said the congressmen, "that those who disarm us in the name of peace might dwell more deeply on their responsibility for the moral character of the peace that would follow our surrender. Peace without justice is moral violence."[19]

Stephen S. Rosenfeld wrote critically of the pastoral letter:

In a democratic society professing to be guided by certain values, it cannot be wrong to demand that public policy be measured against those values. Those who demand, however, must address the practical, political dimension of the problem whose moral dimension intrigues them, and they must look at all aspects of that dimension.

That we have hooked ourselves on a doctrine that "threatens the created order" makes unhooking necessary but not easy. If deterrence does not justify every weapon and war plan hatched in its name, a condemnation of deterrence does not justify every change hatched in *its* name. There is a threat of war. There is also a Soviet threat. Do the bishops have a view of it?[20]

These two points raised by Rosenfeld convey the flavor of the debate which the second draft of the letter precipitated. Archbishop Philip M. Hannan of New Orleans opposed the draft because of what he saw as a one-sided and rather morbid preoccupation with the hypothetical future danger of nuclear war, combined with an unfortunate silence about the very real, concrete and present evil of atheistic Soviet communism and its policies of brutal imperialistic suppression over the peoples of Russia and of neighboring states.[21] On a closely related point, theologian George Weigel of the World Without War Council, formulated a criticism of the pastoral letter which elevated the tone of the debate to a level rarely achieved in human discourse on the problem of nuclear war:

> The second draft, like the first, seems to me to concede far too much to the passions and fears of the present moment, and to a definition of our present danger . . . that is taken from today's headlines rather than from the experience and tradition of the Church . . . . [I]t seems to accept the secular/survivalist entry-point for the discussion that is the hallmark of authors like Jonathan Schell and publicists like Helen Caldicott of Physicians for Social Responsibility. Whatever else may be the merits or defects of their analyses and prescriptions, these people are clearly operating on different ground from that on which the NCCB should be comfortable. Their posing of "survival" as the highest moral value is a teaching that runs directly contrary to our Church's

experience for two thousand years. Their insistence that a nuclear war would cast into question the meaningfulness of the created order (as if we were the measure of the absolute meaningfulness of creation) is another neo-pagan theme that should cause the NCCB great concern: and yet the theme is picked up in the second draft itself, which makes the remarkable claim that "the destructive potential of the nuclear powers threatens the sovereignty of God over the world He has brought into being. We could destroy His work." Indeed, we could. But how does that "threaten the sovereignty of God," which is presumably not a function of our will or our works? We might write off such a phrase as literary excess, and strike it from the document...but I don't think it accidental, in the present political climate, that the phrase found its way into the draft in the first place.[22]

Some radical Catholic pacifists might accuse Weigel of implying an advocacy of nuclear war merely to demonstrate the imperturbability of a Sovereign God, when all that Weigel tried to do was defend a theological truth that is basic to Judeo-Christian belief. Weigel fears that fundamental theological truths are undergoing gradual erosion, like rocks under the continual dripping of water, in an era of mass media communication in which the rational beliefs and assumptions of laity, priests, or bishops are likely to be affected more by the impact of messages emanating day after day from television, radio, newspapers, and magazines, than by a deep, quiet, and studious reflection upon the age-old common teaching of the Church, which blends a faith in Scripture and Tradition with a practical wisdom of an institution whose experience of the good and evil in human hearts has never been matched in the history of the world.

There is much in the prophetic tone of the pastoral letter that can be of great value in the long run for the Church, the nation and the world, despite unfair charges that it represents a politicization of the Gospel. For years, thoughtful and sincere Catholics have been exhorting the bishops to "bite the bullet" (or missile), as it were, and to bring their spiritual judgment into a dimension of contemporary political reality that too long has been considered the private preserve of strategic experts, many of whom, almost out of desperate necessity, have tended to exclude moral and ethical factors from their already complex analysis, perhaps largely because in this religiously and philosophically heterogeneous society it is not feasible to demand that national security strategy be based upon any precisely articulated moral consensus. Those strategists have felt compelled in their thinking about the unthinkable to focus upon nightmarish scenarios which make them seem inhumanly callous, when all they intend is to build a strong defense against war. The bishops are aware that national debates over nuclear strategies in all the Western democracies are becoming intensified as more people become fearful over the potentially catastrophic consequences of deterrence failure— something of which all NATO governments were aware long before the peace activists.

We must remember that leftist Catholics for many years have made Catholic bishops the targets of barbed criticism for being excessively preoccupied with the issue of abortion. Many theologically conservative bishops are sincerely convinced that if their teaching on the sacredness of human life is to be credible with liberal and leftist, intellectual, feminist, and youthful Catholics, they must demonstrate a comparable concern about "respect for life" in regard to the dangers posed by nuclear weapons.

The moral issues are quite different in the two cases, of course. In Catholic moral theology, abortion involves a decision by an individual to terminate an innocent life for one's own private reasons, whereas the decision to invoke the use of nuclear weapons in certain circumstances might be justified by the fact that the common good of hundreds of millions of people may be at stake. Some Catholic leftists and pacifists write as if the use of a nuclear weapon on a military target which indirectly and unintentionally killed fifty thousand innocent human beings is fifty thousand times more immoral than one deliberate abortion. This type of argument, unfortunately, indicates a total ignorance of the entire Catholic intellectual tradition of war and peace, in both its pacifist and just war dimensions. It fails completely to acknowledge the basic difference between the spheres of individual and public morality. One scarcely knows how to carry on any moral discourse with someone who advances this kind of argument and repudiates the historical interpretation of the scriptures according to Catholic tradition.

Undoubtedly many of the bishops are convinced that they bear a special obligation as the Catholic Episcopacy of the only one of the two superpowers which would ever tolerate a free public debate about the government's nuclear policy. Finally, some of them, lacking a sophisticated educational background in history and politics, may have been affected by radical leftist comparisons between the government of the United States and the government of Nazi Germany, as well as by the influential positions of the Church in the two countries. They are now anxious never to be blamable for tacitly blessing an unjust nuclear war by having maintained silence.

The pastoral letter is a lengthy document (more than thirty thousand words) and probably says more than is necessary, partly because of an understandable desire to incorporate "something for everybody" in an effort to maintain a unified ecclesial consensus on an extremely complex subject. Its various drafts have been subjected, therefore, to severe attacks from the right, left and center within the Church. Conservatives were disenchanted with the earlier drafts because they ignored the menace of communism not only to human freedom but to a human environment in which the Christian Gospel can be freely preached. A radical left-wing minority of Catholic clergy and laity has been dissatisfied with those passages that fail to meet its demands for sweeping uncompromising pacifism and absolute condemnation of all nuclear weapons. They were especially disturbed by the final draft, which in their view went too far toward tolerating the role of nuclear weapons in deterring war. The editor of *The National Catholic Reporter* lamented that the third draft "represents a significant retreat from a moral analysis used by the bishops for the past half decade that appeared moving them toward a condemnation of nuclear weapons" and "does not reflect the urgency the bishops have given the nuclear issue."[23] What seemed to disturb Catholic pacifists more than anything else was the fact that the Reagan Administration publicly expressed satisfaction with some changes in the third draft, even though Cardinal Bernardin emphasized its continuity with earlier drafts and insisted that the changes resulted not from Administration pressure but from dialogue within the Catholic community. Moderate Catholics of the center have been upset about many things: (1) the dominant tone of the earlier drafts seemed likely to promote among Catholics and the public at large a sentimental pacifism which the Church historically rejected; (2) the drafts seemed likely to erode Western deterrence by attaching to it, as necessary conditions, serious restrictions and limitations, most of which were not mentioned in Pope John Paul II's message to the Second Special Session on Disarmament of the United Nations General Assembly in June 1982; (3) if the letter should contain an unequivocal demand for an immediate policy of no first use of nuclear weapons under any circumstances, it would expose Western Europe to an increased risk of conventional attack; (4) if it endorsed the proposal for a nuclear freeze, it might preclude all plans for modernization of the West's strategic and Eurostrategic nuclear weapons systems that will be required in the 1980s to maintain strategic political-military stability at both global and European regional levels; (5) this in turn could lock the United States into the older strategy of Assured Destruction which popes, Vatican II, and bishops have often clearly condemned as immoral; (6) it could also pave the way for the further Finlandization of Europe, a process already well advanced; (7) the line of reasoning of the pastoral letter, if carried to its logical conclusion, could eventually stampede many bishops into an intransigent anti-defense mood and into espousing an absolute pacifism as an approach to public policy which runs counter to the common teaching of the Roman Catholic Church for the last fifteen centuries. The Catholic center was more satisfied with the third draft, although some serious difficulties remained.

The pastoral letter, in some of its concrete and specific recommendations, represents a major divergence on the part of the American Catholic hierarchy from the national and international security policies to which the United States has been committed through eight presidencies. This was particularly true of the first and second drafts, but the third also contains some proposals that are bound to be controversial. In view of such serious implications, the late Cardinal Terence Cooke of New York was perhaps not wide of the mark in his ominous prognostication in November 1982 (when the second draft was being reviewed) concerning the great potential inherent in the nuclear issue for deeply dividing the Church and the nation,[24] although fears of this sort were somewhat diminished in Chicago in May 1983.

Those who are critical of the nuclear policy of the United States take it for granted that an antinuclear posture by a unified Catholic Church would have greater political impact than earlier statements made by more diffusely structured Protestant bodies. Protestants have always been known as individualists who were brought up to interpret the scriptures for themselves, without relying on teachers who speak with authority. Accustomed to having a voice in the appointment of their pastors, they are less docile than Catholics were reputed to be in the past. Official pronouncements by the Protestant Church organizations have been received by congregations on their merits, the ability of their arguments to persuade the mind or arouse *Angst* but those statements have not been expected to make the faithful fall obediently into line, and they have had a limited impact upon public opinion and government policymakers. But a proclamation by the largest and most highly organized Church in the United States, characterized by a hierarchical structure of teaching authority, a unified and well-defined set of doctrines regarding faith and morals, and a relatively docile body of fifty million formal but not necessarily "practicing" members, most of them habituated to discipline and loyalty, would be a very different thing, and presumably would have a profound impact upon the policy of the U.S. government.

Paradoxically, for the last two decades the Catholic Church has become progressively less monolithic, less rigid in legal discipline, and much more open and pluralist in its doctrinal and moral theology, especially in areas which combine morality and politics. It is a further irony that some of those Catholics, clerical and lay, who have been most intemperately critical of the Church's traditional "monolithic" teaching regarding sexual morality, marriage and divorce, priestly celibacy, and the ordination of women, would now like to convert the Catholic Church to a pacifist position to which all who consider themselves good Catholics would have an obligation to subscribe.

The pastoral letter is a complex document, not easily analyzed in the brief compass to which the media must usually confine themselves. It contains many concepts which can scarcely be grasped without a basic understanding of the vast historic experience of the institutional Church and the reflection of leading Catholic minds throughout the ages on the problems of war and peace, long before the dilemmas of nuclear weapons technology had given rise to an unprecedented moral challenge to the Christian conscience. Contemporary technology has not rendered obsolete age-old consideration of how the Christian ought to act in the face of enduring and often intractable social-political realities.

Roland H. Bainton once identified three distinctive attitudes toward war and peace in the Christian ethic—pacifism, just war and crusade—which emerged historically in that order.[25] A quarter-century or more ago, several commentators professed to discern in the militant anti-communism of the Church of Pope Pius XII and Francis Cardinal Spellman not only a vestige of the medieval Christian crusading mentality but also an important religious and sociological underpinning of McCarthyism in this country. Whether rank and file American Catholics were any more likely to be rabidly anti-communist than rank and file American Protestants is hardly a relevant issue today. The mood and style of the Catholic Church changed noticeably with Pope John XXIII's *aggiornamento*, the teachings of the Second Vatican Council, and the diplomatic theology Pope Paul VI displayed in his *Ostpolitik* on behalf of the Church in Communist Eastern Europe and his approach to the "liberation theologians" of Latin America. If the earlier drafts of the bishops' pastoral letter were muted in their criticism of the Soviet totalitarian system as a political and spiritual threat to the West and the Church, it was perhaps because the bishops were bending over backwards to avoid the appearance of anti-communism—long defined as a political sin in the American liberal intellectual's lexicon. The final text of the letter is distinctly more critical of Soviet communism.

It is difficult to perceive on the American Catholic scene today any noticeable enthusiasm for a genuine crusade to do battle with the forces of atheistic communism. That mentality no longer seems relevant to the discussion. Hence, it is now appropriate to modify Bainton's older classification and to speak of three distinctive positions in the contemporary Catholic debate over nuclear weapons: pacifism, just war, and nuclear deterrence. These are distinct schools of thought, despite the fact that they intersect and overlap; just war and deterrence overlap more with each other than either does with pacifism. But it must also be noted (and this will be discussed more fully in succeeding chapters) that Catholic nuclear pacifism was originally an outgrowth of just war thinking, even though it is now moving away from its relative form toward a more absolute pacifism which does not condone any use of military force in international affairs or indeed any national defense policy at all, and thus cannot be reconciled with traditional Catholic teaching.

Traditional Catholic teaching with regard to pacifism and just war is fairly well known, but not always clearly understood in a deeper sense beyond formulas that have been recited so often that they may have lost much of their meaning. It has become common for Catholics in recent decades to speak of two "authentic traditions": the first understood as an individual vocation to give Christian witness to the Gospel spirit of peace, the second understood as arising out of the demands of the social common good and known by the light of human reason and experience.

Since the Vietnam War, Catholic bishops, theologians, philosophers, and political scientists have been preoccupied with the debate over the pacifist and just war approaches, though they often argue past each other instead of communicating directly. Many Catholic and other writers have sought to solve most of the dilemmas of war and peace in the nuclear age primarily within the dichotomous intellectual framework of pacifism versus just war, while largely ignoring deterrence as a distinctive analytic dimension.[26] This is unfortunate for at least two reasons.

First, it is a serious error to place the traditional responses of pacifism and just war in an antagonistic relationship, for this pits faith against reason and the law of love against the law of justice. Despite the efforts of ideologues to create a falsely polarizing antithesis, there need be no fundamental contradiction between the call of Christians to work for peace and the obligation of the state to rely upon military power as an instrument to protect the common good for which political leaders are responsible. Actually these two positions, though their advocates often seem to be at war with each other, should stand in a healthy dialectical tension toward each other. In such a dyadic relationship, the two realities need not abrogate or destroy each other. They are not interchangeable positions, but they cannot be completely separated from and opposed to each other. Rather they should support and complement, lend meaning to, and preserve each other from distortion.

Properly understood, both positions have been approved by the Second Vatican Council and repeated statements of the National Conference of Catholic Bishops. Neither pacifists nor those who support national defense policies should hold each other in contempt, as they sometimes do. The community which belittles the value of individual witness to the Gospel is likely to fall short in its quest for justice in its foreign and defense policy, and does an injustice to some of its own citizens who are sincere in their consciences. Conversely, the community which ignores the requirements of legitimate defense will not be able to sustain a framework of social order where political justice can be made to prevail and where the Gospel message can be lived and preached in freedom. Mainstream Catholics respect the soldier who risks his life for the common good and also the person who out of genuine religious conviction refuses to bear arms; but they refuse to acknowledge that Christian pacifism, much less a politicized anti-defense ideology, can ever be made the basis for the public policy of governments in a world of nation-states. Both the just war and the pacifist traditions are quite natural and indeed necessary within the Church and civilized society. The process followed by the bishops of writing three drafts and exemplifying the open Church in practice by inviting comments and reactions from the laity sparked the beginning of a vigorous debate over nuclear deterrence and stimulated a number of moralists and political-strategic analysts to take up the challenge by intensifying their efforts to study and understand the contemporary arms problem. But with few exceptions, consisting of brief allusions rather than sustained treatments, these scholarly undertakings, as well as the pastoral letter itself, fail to give deterrence the attention it deserves as an important and powerful new conceptual factor in international politics.

The second reason that the Catholic debate of recent years must be considered unfortunate is that nuclear deterrence cannot be adequately treated within the "pacifism or just war" dichotomy, and yet for the most part it has been examined in that context. Few Catholic analysts, even among those who regard themselves as Christian political realists, have thought through for themselves the logic of nuclear deterrence in a world where the most crucial decisions must be taken by bureaucratic governments and policy-making units against an internal and external setting of extremely complex and subtle political and psychological factors. Hence, while there is an abundance of modern Catholic writing on pacifism and the just war, there is no body of well-defined Catholic thought on nuclear deterrence to which the bishops were able to turn in their recent effort to come to grips with a profound Christian human dilemma. The bishops realize that if they are to speak credibly to the world on contemporary issues, they must also be willing to learn from the world. With this pastoral letter, they have laid down a challenge to Catholic and other scholars, policymakers and strategic analysts to reassess their own positions and to probe more deeply the foundations and assumptions on which those positions are based, so that the teaching of the bishops themselves may be subjected to critical testing and thereby undergo further refinement.

The concept of nuclear deterrence which has gained ascendancy in the thinking of strategists since the early 1950s requires a radically different mode of analysis from that of either pacifism or just war, yet it has not received it in Catholic intellectual circles. Catholics, no less readily than others, can agree with the Einsteinian truism that in the nuclear age, everything has changed except our way of thinking. They have no doubt that nuclear weapons represent a totally unprecedented phenomenon in the history of warfare and in international relations. For decades, it has been taken for granted that nuclear weapons are not only quantitatively different from conventional weapons by several orders of magnitude, but that they are also qualitatively unique. If so, they must be presumed to have quite an impact upon the decision-making processes of governments, which know at least as much about them as do moral theologians and peace activists, all of whom are compelled to draw, directly or indirectly, upon U.S. government sources for precise knowledge of nuclear weapons effects. Most Catholic writers have drawn negative rather than positive conclusions from the uniqueness of nuclear weapons. Some are grudgingly willing to admit that nuclear deterrence has apparently worked up to now, while others would prefer to argue from no evidence that the Soviet Union would not have committed aggression even in the absence of a nuclear deterrent. Both groups usually hasten to point out that the success of the deterrent policy up to the present time does not lend itself to scientific demonstration. This allegation is quite correct because it is impossible to say why something did not happen. But these groups then often make their own prediction—equally undemonstrable in any scientific terms—that nuclear deterrence is eventually bound to fail, presumably because of the stupidity or wickedness of human nature, especially the human nature of political leaders, which is presumptively of a lower order than that of those who pronounce moral judgment upon them.

Few Catholic theorists have had much to say in favor of deterrence, and that has usually been said grudgingly. Fewer still seem interested in strengthening and stabilizing deterrence for the sake of the future peaceful development of the international community, even though that may be the only practical course available to statesmen. Such a course is a far less utopian goal than others now being proposed with the purest of motives and the innocence of ignorance concerning the enduring realities of international politics. Catholics of a somewhat Manichaean mind are more likely to regard nuclear weapons, given their undeniable potential for horrible destruction, as intrinsically evil, regardless of the purpose and intention for which they are held. Hence, the very concept of nuclear deterrence is taken to be immoral, since no use of weapons—damnable in themselves—could ever be legitimate. Some people even attempt naively to outdo Christ by insisting that there should never be a need for human beings to resort to negative threats designed to dissuade by evoking fear. They believe that the power of love can always overcome evil. This popular heresy ignores the fact that, literally interpreted, Christ apparently perceived some utility in the deterrent effect of the fires of Gehenna.

Catholics who have succumbed to the all-pervasive conditioning process of the peace lobbyists and propagandists currently lionized by the mass media pundits have in some instances abandoned critical thinking in favor of simplistic slogans and shibboleths: "Deterrence will inevitably break down because of human irrationality"; "No weapon has ever been developed which has not sooner or later been used on a large scale in war"; "If the United States has already used two atomic bombs in wartime against Japan, why should it not use them again?"; "The nuclear genie must be put back in the bottle, and the bottle corked up forever"; "We have enough to kill everyone in the world several times over"; "The only way to stop is to stop. Support the nuclear freeze."

So runs the jingle rhetoric of the antinuclear movement. These simplistic and catchy aphorisms are not very penetrating in terms of military strategy or political philosophy, but they can be quite persuasive to large numbers of people in an age of anti-intellectual emotional slogans. Philip F. Lawler, calling for a dispassionate use of reason, prayerful reflection, and reliance on the traditional teachings of the Church in the Catholic debate on armaments, has sounded a warning against superficial interpretations that is worth heeding:

> Bishops, like all other specialists, speak a language that outsiders often do not understand. And political ideologues, both within the church and within the media, seize upon a few Church pronouncements to use them for their

own political purposes. News reports, written under the press of time and space, rarely provide enough background to help people understand the intellectual origins of the Church teachings; nor do they explain the subtleties of a tradition which is, after all, grounded in transcendental truths. So press reports distort the Church position. And if one set of ideological crusaders monopolize the public discussion, the distortion quickly grows.[27]

The present study is designed to probe beneath the contemporary emotional bumper-sticker philosophizing which characterizes much of the current public controversy about the Church and nuclear weapons. When the sacred tenets of faith and the highest moral values cherished by Christian believers are involved in a public issue, the subject deserves to be treated not in a vein of catchphrase political polemicism but with balanced integrity of thought and respect bordering on reverence for others as well as for that truth which one hopes to clarify by posing hard questions. These questions will arise in the course of a review of the Catholic tradition with regard to pacifism in the early Church, the theories of just war and deterrence, the critics of those theories in the nuclear age, recent changes in the Church, the treatment of pacifism, just war and deterrence in the pastoral letter of the bishops, and the implications of their teaching for the strategic policy of the United States and the Atlantic Alliance. It is hoped that such an approach will help not only Catholics but others as well to understand what the bishops intend in their pastoral letter when they distinguish between universal valid moral principles and specific applications of those principles which depend upon the interpretation of changing factual data and the drawing of tentative prudential judgments in areas where honest disagreement is possible.

The bishops have made it clear that they issued the pastoral letter to help guide Catholics in forming their consciences on war and peace matters and also to make a leavening contribution to the public debate over national nuclear policy. They have expressed the hope that their teaching, or parts of it lifted out of context, will not be exploited by political partisans or by extremists on both ends of the ideological spectrum.

2

PACIFISM

AND

JUST WAR

One can find strains of thought or sentiment which reflect the yearnings for peace of such religious prophets, mystics, introspective thinkers, and rulers as Isaiah, Mo-Ti, Lao-Tse and Asoka in the religious and philosophically pragmatic literature of ancient civilizations. These strains might be loosely characterized as "pacifist." Pacifism in the strict sense, however, as the unconditional and conscientious renunciation of war by individuals and like-minded groups, appears in history only with the advent of Christianity.[1]

Pacifism and the Gospel

Down through history Christian scholars and polemicists for either pacifism or the just war theory have scanned the New Testament and the history of the early Church for evidence that might support one position or the other. Christian pacifists have never taken their stand on any New Testament texts explicitly condemning warfare or the soldier's profession, for there are none, apart from a few cryptic remarks and episodes.[2] Generally, the Church has warned Christians against trying to construct whole political theologies out of single sentences lifted from the Gospels to prove a point. One can scarcely argue that Christ gave the signal for all Christians to be pacifists when he told Peter to put his sword in its scabbard; nor can one conclude from the "whip of cords" incident that, since Christ resorted to the use of force, it is perfectly appropriate for Christians to do so. Catholic political thought is not that simplistic.

Christ taught no specific theology of politics except to assert that political power comes from God, that His kingdom is distinct from all early states, and that man owes obedience to two distinct jurisdictions, but must obey the higher in case of conflict. He never denounced civil authority as such. Indeed, he did not seem to be keenly interested in political issues. He sometimes employed political similes in his teaching, but it is doubtful that his political attitudes can be deduced from them.[3] On the subject of war and the military, he was generally silent or paradoxical, but the Roman centurion who likened Jesus' authority to his own military power of command was praised for doing so. Roland Bainton comments: "The centurion was commended for his faith rather than for his profession, but was not called upon to abandon his profession."[4]

Most Christian pacifists, instead of relying upon isolated scriptural texts of dubious relevance, have based their position on what they interpret the mind or spirit of Christ to be. They look not to his political teaching, which was sparse, but to his emphasis on reconciliation and love of enemies instead of the law of the talon from which our word *retaliation* is derived. Their favorite Gospel passages are the Sermon on the Mount and the admonition to "turn the other cheek." Above all they point to the fact that Christ never approved a resort to force either to protect himself or to advance the nationalist aims of Jewish zealots against the Romans. His kingdom was not of this world. Concerning genuine Christian pacifists, the author of this study has written elsewhere as follows:

> Throughout the history of the Church, a minority of radical Christians, stronger at certain times and weaker at others, but always tending toward an apocalyptic or eschatological vision, has insisted that the Christian, so far as his action in society is concerned, should always emulate the submissiveness of Christ, regardless of the consequences for the State. According to this school of thought, the moral-juridical order cannot be defended by physical force without being undermined. Under all circumstances, the Christian must respond to injury by turning the other cheek. At

times, the more extreme pacifists have questioned the purity of the Church's traditional teaching on the subject of war .... The more orthodox writers who have approved the performance of military service by Christians and who have defended the legitimate use of force in interstate affairs have sometimes been accused of placing the *raison d'état* above the Christian ethos....[5]

The history of the Church in the first three centuries has been scrutinized frequently for an understanding of authentic Christian practice, because it has always been taken for granted that the Church in that period was closest in time to the apostles and disciples who best knew the spirit of Christ. This makes a great deal of sense, at least at first glance, but a Catholic perhaps can be justifiably chary of the implicit assumption that with the passage of historical time and cumulative contact with a sinful world, the Church underwent a progressive corruption from its original pristine purity. That was a fundamental conviction of the Protestant Reformers. It is a fundamental conviction of many contemporary Catholics of the extreme left. But apart from the debatable assumption that the world corrupts the Church more than the Church sanctifies the world, which is a matter for the discernment of bishops and theologians rather than political scientists, it would seem logical, in any effort to appreciate the historical evolution of an issue that is so salient today, to go back to the beginning.

It is no simple task to determine exactly the attitude of early Christians toward war and military service. No one doubts that there was a strong intellectual sentiment in favor of a pacifist position in the primitive Church. There is much more disagreement as to whether pacifism was the official position of the Church (assuming that such a term has a definite meaning), whether the pacifism was doctrinal or pragmatic, absolute or relative, whether Christians did generally shun military service, and if so, whether they did so for doctrinal or other reasons. Two historians of the early Church call it "a great exaggeration to say that the ordinary practice of Christians was to refuse military service" and they conclude that such refusal "was, for a century, a theory of moralists, not the teaching of the ecclesiastical magisterium, and not the ordinary reaction of the faithful to the question when it arose."[6] But to the contrary, Bainton observes that from the end of the New Testament period to 170 A.D., there is no evidence of Christians serving in the army. Catholics often explain this absence by referring to Christian aversion to emperor worship in the army and to Rome's persecutions. Protestant nonpacifists maintain that the avoidance of military service was due to an eschatological expectation that the Second Coming of Christ was imminent.[7]

Jesus, as we have seen, did not censure the military life when he cured the centurion's servant, nor did he advise the soldier to abandon his profession. The extent to which Jesus' revelation was intended to be purely a message of individual sanctification and salvation beyond the temporal order or to lead toward the reform of social institutions has always been a matter of debate in the Church. When Jesus said that His kingdom was not of this world, was He preaching a Gospel message of personal salvation through renunciation of and flight from the world—a message directed to individuals and not to social collectivities, much less governments? G. I. A. D. Draper, an English Catholic historian, has presented the following interpretation:

> Christ would seem to have been primarily concerned with the entry of the individual soul into the kingdom of his Father and the imminent realization of the kingdom in the second coming. War is essentially a group activity. Groups have no soul. As such, groups are candidates neither for entry into, or rejection from, the kingdom of God. Private killing of man by man was already expressly proscribed by the Law of the Old Testament which Christ came to fulfill and not to destroy.... It was left to the Christian theologians and apologists to make the bridge of moral doctrine between the condemnation of private killing and the killing by a soldier in a public war.[8]

The question as to whether the Christian should shun the world and adopt a passive attitude toward social institutions or try to build the kingdom of God on earth by reforming those institutions is a difficult one. There does not appear to be a single answer capable of satisfying Christians in all times and places. Eastern and Western Christianity have differed in their dominant attitudes, as have eschatologists and incarnationalists.

We must remember that nearly all of the writings that have come down to us from the patristic period represent the thought of well-educated intellectuals, who in most ages manifest an antimilitarist bias even in the absence of pacifist doctrine. It is also necessary to distinguish between absolute, uncompromising pacifism which condemned any relationship whatever between the Christian and the Roman Empire (seen as diabolical) as well as all military service by Christians and military activity by the state, and the more relative pacifism of those who preferred to see Christians follow a higher way of nonviolence but who also appreciated the *pax Romana*, based on military power, and the freedom which a protected social order provided for the peaceful work of Christian evangelism. Finally, it is important to recognize the fact that several texts of less-than-absolute pacifists were addressed to Christians as guides to individual choice rather than political action.[9]

Pacifists in the patristic era included Marcion, Tatian, Arnobius, Origen, Justin Martyr, Cyprian, Minucius Felix, Tertullian, Hippolytus, Maximilianus, and Lactantius. Not all of these could be called absolute pacifists by any means, and not all of them postulated an implacable hostility between Christians and a Roman Empire that depended upon military force to preserve order in the Mediterranean. Before we look at some of these writers and examine actual Christian practice with regard to military service, we should attend briefly to the Old Testament experience of the Israelites, with which many of the Christian Fathers were thoroughly familiar.

War in the Old Testament

The Israelites were Yahweh's beloved chosen people. He and they entered into a covenant (*berith*) by which the land of Canaan was promised to them, but they had to take possession of it by force, make war against the unbelieving occupying tribes, and drive them off, because idol worshippers had to be banished from the territory which had been invested with a specific holiness. If Israel refused to fight such wars, the Covenant would be broken, and Israel would suffer for its sins. The wars of Israel were the wars of Yahweh, who was present in their camp as a warrior, and who would deliver the enemy into the hands of Israel. But in the period before the rise of political kings, it was the prophets and judges who called the people to arms, and they never lost sight of the fact that it was not the strength of numbers, but Yahweh who guaranteed the victory.[10] Deuteronomy 20 sets forth the fundamental scriptural regulations concerning how the Israelites were to prepare for the waging of war:

> When you go out to battle against your enemies, and see horses and chariots, forces greater than your own, you must not be afraid of them; for the LORD your God who brought you up from the land of Egypt is on your side. When you are on the eve of a battle, a priest must come up and speak to the people. He shall say to them, "Listen, O Israel; today you are on the eve of a battle against your enemies; do not be faint-hearted, nor afraid, nor alarmed, nor stand in dread of them; for the LORD your God is going with you, to fight for you against your enemies and give you the victory." Then the officers shall say to the people, "Whoever has built a new house, but has not dedicated it, may leave and return home lest he die in the battle, and another dedicate it. Whoever has planted a vineyard, but has not had the use of it, may leave and return home, lest he die in the battle, and another get the use of it. Whoever has betrothed a wife, but has not married her, may leave and return home, lest he die in battle and another marry her." The officers shall say further to the people, "Whoever is afraid and faint-hearted must leave and return home, so that his fellows may not become faint-hearted like him." As soon as the officers have finished addressing the people, the army commanders shall place themselves at the head of the people.

In a later historic phase, after the emergence of the kings,[11] the traditional call of the prophet to arms gave way to a system of royal mobilization, based on a form of conscription. Thus, when King David conducted a census of the people for military purposes, he was filled with remorse because he realized that he was thereby placing heavier reliance on numbers than on the Lord.[12] In the age of the kings, wars were no longer the "holy wars" aimed at the conquest of Canaan, but became more imperialistic. They were waged against faraway cities, rather than against the cities of the peoples who occupied Canaan. In the holy wars for Canaan, it was not a case of Israel fighting for Yahweh, but rather Yahweh fighting for Israel. These were the extermination wars of *herem,* the principles of which were codified in Deuteronomy:

> When you march up to attack a city, you must offer it terms of peace. If it agrees to make peace with you, and surrenders to you, then all the people to be found in it shall become forced laborers for you, and serve you. But if it will not make peace with you, but wages war with you, you are to besiege it, and when the LORD your God delivers it up to you, you must put every male in it to the sword; but the women and children and live stock and everything that is in the city, that is, all its spoil, you may take as your booty, and yourselves use the spoil of your enemies which the LORD your God gives you. So shall you treat all the cities that are very far away from you, that do not belong to the cities of the nations here. However, in the cities of the people here, which the LORD your God is giving you as a heritage, you must not spare a living soul; but you must be sure to exterminate them, Hittites, Amorites, Canaanites, Perizzites, Hivvites and Jebusites, as the LORD your God commanded you, so that they may not teach you to imitate all the abominable practices that they have carried on for their gods, and so sin against the LORD your God.[13]

A few early Christian thinkers, notably Marcion, when confronted with Old Testament history in which Joshua, Gideon, David, and the Maccabees waged war ruthlessly, giving no quarter to enemies who refused to surrender, and believing themselves to be acting in observance of Israel's covenant with Yahweh, concluded that the Old and New Testaments were irreconcilable. Marcion ignored the themes of compassion, mercy, justice for the poor, and the yearning for peace which run through the Hebrew Scriptures. Marcion saw Yahweh only as a God of war, whereas for Israel he was a God of love and peace as well, although the Israelites recognized that peace was not a reality knowable in the present, only a dream for the future. If the early prophets summoned the people to holy wars for Canaan, several later prophets, especially the second Isaiah,

Jeremiah, Amos, and Hosea explicitly renounced war and preached that Israel survive through faith and not military power.[14]

Marcion apparently overlooked these tender aspects of Yahweh. Focusing only upon his fierce countenance, Marcion did more than any other Christian writer to separate the Old dispensation from the New. He postulated two Eternal Gods—the stern God of Justice revealed to the Israelites, a jealous vindictive instigator of wars, and the merciful God of Love shown to the disciples of Christ. For him, the grace of the Gospel erased the punitive law of justice.[15] Marcion merely stated explicitly what many radical Christian pacifists throughout the ages come close to assuming implicitly. There can be litle doubt that some contemporary Christian pacifists harbor negative attitudes toward the State of Israel because of its avowed determination to defend itself militarily and because of what they regard as a recurring tendency to act in excess of what they regard as the requirements of defense. The orthodox Fathers completely rejected Marcion's interpretation. Moreover, their acquaintance with the Old Testament made them extremely cautious about condemning the use of military force as intrinsically evil. They knew that Isaiah, however weary of war he may have been, was not a pacifist, for he believed in self-defense.[16]

The Early Christians and the Question of Military Service

The Apostles and Fathers did not adopt a stance of absolute opposition to any of the institutions of the world in which they found themselves, e.g., the empire, private property, slavery, war, or marriage.

Generally speaking, most of the Apostolic Fathers adopted a deferential view toward political authority, although it is not correct to say, as do several standard works in the history of Western political thought[17] that the political ideas of the Church Fathers were substantially the same as those of Cicero, Seneca, and other later Stoics. The patristic conceptions of natural law and the obligation to obey political authority were quite different, despite similarities of language, because the Christian context differed profoundly from the pagan one. The Fathers, far from excoriating the Roman Empire and the *pax Romana*, supported them. Peter and Paul, perhaps partly to counter the charges that Christians were subversive, exhorted a proper respect for duly constituted political authority as the legitimate preserver of law and order.[18] They also recalled Christ's instruction concerning "the things that are Caesar's."

The attitude of the patristic Church toward the political order is important for an understanding of its attitude toward military service, which cannot be fully grasped merely by quoting passages about military service itself. Most of the writings which have survived are unfavorable or hostile toward the soldier's profession. Undoubtedly many Christians were advised or warned not to enter the military for a variety of reasons. Undoubtedly numbers of Christians refrained because of their religious beliefs. But one cannot conclude that the early Church was pacifist. Soldiers who became converted to Christianity were not required to abandon the profession of arms.[19]

Later, some of the most eminent Christian intellectuals took a more absolute pacifist position, none more than Tertullian. At one time he eloquently defended the Christians against the charge of disloyalty to the empire by attesting to their presence in the palace, Senate, forum, and army, but later he became an uncompromising pacifist while en route to Montanism. In the following famous passage Tertullian fixed an unbridgeable gulf between Church and Empire:

> The issue now arises whether a believer may take to military service, and whether a member of the armed forces may be admitted to the Church. We may even ask whether the Church should admit a private or any of the inferior ranks who are under no necessity of joining in sacrifices or in trials which involve the punishment of death. There is no agreement between God's sacrament and the sacrament of man (i.e., the oath of service to God and the oath of service to Caesar); between Christ's standard and the Devil's; between the camp of light and the camp of darkness. One soul cannot be bound over to two masters—God and Caesar.[20]

Although Tertullian was still a Catholic when he wrote this, his views of the empire were not those of the apostles, who regarded political authority as a divinely instituted remedy for sin and a positive benefit to human society.[21] One can readily understand how

Tertullian might be carried away by the power of his own rhetoric, especially at a time when the Empire was persecuting the Christians.

Other writers who are often regarded as pacifist in general inclination were less absolute and intransigent than Tertullian. They seemed to understand the need for the Empire to provide military security. Origen, who wrote in the first half of the third century, was along with Augustine one of the most profound of all the patristic writers, even though he was not always considered orthodox. It was Origen's task, among others, to play the role of apologist against the effective barbs which the talented Platonist Celsus had aimed against the Christians, whom Celsus accused of taking no interest in the state:

> If all men were to do the same as you [Christians], there would be nothing to prevent the king from being left in utter solitude and desertion, and the forces of the empire would fall into the hands of the wildest and most lawless barbarians.[22]

Commenting on that charge, Jean Danielou writes:

> There is something moving in this cry from the heart. It seemed to Celsus that the whole of the ancient world, the entire civilization of Greece and Rome, a thing at once religious, political and cultural, was in danger; and his grievance against the Christians was that they would not exert themselves in its service.[23]

Origen offered the following defense of those who adopted a pacifist position:

> In so far as we conquer the demons who stir up war and derange the peace, we perform better service for our ruler than do they who bear the sword. We fight for the Emperor more than any others. We do not indeed enter the field with him, not even though he order it, but we fight for him in so far as we are setting up a camp of our own, a camp of godliness, from which we send our prayers to God.[24]

There is a slight touch of Christian triumphalism here, mixed with a faint air of moral superiority; but at least Origen does not appear to be imposing his own pacifist preference upon all Christians, and he certainly does not condemn the Emperor outright for taking up the sword. Thus Origen qualifies in this passage as a Christian pacifist, not a fire and brimstone preacher ready to anathematize all who do not see things his way. St. Cyprian, too, showed himself to be more relativist than dogmatic in his pacifism when he listed among the calamities of his day the fact that the army was decreasing in numbers and in efficiency.[25]

Several other antimilitarist statements less well known than those of Tertullian, Origen, and Cyprian, can be cited, dating from 170–180 A.D. onward, when the references to Christians serving as soldiers also begin to increase. Objections to military service seem to have been greater in the Hellenistic East than in the West. Bainton notes that Rome, which had taken the lead in forgiving sexual offenders and apostates, probably anticipated other communities in relaxing opposition to the military profession.[26] The Church Order of Hippolytus, written a generation or so after Marcus Aurelius, contained this statement: "If a catechuman or baptized Christian wants to become a soldier, he shall be excommunicated, because he has disdained God." But early in the fourth century, the Canons of Hippolytus contained a more moderate instruction: "A Christian must not voluntarily become a soldier unless he is obliged to."[27] In the year 295, the 21-year-old Numidian Christian Maximilian, in refusing to be measured for the army, declared: "I cannot serve in the military, I cannot commit a sin. I am a Christian." When the proconsul Dion reminded him that there were Christian soldiers in the army, Maximilian replied: "They know what is best for them. But I am a Christian and I cannot do any wrong." Knut Willem Ruyter, who records this exchange, calls this the only clear pacifist witness in the acts of early martyrs.[28]

Actually the lives of the saints as traditionally received do not provide, even as late as the third and fourth centuries, a clear resolution of these ambiguities and apparent contradictions. St. Sebastian suffered martyrdom as a soldier; St. Martin of Tours left the army after his conversion.[29]

It has never been possible to reduce the issue of Christians and military service to a simple question of entering or refusing to enter the army or leaving the service for reasons of conscience. We know that there were some Christians in the army, and their numbers were not large. Not too much should be inferred from the fact, however, since the numbers of Christians in the total population were not large. From the accusations of Celsus, we might conclude that the number of Christian soldiers was less than proportionate, and that Christians generally had a reputation for avoiding military service. But the question is whether Christians refrained from military service primarily from reasons of doctrinal pacifism or because of other factors. Christians, after all, did not usually confront the possibility of being conscripted into military service. People could be impressed into the army under conditions of near emergency in the vicinity of frontier outposts. But in the early centuries, Christians were rarely to be found there, since Christianity was largely an urban religious movement. Rome's security needs had not yet become critically urgent. The empire preferred to recruit from the sons of soldiers whose loyalty and reliability had already been demonstrated. We should not forget that the Romans looked upon the Jews as a particularly troublesome people who were not wanted in the army, and for a long time the Romans had difficulty distinguishing between Jews and Christians, who were regarded at times as one more troublesome Jewish sect subversive of established authority. For these reasons, it is important to realize that entry into the army was for Christians normally a matter of free choice, not a political or legal obligation.

Besides doctrinal pacifism, there were other good reasons for Christians in the early Church to avoid military service. The service period was for twenty-five years, usually with no exit except desertion, for which the penalty was death or loss of all benefits and citizen privileges. The Christian who entered the army after conversion risked having his faith undermined by the corrupt life of the military. (This danger, not doctrinal pacifism, is the reason why many bishops in the modern period, and especially in the United States, have been opposed to a peacetime draft.) In ancient Rome, the soldier was not allowed to marry. A Christian soldier, therefore, facing a choice of chastity or fornication with camp followers, had to ponder the Pauline counsel with respect to marrying or burning.

As he rose higher in the military ranks, he came under increasing pressure to engage in idolatrous emperor worship or other cultic and symbolic practices which violated his religious conscience. (Some contemporary Christian pacifists argue by analogy that this dilemma still confronts the Christian in the armed forces.) Finally, the Christian soldier in the early centuries might find himself in a military unit which was ordered to persecute his fellow Christians, or else he would find himself, once discovered as a Christian, running a greater risk of being persecuted than if he had stayed out of the army. These reasons are no less compelling than doctrinal pacifism in the explanation of why many early Christians avoided military service.[30]

Undoubtedly some Christians were advised by pious counselors, convinced in their consciences that war must be shunned by the Christian, not to enter the service because of their religious belief. But the Church itself did not forbid military service. St. Basil the Great, who came to be known as an Eastern Father of the Church, wrote in a canonical letter the following advice, which shows that the problem was a profound one that did not lend itself to absolute or glib solutions:

> Our Fathers did not reckon killings in war as murders, but granted pardon, it seems to me, to those fighting in defense of virtue and piety. Perhaps, however, it is well to advise them that, since their hands are not clean, they should abstain from communion alone for a period of three years.[31]

This is perhaps the earliest authoritative statement of the just war doctrine to be found in patristic literature, written in the third quarter of the fourth century. It reflects a certain Christian sense of the tragedy of the human condition.

The Church refrained from laying down monolithic rules on the subject which would be binding upon all. The early Christians drew distinctions between what Christians and non-Christians might do, between what the laity might licitly do and what the clergy were forbidden to do, between noncombatant "soldiering" in peacetime (*militare*), which involved socially useful police functions, and actually waging war (*bellare*), and between fighting in unjust wars of imperial aggression and fighting in more justifiable wars of defense or vindication of rights. They also appreciated the distinction between what would come to be called, in a somewhat more legalistic era of Church history, the "laws of the Church" which obligate all and the "counsels of Christian perfection" which not all, and perhaps not most, who sincerely seek salvation are thought capable of observing.

The patristic writers also understood the subtle differences among motives, intentions, and actions, as well as between the morality of the individual Christian person and the necessities of the state.

Throughout history, eschatological Christian pacifists have tended to manifest impatience with most of the distinctions mentioned above. They have regarded them as instances of worldly hairsplitting or watering down the Gospel message, irrelevant to anyone who takes Christianity seriously. Yet the Church recognized those distinctions and displayed a rather remarkable tolerance of the tensions and ambiguities which often confront the Christian of this world, as Christ Himself had done.

From the foregoing, it can be suggested that it may be an exaggeration to call the early Church pacifist, although there were many Christian pacifists. Not even in the first two centuries, when doctrinal pacifism is presumed to have been strongest, did the Church impose a burden upon the soldier's conscience by requiring him to abandon the military profession upon his conversion to Christianity. Looking back to the early Church from the fifth century, St. Augustine wrote: If Christian practice condemned war in general, then the soldiers in the Gospel who asked how they were to be saved should have been given the advice to throw down their arms and give up the military service entirely.[32]

Bainton, Brock, and Ruyter are all entitled to reach the conclusion that primitive Christianity was pacifist from their research into the surviving texts of individual writers. But one is equally entitled to arrive at a different judgment—namely, that there were two discernible tendencies in the early Church, one of pacifist witness to the Gospel as an individual vocation and one of honorable military service as a civic duty. L. L. McReavey sums up the question as follows:

> For the first three centuries of the Christian era, the general exclusion of Christians from public life removed the moral problem of war from the area of their immediate responsibility and concern. Only in regard to service in the imperial forces did a practical case of conscience arise. Many converts continued in fact to serve, and those who left the army seem to have done so in order to avoid being involved in idolatrous practices, or to devote themselves

more directly to the service of God, rather than from any conscientious objection to war as such. Some, like Hippolytus ... , condemned voluntary military service by Christians ... ; and, a century later, after the Emperor Licinius had imposed idolatry on all his forces, canon 12 of the First Council of Nicaea (325) enacted a severe penalty against Christians who reenlisted in the imperial army; but only Tertullian ... and Lactantius ... condemned military service outright. None of the accepted Fathers of the Church ever accepted this extreme position.[33]

As Christians in the West began to assume an increasing degree of responsibility for the social order, instead of fleeing from it, reminding themselves that there was here no lasting city, and as the hope of the Second Coming faded, they became more willing to work out an adjustment between their faith and their political and social roles in an empire which was no longer persecuting them but which was growing increasingly dependent upon their numbers, intelligence, vigor, and leadership potential. Church leaders saw no contradiction between an individual vocation to give witness to the love of Christ and the evangelical spirit of peace on the one hand and, on the other, a natural impulse to fulfill the demands of social order, issuing not from charity but from a concern for justice in the public policy of the state as arrived at by reason.

From the time of Constantine onward, the military career was looked upon less and less as a peril to Christian faith and morals. The Catholic Church in the era of St. Ambrose and St. Augustine would move to an official doctrine of just war which was to dominate Catholic thinking and place Catholic pacifism in shadow for nearly fifteen centuries, except as a rule for priests and monks because of their special commitment to follow Christ in the quest for perfection. Apart from Franciscan criticism of the Crusades, we find that in medieval and early modern Europe, Christian pacifism was usually associated with sects that were often regarded by both Catholic and major Protestant Churches as unorthodox and subject to harassment, isolation, or persecution, e.g., the Waldenses, Anabaptists, Hussites (particularly Taborites), Brethren, Mennonites, and Quakers. Not until the twentieth century did Catholics, Lutherans, Calvinists, and other large Protestant groups begin to exhibit a renewed interest in religiously motivated pacifism, whether absolute or relative. It is safe to conclude that just war, not pacifism, has been the common teaching of the Catholic Church throughout most of its history, and remains so today, although pacifism is recognized as an individual option for those Christians whose conscience demands that they give special witness to Gospel values. As we shall see, however, the Catholic Church does not regard pacifism as a public policy to be urged upon the state as an imperative of the Gospel or of Catholic faith. The Catholic Church works for peace, but it is not a pacifist Church.

The Christian and the State

The Fathers of the Church discouraged Christians from entering the army when the practice of emperor worship endangered their faith, but they did not condemn war under all circumstances, nor did they forbid military service for reasons of doctrinal pacifism, despite the fact that many Christian intellectuals were undoubtedly absolute or relative pacifists in the attitudes preserved in their writings. Their knowledge of Old Testament history made it impossible for them to believe that the waging of war was evil by nature. They were also aware that nowhere in the Gospel was the military profession censured. The Founder of Christianity had pointedly disdained the use of force in His own mission. But the question then, as now, was whether Christ's example of self-abnegation was intended to have an explicit significance for the political order.

In all ages, radical Christian pacifists have been inclined to make Calvary a luminous guide for the action of citizens in states facing the problem of power and external aggressive threats. But it would seem that the orthodox Church Fathers looked upon Christ's sacrifice on the cross as a spiritual act so sublime, unique, and transcendent that it could never serve as an appropriate model for the action of a political community. To be sure, coercive power was a divinely appointed remedy for human sinfulness, but the coercive power itself was deemed good, not sinful. Christ disdained the use of force, because of the purely spiritual mission He had to perform, not because physical power in God's creation was intrinsically evil.

The Fathers took it for granted that the individual Christian seeking perfection should turn the other cheek when his or her own private rights are violated. One who looks for complete fulfillment beyond the historical order need not egoistically assert any personal claims to justice in this world of pilgrimage. But the organized political community, charged with safeguarding a human common good, however imperfect, which has meaning only within the temporal sphere, cannot seek moral perfection in the same way as one person might. *The state, therefore, cannot turn the other cheek.* Having no destiny hereafter, the state has no choice but to uphold its order of justice and to protect its people when threatened or attacked, internally or externally.[34] Law and domestic peace require the backing of force. If the state becomes a fountain of love, mercy, compassion, forgiveness, and humble submission, it quickly ceases to be. Thus the Christian who believed that "the powers that be are ordained of God," as St. Paul had said, could not deny the obligation of the state to protect itself by the threat or use of force when necessary. For the Fathers, the Christian love of peace could not be erected into a monolithic dogma which would prohibit Christians from supporting the military defense policies of their state and be binding in the same manner upon all. The individual Christian may voluntarily choose martyrdom, but no one has the right to impose martyrdom on the whole community.

The Catholic doctrine of the just war is usually traced to St. Ambrose (c. 334–397) and St. Augustine (354–430). Like St. Basil, who wrote his canonical letter fifteen years before St. Ambrose's *De Officiis* and at least forty years before St. Augustine wrote *Civitas Dei*, they deemed it wise for the Church to refrain from laying down rules which would create a basic enduring conflict between Christian faith and citizenship in a political community. All of the Christian Fathers appreciated the distinction between the laws of the Church and the counsels of Christian perfection,* between the moral choices of the free Christian person and the necessities of the

---

* It should be noted that the Christian who, like St. Francis of Assisi, wishes to live a life of heroic witness to the spirit of Christ must strive for perfection in several dimensions—e.g., humility, poverty, chastity, devotion to truth, obedience to the will of God, and the renunciation of force in self defense. One cannot be selective. Nor is denouncing every use of force by the state a hallmark of Christian sanctity.

state. Ever since the patristic age, thinkers in the Catholic intellectual tradition have treated the problem of war primarily within the context of social rather than individual morality. War is an action of states, not individuals. The doctrine of the just war, therefore, belongs properly and initially to the province of Catholic political philosophy, and only derivatively to the province of moral theologians and philosophers who are concerned principally with what individuals acting in a private capacity may or may not do. According to the Catholic tradition, the state is authorized by God, for the sake of the common good (which excessively individualistic moralists deride), to do things which an individual is forbidden to do. To restrain and punish evil deeds which threaten the order of justice and peace, the state may take human life—internally in the application of capital punishment, externally by waging a just war. Regardless of how substantially the attitudes of Catholics on these subjects may have changed in the last few decades, no one can honestly deny what has been held historically in the Catholic tradition and in official Church teaching for more than sixteen centuries. Within recent years, the author has heard devout Catholics argue that there can be no just war doctrine for the Christian because God said: "Thou shalt not kill." They will remind you that He made no exceptions. When one reminds them what the common teaching of the Catholic Church has been, and that it is reiterated in the pastoral letter, they rejoin quickly that the common teaching of the Church has been wrong, and that the bishops are wrong now because they are thinking politically, not evangelically. An orthodox Catholic can only wonder: If the Church can be wrong in this common teaching, how do we know it must be right in any moral teaching?

Christian Faith and Pagan Wisdom

Just war theory as we know it in Western civilization is by no means distinctly Christian or Catholic in its foundations. Its roots are found in classical pagan antiquity, in the tradition of reason which was embodied in Greek philosophy and Roman law. For some Christian critics, the theory is suspect precisely because it is traceable to pre-Christian pagan thought. One of the earliest and most profound intellectual controversies in the Church pertained to the relationship between Hellenistic metaphysics and Christian belief.

The same fundamental dichotomy postulated then by some writers between the Gospel and Graeco-Roman "worldly wisdom" has appeared repeatedly throughout the dialectic of Christian history. Pacifists in particular have been inclined to disdain what they regard as the "logic chopping" of those philosophers who interpret the Gospel according to the principles of natural reason instead of reading it with a simple childlike faith. Tertullian, who had received an excellent classical education and used his rhetorical skill with great effect to defend the Christians, nevertheless came to harbor hostility and suspicion toward Greek metaphysics. He regarded pagan wisdom and Christian faith as incompatible, for he traced to Greek philosophy all the heresies which threatened to scandalize the humble and illiterate body of the faithful.[35]

The more orthodox tendency was to incorporate classical knowledge into the Christian worldview. St. Justin Martyr, himself a pacifist, who has always been renowned for noting the identification of the divine Word with the *logos* of the ancient Greeks in the first sentence of St. John's Gospel, concluded that everything rational belongs to Christianity: *nihil humanum alienum mihi*. Those who lived by reason, such as Socrates and Heraclitus, were considered to be Christians even though they might be pagans or atheists.[36] St. Clement of Alexandria (150–215?) insisted that Greek science was a salutary gift from God, equally valid as a rational view of the universe for Christians and pagans. All the truths attained by man in different parts of the earth, said Clement, were seeds of the Word and thus emanated from the same source as Christian revelation, although they were inferior to the latter because they approach truth from a distance, while the Gospel of Christ is perfect and complete.[37] St. Ambrose and St. Augustine were thoroughly steeped in Greek and Latin learning. It was quite natural for them to look to the Greeks and Romans for ideas about the state and war.

Limited and Just War in Graeco-Roman Antiquity

The Greeks believed in limit or measure as fundamental keys to perfection. Both Plato and Aristotle deplored the tendency of states to pursue policies which exceed the limits of necessity. For both, war was essentially a matter of defense, not of conquest and annihilation. Ernest Barker has summed up their thought by asserting that the ideal state "will train its sons for war, without forgetting that war is for the sake of peace . . . . It will do the things which are not themselves the things of reason for the sake of the things which are."[38]

The Greeks did not have a highly refined concept of the just war, but they were convinced that certain uses of military force were justifiable while others were not. That is the essential formulation of the just war theory. There should be a reasonable cause for resorting to war (later called *ius ad bellum*) and the war should be waged justly (*ius in bello*). The latter idea was not too well developed except for wars among Hellenes. Like most peoples through history, the Greeks assumed that poliical communities which share cultural values should be less ready to resort to war as a means of settling disputes among themselves, and should strive the more to attenuate the destructiveness of "intramural" war. Thus they placed as much emphasis upon negotiation and arbitration as upon war. They also believed that when war came the amount of force to be employed should be proportionate to the objectives sought and should, therefore, be confined within the limits of necessity. One notable achievment was the Amphictyonic League of Delphi, based on a treaty which laid down these rules: there should be no war among signatories except for a good cause; fellow Greeks should never be reduced to slavery following defeat; there should be no wanton destruction of civilian populations; and no member city should be destroyed or have its water supply cut off in peace or war.[39]

The refinement of the idea of the just war was left to the Romans, who were avowedly more moral and legal in their approach to war than the Greeks had been. Before Rome became an empire, it was quite meticulous in observing its rules of war. During the sixth century of the pre-Christian era, there had developed a *ius fetiale*, that part of the sacred law which regulated the declaration of war, the solemn swearing of treaties, and the settlement of international disputes. It was the function of a religious and political college of priestly officials, the *Fetiales*, to determine whether a foreign community had so wronged Rome as to justify a resort to force. The Romans apparently felt compelled in conscience, as it were, to convince themselves before embarking upon war that their case was "just and pious" (*justum et pium*). Before Rome was entitled to go to war, satisfaction had to be demanded and denied. The demand for formal compensation from the wrongdoing community was supported by an oath of the Fetial Judges, formally committing the Roman gods to the justness of Rome's cause. Here is Draper's interpretation:

> Conversely, and no less important, the execration of the Roman gods was invoked should it transpire that the cause of the Roman people was unjust or that a just cause did not exist. It can thus be seen how the intimate relationship between the 'just' and 'pious' war became established under this practice.... Bearing in mind that the wrath of the Roman gods had been invoked ... a defeat of the Roman armies would be taken as the clear answer of the gods to the justness of the Roman cause.[40]

The Romans, even more so than the Greeks, believed at least in theory, although not always in practice, that no greater force should be used in war than was required by legitimate military necessity. Phillipson writes: "The methods of Roman warfare indicate a distinct advance on those of the Greeks, and of all other ancient nations. On the whole, we perceive further mitigations, and more deliberate attempts to regularize belligerent proceedings."[41]

One other contribution of the Romans to the Western idea of the "just war" must be mentioned, the development during the two centuries before Christ of a law common to all peoples, the *ius gentium*. This body of law grew empirically; it was not the product of abstract philosophical reasoning. As it developed, jurists noted some congruence between it and the philosophical *ius naturale* which the Roman Stoics were taking over from the Greeks, and whose commands and prohibitions were intellectually necessary and morally binding. In contrast, the *ius gentium* was existential, not essential, and was based on experience, not philosophy. It had made its way into history as a result of the free consent of human beings organized in nearly all political communities with which Rome was in contact.[42] This "law of peoples" and its most fundamental principle—"treaties must be observed" (*pacta sunt servanda*)—became the basis of modern international law as it developed in the Western nation-state system. Under modern international law, and especially in its classical period from 1648 to 1914, it was always taken for granted that the state has a right to make war in order to defend itself against attack, to rectify wrongs committed against it, and to vindicate its juridical rights, even by initiating the use of force if necessary. The right of the state to use armed force as an instrument of foreign policy has undergone curtailment in the era of the League of Nations and United Nations, but the legal nature of the modification remains a matter of disagreement.[43]

Ambrose, Augustine, and the Just War Doctrine

The just war doctrine in its Christian context was developed and refined by patristic writers, medieval theologians, philosophers, and canonists, and later Scholastic systematists, all of whom reflected upon the Old Testament, the Gospel, the traditional teaching of the Church, classical political and legal thought, the canon law, and the requirements of social and political order. As we have seen previously, most of the early Christians felt no responsibility for the defense of the existing social order. But the Christian Fathers had upheld the political order as divinely instituted long before they elaborated the doctrine of the just war.

With the Christianization of the empire under Constantine, doctrinal pacifism, which had never been the authoritative teaching of the church, suffered a substantial setback.[44] Once the Christian community became responsible for the maintenance of social order and imperial security, at a time when barbarian pressures on Rome's borders were increasing rapidly, the Church moved quickly toward a just war doctrine which left little room for doctrinal pacifism, even though pacifism would continue to reappear throughout Christian history, both in the lives of individuals with a special vocation to bear witness to the evangelical spirit of peace and in the ideology of radical or unorthodox sects which became alientated from the political order in which they found themselves.

The distinctive Christian doctrine of the just war was elaborated in the late fourth and early fifth centuries. The process began with St. Ambrose, a great ecclesiastical administrator learned in Greek philosophy and Roman law, who had been made bishop of the important See of Milan by acclamation while still an unbaptized catechuman. Although he is often unjustly accused of equating the good Christian with the good Roman citizen, he never placed the empire ahead of his faith. After Emperor Theodosius ordered the massacre of the Thessalonians in 388, Ambrose charged him with sinning atrociously for killing the innocent and compelled him to do public penance in the Basilica at Milan[45]—something that no modern bishop would require an erring Catholic head of state to do for an action performed in his official capacity.

St. Ambrose, like St. Augustine after him, had a profound and sensitive understanding of the tensions between Christian piety and public responsibility, as he demonstrated in his anguished reply to an inquiry from a Christian magistrate who wished to know whether the Church allowed a judge who handed down a sentence of capital punishment to receive Communion.[46] Yet the same Ambrose at about the same time taught that not only does the state have a right to make war, but under certain circumstances there may even be a positive moral obligation to undertake it. "Man," he said, "has a moral duty to employ force to resist active wickedness, for to refrain from hindering evil when possible is tantamount to promoting it." But he insisted that war may be waged only for a just cause and only by fair methods, and that punishment meted out to an adversary should be proportionate to the degree of injustice perpetrated by him.[47]

The doctrine received its principal theological justification from St. Ambrose's most illustrious pupil, St. Augustine—intellectually the most brilliant and comprehensive of all patristic writers. This man, of whom Bainton says that "the Sermon on the Mount had burned into his heart," but whose outlook "was much more somber than that which had prompted the pragmatic pacifism of Origen" because he deemed neither Christian perfection nor genuine peace on earth to be possible, could never be called an apologist for the Roman Empire, built as it was on pride, idolatry, fear, lust, and blood.[48] Nevertheless, in his day the empire was being ruled by Christians, and could not be held to be unjust as it had been in pagan days.

As the Bishop of Hippo, Augustine branded as a Manichaean heresy the proposition that waging war is intrinsically evil and contrary to Christian charity. At the same time, he keenly appreciated the tragic aspects of human warfare. Few writers have condemned its gladiatorial features as scathingly as he did. Nevertheless, he reluctantly conceded that there are times when responsible rulers have no other choice except to resort to war. "War and conquest . . . are a sad necessity in the eyes of men of principle . . . . [Yet] it would be still more unfortunate if wrongdoers should dominate just men."[49] The good ruler, said Augustine, will bewail the necessity of waging even just wars. He assigned to war a deep spiritual meaning, because he saw that war reflects both a profound restlessness in man and a fundamental craving for peace. If men are willing to take up arms, he said in one of his memorable passages, this does not necessarily mean that they love peace the less, but rather that they love their own kind of peace the more.[50]

St. Augustine was convinced that Christians were under a strong social obligation to defend the civilization of the Roman Empire, despite all of its imperfections, against the invasions of the barbarian Vandals. When Boniface, the Roman general in North Africa, wished to retire and become a monk, St. Augustine urged him to postpone his vocation and continue to perform his duties as a soldier.[51] But he always insisted that war has to be waged not merely for the sake of victory but for justice and a better peace. Those who wage war must do so in the spirit of peacemakers. When war does come as an unavoidable necessity, it must be conducted justly. Gustave Combès summarizes the Augustinian teaching on just conduct by saying that there should be no wanton violence, profanation of temples, looting, massacre, conflagration, vengeance, atrocities, or reprisals.[52]

Finally, St. Augustine insisted that for a war to be just, it must be waged with the proper inner attitude, a spirit of Christian love (*caritas*). This aspect of his doctrine often scandalizes people today. Yet he held that Christian love dictated the duty of protecting the innocent against unjust attack, and if the Christian was compelled to kill an enemy it had to be done with a proper interior disposition, free of all traces of hatred and vindictiveness. He wrote:

> Love does not preclude a benevolent severity . . . no one indeed is fit to inflict punishment save the one who has first overcome hate in his heart. The love of enemies admits of no dispensation, but love does not exclude wars of mercy waged by the good.[53]

It must be emphasized that in Augustine's view, killing by the Christian can be justified only on behalf of the common good, never for the personal defense of the individual Christian person, who cannot defend himself without selfish passion and hatred.

> As to killing others to defend one's own life, I do not approve of this unless one happens to be a soldier or a public functionary acting not for himself but in defense of others or of the city in which he resides.[54]

Development of the Doctrine in the Middle Ages

The just war theory was accepted as a given by the writers of medieval Christendom. The medieval doctrine has been thoroughly researched and analyzed by such scholars as Joan D. Tooke, William V. O'Brien, James Turner Johnson, Paul Ramsey, and Frederick Russell.[55] Johnson in his latest book notes that the just war doctrine resulted from the confluence of several separate streams of thought and practice in the late medieval period: the Old and the New Testament, the canon law tradition after the twelfth century *Decretum* of Gratian, to whom Johnson assigns great significance, Thomistic theology and philosophy, the work of civil lawyers in reconstructing the Roman Law, with inputs from Roman political and military theory and practice; and the chivalric code, which drew upon Germanic traditions regarding warfare, manliness, and soldierly ideals.[56]

In the thirteenth century, St. Thomas laid down three necessary conditions for a just war: declaration by proper authority with legitimate responsibility for the common good, just cause, and right intention.[57] With regard to just cause, O'Brien holds that the substance of the cause must be just; the forms of pursuing the just cause, whether by defensive or offensive warfare, must be just; there must be proportionality between the just ends and the means used; and war should be resorted to only as a last resort after peaceful alternatives have been exhausted. St. Thomas himself quoted St. Augustine:

> Those wars are generally defined as just which avenge some wrong, when a nation or a state is to be punished for having

failed to make amends for the wrong done, or to restore what has been taken unjustly.[58]

The justice of self-defense, says O'Brien, is generally considered axiomatic, so much so that "the requirement of probable success . . . is usually waived."[59] One can argue that the medieval just war doctrine was developed principally to apply to cases in which the use of force could be justly initiated, not to wars of self-defense, which were always presumed to be just. The right to wage offensive warfare for the purpose of vindicating wrongs done has been severely curtailed in the twentieth century, under both the just war doctrine and positive international law, until it is now virtually limited to a right of extended self-defense against aggression or the direct results of aggression. Under the natural law, it is always lawful to repel force with force (*Vim vi repellere omnia jura permittunt*).

To sum up the medieval doctrine concisely: War had to be declared by public authority—an important requirement in a feudal age when private wars abounded. Rulers had to be morally certain that there was a sufficiently grave cause involving a serious violation of the juridical order. War could be declared only after negotiation, arbitration, and other peaceful means had been tried and failed. There had to be proportionality between ends and means. The purpose of war had to be sufficiently important to warrant killing in a just war as a permissible exception to the divine prohibition against murder. There also had to be a reasonable expectation or probability that the war would be successful, not in the sense of merely winning, but of producing more good than evil and restoring the order of justice by bringing about a better situation than that which would prevail if war were not fought. The war had to be fought with a right intention to restore peace and justice, not with a desire for revenge or booty. And, finally, the party waging a just war needed more than the *ius ad bellum* (the right to go to war). It was obliged to observe the *ius in bello*. That is, while waging the war, it had to abstain from using means which were intrinsically immoral, such as deliberately spreading false propaganda, entering a truce with the intention of deceiving the enemy, and, most important of all, engaging in military operations which involved direct killing of innocents. This last requirement, which is often called the principle of discrimination, received its full theoretical elaboration only from the Spanish Late

Scholastics Victoria and Suarez toward the end of the sixteenth and the beginning of the seventeenth centuries. They also developed the principle of proportionality as it relates to the conduct of military operations in the course of war.[60]

Discrimination and Proportionality

The principles of discrimination (noncombatant immunity) and proportionality, and their relationship to each other, undoubtedly pose more complex problems of judgment than do any other elements of just war theory, precisely because they involve not only qualitative but also quantitative assessment. These principles pertain to how just and important the state's cause is, and how much military force and human suffering may be justified in defending that cause. O'Brien brings together the high interests of the state (*raison d'état*) and the use of the military instrument (*raison de guerre*) in the following passage:

> To begin with, the ends held out as the just cause must be sufficiently good and important to warrant the extreme means of war . . . . Beyond that, a projection of the outcome of the war is required in which the probable good expected to result from success is weighed against the probable evil that the war will cause . . . . Manifestly, the task of performing this task effectively is an awesome one . . . . Moreover, the calculus of proportionality between probable good and evil in a war is a continuing one.[61]

Before proportionality can be examined more closely, it is necessary to look at the origin of the Western notion of noncombatant immunity. Limits on the prosecution of the war were derived mainly from the canon law of the medieval Church and from the chivalric tradition. Through its Truce of God and Peace of God, the Church attempted, with meager success, to define certain times (days of the week and religious festivals) when fighting was illicit for Christians, and to outlaw certain types of weapons. Ecclesiastical efforts at the Second Lateran Council in 1139 to ban (only in warfare among Christians) such weapons as the crossbow, bows and arrows generally, and siege machines, ended in utter failure, so much so that Gratian, writing only a decade or so after the Council, did not even bother to mention the proscription.[62]

Johnson also shows that under the Peace of God the Church proved more successful in spreading a mantle of protection over specific classes of persons who were entitled to full security against the ravages of war: clerics, monks, friars, pilgrims, travelers, merchants, and peasants who cultivated the soil. This was not a prescription for general noncombatant immunity. It protected only those classes of persons whose social function had nothing' to do with warmaking. Other obvious groups such as women, children, the infirm and the aged were not mentioned, for the immunity of these classes was taken for granted in the chivalric tradition, as they were too weak to bear arms. Under canon law, persons named as noncombatants had immunity bestowed upon them as a *right*. According to the chivalric code, immunity and protection were conferred by the knight as a *gift*, an imperative of his professionalism, deriving from a sense of noblesse oblige. By the fourteenth century, the two lists of noncombatants—one mandated by the Church, the other granted by the knights—coalesced into one and became the basis for a general concept of noncombatant immunity.[63]

Neither Johnson nor O'Brien thinks that it is possible to observe noncombatant immunity as an absolute principle under conditions of modern war, although they agree that it is to be striven for to the fullest extent possible by matching force to force as economically as one can and by refraining from the use of any more force than is required by legitimate military necessity to achieve the specific strategic or tactical objectives of a just war. There must be compromises between military necessity and the dictates of humanitarianism and civilization. The use of force in the modern world, given the state of weapons technology, cannot be finely calibrated to the higher dictates of Christian love, compassion, and mercy as absolute moral imperatives.

At this point it should be noted that we are dealing here with two distinct yet closely related concepts in the Western tradition—just war and limited war. Both are opposed to the idea of unlimited and total war, and both place emphasis on the principles of proportionality and discrimination in the use of force. Just war theorists, who are concerned about these questions from the standpoint of

Christian moral theology and political philosophy, insist that the direct killing of innocent people (a status difficult to define in view of civilian contributions to military production and the war effort) can never be deliberately intended, although unintentional killing may be unavoidable. Limited war theorists, by contrast, are more interested in placing restraints upon the conduct of war out of secular considerations of civilization or humanitarianism.[64]

In treating the principle of proportionality, O'Brien follows the teaching of the eminent Jesuit theologian, John Courtney Murray, who often argued that war should never be waged for trivial causes, but that when ultimate human and spiritual values are at stake on a large scale the principle of proportionality might justify a large amount of death, suffering, destruction, and sacrifice. O'Brien quotes one of Murray's memorably eloquent passages, in which he expounds the teachings of Pope Pius XII on the question of proportionality in just war:

> [T]he standard is not a "eudaimonism and utilitarianism of materialist origin" which would avoid war merely because it is uncomfortable, or connive at injustice simply because its repression would be costly. The question of proportion must be evaluated in more tough-minded fashion, from the viewpoint of the hierarchy of strictly moral values. It is not enough simply to consider the "sorrows and evils that flow from war." There are greater evils than the physical death and destruction wrought in war. And there are human goods of so high an order that immense sacrifices may have to be borne in their defense. By these insistences Pius XII transcended the vulgar pacifism of sentimentalist and materialist inspiration that is so common today.[65]

There is no doubt in O'Brien's mind that when a just, free, and self-correcting political system is responsive to the popular will and finds itself threatened by aggression from an unjust, totalitarian policy, defeat of the former in war (or surrender without war) will probably lead to having an unjust social order and alien system of values imposed upon it forcibly. Such a prospect creates a strong *ius ad bellum* and justifies the use of considerable military force, if necessary, to ensure a just peace. We should not forget the appalling magnitude of the casualties and destruction which belligerent states and their populations were willing to sustain in World War II. The leaders of the Soviet Union, whose total losses have been estimated in excess of 15 million people,[66] never thought of suing for peace on the grounds that the cost of war in terms of life was excessive.

The Just War Doctrine from the Medieval to the Modern Period

Many circumstances of medieval culture, including feudalism, prevailing economic conditions, and the crude state of the military sciences, reinforced the moral efforts of the Church to mitigate the harshness of "intramural" warfare during this period. To the extent that the chivalric code was observed, warfare took on the aspect of a tournament. This was possible in an environment in which legal and political institutions, as well as religious beliefs and cultural values, were relatively homogeneous.

The ideological differences which can provoke absolute struggles to the death were lacking in Europe prior to the fourteenth century. The outcome of a feudal war often determined *who* should wield authority over a particular piece of territory, but it seldom affected the *how* of life. In that age and place, it was difficult for most people to become passionately involved in the issues over which feudal wars were fought. Thus, although difficult, it was not impossible to limit war. When a cherished set of values or a way of life was thought to be at stake, however, as in the Crusades, the Hundred Years' War between the nascent nationalisms of the French and English, and the religious wars following the Reformation, war became an all-consuming religious, political, or cultural, ideological and psychological experience. Hence the battles of Antioch, Acre, Crécy, Poitiers, Agincourt, and Magdeburg were bitter and bloody in the extreme. No holds were barred, no limits observed.

At the time of the Crusades and Reformation wars, there was a widespread tendency in Christian Europe to assume that religious differences by themselves constituted a just cause for "holy wars." But during the seventeenth century a more tolerant policy of "live and let live" came to prevail, primarily the result of practical political consid-erations of what was good for the state rather than from any strong theological convictions that it was wrong for believers to kill each other. The violence of the religious wars subsided after the Peace of Westphalia of 1648, which ushered in the modern era of balance of power, diplomacy, and international law. For the Late Scholastics and also for the earliest systematic expounders of secular international law such as Grotius, Ayala, Gentilis, Vattel, Wolff, Pufendorf, and others, the medieval *ius ad bellum* emerged as a substitute juridical proceeding—a cross between judgment by ordeal and a lawsuit in defense of the legal rights of the state, prosecuted by force in the absence of an effective international judicial superior. War came to be spoken of as the "final argument of kings" (*ultima ratio regum*), but the Europeans were too intelligent to assume that justice had to be all on one side in war. They certainly did not believe that the side which prevailed necessarily had the more just cause, for that was tanta-mount to thinking that "might makes right."

The dissolution of the religious consensus in Europe occurred during the emergence of the modern sovereign state (which had no superior legal judge) and rendered the task of legally assessing the justice of each party's cause an increasingly complex and irrelevant one. Eventually, international legal publicists found it necessary to assume that each sovereign was judge of the justice of his own cause, and that international law must prescind from that question. It was always an imperative of international law, however, that war be limited and restrained by a rational calculus of ends and means, costs and benefits.[67]

In the latter half of the seventeenth century, the pendulum swung back toward more moderate warfare, which was less ide-ological and more instrumental in the traditional sense. The rise of the bourgeoisie buttressed pacifist more than militarist sentiments, for the bourgeoisie desired an orderly international community in which the conditions of business and trade would be predictable. Land warfare became marked by skirmish and adroit maneuver, surprise, march and countermarch, and rapier thrusts at the enemy's supply lines. In an era of rising comfort levels and improved manners, there was a growing distaste for violence among aristocrats who admired subtlety more than brute strength in battle. The growth of the fine arts and the intensified efforts to apply reason to human affairs reinforced the trend toward limited war. Encounters between armies in the field were often looked upon as mere adjuncts of the diplomatic process, and were designed to reinforce the bargaining positions of envoys during prolonged negotiations. The development of naval power, insofar as it permitted hostile engagements without directly involving land populations, also helped to soften the effects of warfare.[68]

Under such conditions, the Catholic Church felt no pressing need to modify the traditional concept of the just war. Church teaching was not affected by the pacifist writers Erasmus, More, Crucé, Fenelon, Penn, Voltaire, and Rousseau, who took their stand either on Stoic and early radical Christian positions or on the newer European Renaissance and Enlightenment ideals of cosmopolitanism, humanitarianism, and bourgeois internationalism. Unfavorable comparisons were drawn between the destructive life of the soldier and the useful life of the merchant. The quest for human happiness unmarred by any trace of the tragic became for most intellectuals the great goal of life.[69]

The *philosophes* were not agreed among themselves whether happiness was to be achieved through the application of scientific and technical reason or through man's return to nature and rediscovery of the state of original simplicity. But rationalists and romantics alike were convinced that society was about to burst the chains of traditional authority and superstition, dispel the historic curses of ignorance, disease, and war, and embark upon the indefinite perfectibility of humankind. The transition from monarchical to republican and more democratic institutions it was thought, would certainly be accompanied by a shift from war sentiments to the peace spirit. The hypothesis of inexorable human progress, however, did not win the assent of the Catholic Church.

The French Revolution and its Napoleonic aftermath contributed to an intensification of warfare on the part of citizen armies, backed by a growing industrial base and infused with powerful nationalist ideals. A weakened Church was in no position to preach homilies to governments on the subject of war. The conservative reaction of 1815 produced the Concert of Europe and thereby minimized the harsh effects of developing war technology. But at the theoretical level, the Clausewitzian idea of absolute war made its appearance. The latter part of the century witnessed the spread of universal conscription in Europe, the mass production of automatic weapons, the creation of alliance systems, and increasing imperialist rivalry and armaments competition among the powers. In 1889 Pope Leo XIII declared:

> Large standing armies and unlimited warlike preparations may indeed for a time commend the respect of an enemy disposed to attack, but they cannot bring about a secure and stable peace. Armaments that are built up with aggressive intentions tend rather to increase than to diminish rivalries and enmities.[70]

The outbreak of World War I found the papacy a helpless onlooker without any friendly Catholic governments in Europe through which it could wield influence. Benedict XV, attempting to steer an impartial course, called for a negotiated peace, the amicable settlement of disputed territorial claims, and a simultaneous reciprocal reduction of armaments—for which he was called the French pope by the Germans and the German pope by the French.[71]

In the cynical intellectual atmosphere that followed the first world war, many Catholics became more pacifist and began to argue that in view of modern technological developments the conditions for a just war could no longer be met. Nevertheless, Catholic treatises *de ethica sociali* continued to discuss throughout the interwar period the traditional theory of the just war and the criteria for it,[72] because, as noted in the Malines Code of International Ethics, there was an absence of any "effective juridically constituted international authority."[73]

Long before the onset of the nuclear age, virtually all writers on the morality of war and just war theory realized that changes in the structure of society, the character of warfare itself, and weapons technology had wrought havoc with the traditional principle of discrimination. The late nineteenth and early twentieth centuries had witnessed a gradual erosion of the distinction between combatants and noncombatants, military and nonmilitary targets. Industrialization brought pressures upon military establishments to wage war not only against soldiers, but also against the production sources of guns, shells, bombs, tanks, planes, and submarines. Power plants, ports, and railheads came to be listed as military targets because they directly supported the war effort. Just war moralists did not accept the arguments of Giulio Douhet and other advocates of air power that modern warfare necessitated the strategic bombing of industrial centers and even residential neighborhoods, so that hitting the home front would break the enemy's will to fight in the Clausewitzian sense. Still, even moralists who unequivocally condemned the obliteration bombing of cities were compelled to admit that under conditions of a modern total war such as World War II, not all persons in the "civilian sector" could claim noncombatant immunity solely because they did not wear military uniforms.

The Second World War was widely regarded by Catholics in the Western democracies as the most just war in modern history, because of the Nazi-Fascist militarist systems against which it was waged. Nevertheless, during the course of that war, a Jesuit theologian rejected the ethical principle of "double effect" as a justification for obliteration bombing. He contended that bombing whole cities with the intention of destroying targets of military value while withholding the intention of killing "innocents," is morally untenable.[74]

Toward the end of that war, when Pope Pius XII said that "war as an apt and proportionate means of solving international conflicts is now out of date,"[75] he apparently meant that governments should no longer contemplate the initiation of offensive wars even if they had a just grievance. According to John Courtney Murray, S.J., it was not the pope's intention to proscribe either defensive war or defensive preparations:

> A defensive war to repress injustice is morally admissible both in principle and in fact. In its abstractness this principle has always formed part of Catholic doctrine; by its assertion the Church finds a way between the false extremes of pacifism and bellicism. Moreover, the assertion itself, far from being a contradiction of the basic Christian will to peace, is the strongest possible affirmation of this will. There is no peace without justice, law and order. But "law and order have need at times of the powerful arm of force."[76]

Skeptical and even hostile critics have pronounced many funeral orations over the just war theory as its remains were being lowered into the grave of quaint but archaic ideas. It is important to realize the extent to which some radical Catholic pacifists loathe the

theory as a perversion of the Christian ethic. The position of the
radical Catholic pacifists goes beyond that of those nuclear pacifists
mentioned briefly in Chapter 1. It also goes beyond that of Catholics
who, earlier in this century—even prior to the advent of nuclear
weapons—seriously doubted whether, given the nature of modern
weapons technology, the traditional criteria for a just war could ever
be fulfilled. Rather, the radical pacifists have rejected outright the
traditional doctrine of the just war. James W. Douglass has attributed
just war thinking to a historic infidelity to the Gospel message:

> Inasmuch as war's central action of *inflicting* suffering and
> death is directly opposed to the example of Christ in *endur-
> ing* these same realities, the Church has reason for repent-
> ance in having allowed herself to become involved since the
> age of Constantine in an ethic which would justify what
> conflicts with the essence of the Gospel.[77]

Richard T. McSorley, S.J., also insists that the Gospel itself is
pacifist even though the Catholic tradition has not been. He notes
that St. Augustine saw a threat to the whole Church from the barbarians, once the Church had become allied to the Roman state, and
taught that under certain rigorous conditions, every one of which
must be continuously fulfilled, the waging of a just war could be a
permissible exception to rather than a violation of the Gospel.
Although the just war idea may be acceptable in pure theory,
McSorley concedes, it is unacceptable because it has not worked in
practice. "We have never yet had a war in history which has been
condemned by society at large at the time as a violation of the just war
theory; nor has any such war been condemned retroactively."[78]
Christ's love ethic and life example, he goes on to contend, have
nothing to do with the philosophical arguments of Aristotle, Cicero,
and Plato from which the just war theory is partly derived.

One more instance of a Catholic repudiation of the just war
theory will suffice. At the height of the Vietnam War, Peter J. Riga
excoriated the doctrine in the following passage:

> There has never been historically any large Christian com-
> munity or national hierarchy which has refused to serve its
> nation-state because a particular war was considered to be
> unjust. This theory was a concatenation by theologians who

realized that, from a theoretical point of view, the raison d'etat was not sufficient for the Christian to engage in war. This theory was invented to soothe his conscience even though there is no place in historical record where it was really taken seriously.[79]

This language shows that Father Riga's rejection of the theory was due not to a conviction that the conditions of the just war could no longer be met, but from a deeper contempt for the Augustinian-Thomistic doctrine as being little more than a rationalization for nationalistic passions and propensity to war.

At this point, a few summary comments are in order: (1) In our contemporary mass media culture, it is easier to ridicule the just war theory with clever but specious arguments than it is to defend it with carefully reasoned theological and philosophical ones. (2) The fact that a set of norms is frequently violated does not destroy its validity. Were this true, the Ten Commandments would have been obsolete long ago. (3) It is an extremely inaccurate and imprudent judgment to say, in view of all that has been written by Catholic thinkers and pondered by Catholic political and military leaders for fifteen centuries, that the theory has never been taken seriously. Such a sweeping statement is unprovable and improbable. (4) The fact that states since the time of Rome have seldom gone to war without a conviction concerning the justice of their cause does not in any way vitiate the just war theory, nor does it prove that genuine justice is never at issue in war. It merely demonstrates that in all ages civilized peoples find it difficult or impossible to sustain the horrors of warfare without a belief that their cause is just. Indeed, the theory itself provides for the possibility that both contesting parties in a war might perceive a just case for resorting to war from their unique and limited perspectives, especially if it is seen as defensive by both sides. Both might conceivably try to wage such a war as justly as possible. This can only be attributed to the tragedy of the human condition, which ought not to be lightly dismissed, as it is by some Catholic pacifists, with the superficial argument-begging assertion that there is no such thing as fighting for a just cause. (5) The just war theory, despite the obsequies which have frequently been intoned over it, keeps reappearing in history simply because the real world in which morality and politics have to remain intermixed cannot do without it. Even though some but not all Catholic moralists reject the relevance of the theory to nuclear war, there have been and will continue to be in the nuclear age countless subnuclear military conflicts to which its principles are readily applicable. There is an exquisite irony in the fact that the very intellectuals who scoffed most contemptuously at the doctrine during the Vietnam War employed its essential categories and criteria to condemn United States involvement in that conflict. Others, like John Courtney Murray, used the same set of criteria to make a marginal case for U.S. participation.

It is not inappropriate here to reiterate that any Catholic who contends that waging war under any circumstances is incompatible with the Gospel is abandoning the traditional, consistent, and common teaching of the Catholic Church. Some do so with unquestionable sincerity and great circumspection. The Jesuit David Hollenbach, for example, admits that the theological argument that commitment to peace must rest upon an active struggle for justice—an important argument in the confrontation between a free West and a totalitarian communist East—possesses plausibility. Yet, he says, it raises a question because it fails to account for the fact that Jesus did not resort to violent force in self-defense against unjust attack.[80] The author of this study has sought to deal with that question earlier in this study by pointing out that the Fathers of the Church sharply distinguished between the Christian person and the state, and never held up Calvary as a model for Christian action within the state. Most contemporary radical Catholic pacifists, however, including Gordon Zahn, James W. Douglass, Joseph Fahey, and many of the bishops who are members of the organization Pax Christi are quite candid in placing distance between themselves and the Catholic just war tradition, preferring over St. Augustine and St. Thomas such pacifist models for our present environment as Gandhi, Martin Luther King, Dorothy Day, and A. J. Muste.

One final point needs to be made. Many Catholic members of the Christian New Left, including not a few "pacifists," present an ironic paradox. Under the traditional just war doctrine, only legitimate governing authorities were allowed to declare war, and they usually enjoyed the presumption that their resort to force was justified. During the last three decades, the traditional just war doctrine has been transmuted by Christians of the left into a doctrine of just revolutionary violence in "wars of national liberation" against "oppressive capitalist-imperialist systems" whose institutions themselves are branded as a form of violence. The new presumption is that only revolutionary violence against unjust social and political structures can now be viewed as morally defensible—indeed, as a necessary "holy war"—while the use of force by incumbent governments is presumed to be evil in itself. Such is the ideological conviction of those Catholic and Protestant liberation theologians for whom salvation becomes equatable with revolutionary struggle.[81] Paul J. Weber, S.J., pointed out fifteen years ago that "there are few, if any, recorded instances in which the church has joined a revolt against a government—no matter how unjust—under which she had a relatively secure institutional position," but the New Left theologians who advocate "Christian violence" were "pressing for church involvement in revolution against the very societies that guarantee its peaceful existence."[82] A pacifism which makes an exception only for anti-Western revolution is clearly problematical.

3

DETERRENCE OF WAR

IN THE

NUCLEAR AGE

Pope Pius XII was appalled at the thought of the catastrophe which might be inflicted upon the human race and the planet by large-scale nuclear warfare. Yet, he refused to condemn nuclear weapons as immoral in themselves and label every use of them, regardless of circumstances, as illicit. He insisted that their use would be lawful only when indispensable for self-defense, when forced upon a people by an extremely serious and unavoidable injustice, and when rigorous limits were imposed upon their use. Pius XII was convinced that one can conceive of greater evils than the death and destruction caused by war, and that there are times when the danger of war must be accepted, especially when there is a probability of success in employing forces against injustice. He was favorably disposed toward the Atlantic Alliance as a means of defending Western civilization against Stalinist totalitarianism and of deterring war in a Europe still recovering from the costliest and most tragic conflict in its history. Deeply disturbed by the suppression of the Hungarian uprising in late 1956, Pius XII strongly reiterated the traditional just war doctrine of the Catholic Church:

> If, therefore, a body representative of the people and a Government—both having been chosen by free election—in a moment of extreme danger decide, by legitimate instruments of internal and external policy, on defensive precautions, and carry out the plans which they consider necessary, they do not act immorally;

so that a Catholic citizen cannot invoke his own conscience in order to refuse to serve and fulfill those duties the law imposes.[1]

There is more continuity than innovation in the formal teaching of Pius XII and John XXIII, despite the popular impression that a profound change occurred in the papacy in 1959. Certainly there was a remarkable difference in the personal styles of the austere, aloof Pacelli and the warm, jovial Roncalli. The international environment was also undergoing a transition from Cold War to detente. Rome both reflected and helped to accentuate a more hopeful mood in ecumenical and international relations brought about by improved communications, the recovery and unification of Western Europe, and the complex process of strategic stabilization and tension reduction to which Kennedy and Khrushchev contributed in the wake of the Cuban missile crisis. Pope John's 1963 encyclical *Pacem in Terris* was highly and rightly praised as a spiritual keynote of the new era. Although it warned against an overly heavy and lengthy reliance upon a mechanistic balance of power for the preservation of genuine peace, it far from constituted an endorsement of nuclear pacifism as a political policy. John XXIII followed his predecessor in insisting that, given the destructiveness of modern military technology, it is contrary to reason to hold that war is now a suitable way to restore rights which have been violated. This must be viewed in the light of the traditional Catholic doctrine of the just war, which permitted a government under some circumstances to launch an offensive war to correct an injustice in the juridical order. The pope, however, did not deny the right to deploy nuclear weapons in defense against the threat of unjust attack, in hope of deterring such an attack.

The pope regretted the fact that the industrially advanced countries, by accumulating "enormous stocks of armaments," used economic resources which might otherwise be allocated to the task of developing poorer countries. Nevertheless, he did not attribute evil motives to governments which maintain nuclear deterrent forces. He deemed it unfortunate, however, that "the law of fear still reigns among peoples, and it forces them to spend fabulous sums for armaments, not for aggression they affirm—and there is no reason for not believing them—but to dissuade others from aggression."[2] In this one sentence, John went further than any pope in the nuclear age in expressing at least a vague Christian existential appreciation of and sympathy for the rationale underlying the military policies of the United States and the Soviet Union. He went even beyond Pius XII, who did not speak of deterrence, probably because the secular strategic concept of deterrence was not yet clearly comprehended by Rome during his pontificate. It is not surprising that nuclear and absolute pacifists, in their antideterrence literature, never reprint the passage just quoted. The pope warned that even though the deliberate initiation of war seems unlikely, there still remains the possibility of a conflagration by unpremeditated act.

> Justice, then, right reason and consideration for human dignity and life urgently demand that the arms race should cease; that the stockpiles which exist in various countries should be reduced equally and simultaneously by the parties concerned; that nuclear weapons should be banned; and finally that all come to an agreement on a fitting program of disarmament, employing mutual and effective controls.[3]

The late 1950s and early 1960s witnessed an intensification of the debate among advocates of pacifism and the just war. Confusion surrounded the "just cause" criterion for going to war. There arose in the West a skepticism about our human ability to determine which party in a war has justice on its side. The skeptics pointed to the unhappy experience of the historians during the interwar decades who tried to fix blame for the outbreak of World War I. There was an erroneous tendency to assume that whichever side initiated the war must have been in the wrong. But that had never been true either under the traditional just war doctrine or under positive international law—at least untrue prior to the experience of World War II, which led to the modification of the just war doctrine by Pius XII and the adoption of the United Nations Charter (which curtailed the historic right of the state to initiate offensive warfare in order to correct a wrong for which no other compensation or remedy could be obtained). Neither under the just war doctrine nor under secular international law has the right of a state to engage in preparations or, if necessary, operations for self-defense against attack ever been at issue. It is not at issue today, nor can it be in the future as long as power and law remain decentralized in the international system, and as long as there is no effective central authority which can enforce the peaceful settlement of disputes or guarantee the rights and security

of states against aggression. The United Nations in its present structure (which appears for all practical purposes to be irreformable)
cannot be expected to formulate a fully satisfactory and workable
definition of "aggression," must less "unprovoked aggression," "indirect aggression," "the direct effects of aggression," or the "threat of
aggression" to which a response may be justified.[4]

The contemporary debate over war and peace has been hope-
lessly confused by a chronic and widespread failure to recognize the
fundamental distinction between illegitimate, unprovoked, unjust,
and offensive aggression and a war of self-defense which, as Suarez
realized clearly, is a matter not of choice but of necessity.[5] Whether we
like it or not, in the existing international system, states remain the
final judges of what measures are required for their own defense and
the deterrence of war. The Second Vatican Council recognized this
inescapable fact.

The relevance of the traditional just war theory incurred even
more telling criticism in regard to the criteria of "morally permissible
means" of waging war. In other words, the debate has focused greater
emphasis upon *ius in bello* than upon *ius ad bellum*. As early as 1948,
Alfredo Cardinal Ottaviani, long regarded by Catholic liberals as the
archetype of ecclesiastical conservatism, pronounced the surprising
maxim that "war is to be altogether forbidden as immoral" (i.e.,
unreasonable in the Thomistic sense).[6] In the mid-1950s, Father
Francis M. Stratmann, O.P., a leading German Catholic student of
the problem of war, argued that full-scale military conflict between
major powers in the modern world is bound to end in total war and
must be condemned as immoral because it obliterates not only the
distinction between combatants and noncombatants but also the
whole social order. Thus, he said, the natural law teaching on which
the just war doctrine is founded now offers a solid basis for repudi-
ating modern war, since the conditions specified by the doctrine can
no longer be fulfilled.[7] An English Catholic historian, Christopher
Hollis, conceding that the general mind of the Church throughout
history favored a commonsense interpretation of the New Testament
and rejected unconditional pacifism, nevertheless contended that
modern weapons have created a new case for pacifism.

One of the traditional arguments for a just war has always
been that a war can only be just if, *inter alia*, it has a

reasonable chance of achieving its purpose.... Whatever
emerges from a new international war, nothing remotely
like any of the institutions that began that war would
emerge. It is therefore absurd to invoke the argument of
self-defence, because self-defence in international affairs
means the defence of institutions, and the institutions
would be committing suicide by going to war.[8]

Other Catholic writers pursued a similar line of reasoning in the
early 1960s. The Canadian Leslie Dewart argued that when war is no
longer waged for legitimate defense but for the annihilation of the
enemy, it becomes antihuman and instrinsically immoral. If the
Christian ethic excludes "peace at all costs," he asserted, it also
excludes "survival at all costs." He therefore condemned preparations for a future war based on the "assumption that our survival is
the highest value to which every other value must be subordinated."[9]
In an article frankly apocalyptic in tone, the American Trappist
Thomas Merton called it "pure madness to think that Christianity
can defend itself with nuclear weapons" and a serious error to
identify the cause of the West (which in his view was no longer really
Christian) with the cause of God.[10]
These reactions were typical nuclear pacifist commentaries of
that time. All of the moral critics were quite correct in their assessment (with which secular strategists did not disagree) that total
unlimited war fought with nuclear weapons would be the most
horrible catastrophe in history. It would produce megacorpses—
millions of dead—destroy the social fabric of the two principal
antagonists, and possibly threaten life over large segments of the
earth's surface. They argued that if the indiscriminate annihilation of
millions of helpless, innocent people is wrong to initiate, nuclear
retaliation is no less wrong according to the Christian ethic. At about
the same time, such secular strategic analysts as William Kaufman,
Henry Kissinger, Robert Osgood, and Generals Maxwell Taylor and
James M. Gavin were saying that all-out nuclear war made neither
political nor military sense, and that the United States and the West
needed a strategy of limited war.[11] But whereas the secular strategists
were generally convinced that nuclear war could be successfully
deterred, the moralists focused upon its probable immorality if it
should occur. Virtually all the pacifists concluded that a nuclear war

could never meet the conditions of a just war. For most types of nuclear war which the human mind normally envisages in its imagination, they were probably right. But they went too far in ruling out every possibility of the just use of nuclear weapons.

The passionate eloquence of those Catholic writers still has power to move the reader even today. Indeed, the arguments of the antinuclear pacifists have not changed much at all in the last twenty-five years. Yet one cannot avoid the conclusion that there is a fundamental lacuna in their thinking, an intellectual chasm of vast proportions. Speaking with the deepest sincerity in the name of Christian reason, they employ language calculated to appeal primarily to the emotions and fears of their audience. Their case is not without a certain compelling logic of that exaggerated sort which perhaps belongs in the theater of the absurd, but has no proper place in the realm of public political discourse, even though it has virtually seized and occupied that realm in the politically irresponsible mass media.

The lacuna in the thinking of the nuclear pacifists is the absence of any proper appreciation of deterrence, for which they do not have a single favorable word. Instead of inquiring into the validity of the assumptions on which stable deterrence rests and asking what steps might be taken to strengthen those assumptions, they proceed from such a visceral aversion to the whole concept of deterrence that they are inclined to take it for granted that sooner or later nuclear deterrence is bound to break down and bring on the catastrophe that all sensible people dread. They outdo each other in their lurid depiction of the holocaust which all-out nuclear war would undoubtedly be. Few of the most hawkish generals or strategists would deny that such a conflict would be inhumane, unreasonable and immoral, and therefore could never qualify as a just war by any standards. The nuclear pacifists for the most part are unwilling to entertain the thought that the strategy of nuclear deterrence can be prolonged in its effectiveness for an indefinite period by intelligent, restrained, and prudent policy making and decision making on the part of the two superpowers. Instead, they choose to think, almost as a matter of faith, that political and military leaders in Washington and Moscow—and especially in Washington, according to the prognostications of not a few Catholic pacifists—can hardly wait to plunge into the excitement of launching a nuclear war.

Films from *Dr. Strangelove* and *On the Beach* to *Gods of Metal* and

The Day After have not been without effect in arousing fears concerning the irrationality of political leaders and the imminence of nuclear war. Thus, in one of the most remarkable non sequiturs in the history of Western thought, the condemnation of a hypothetical all-out nuclear war as the final travesty of the traditional just war doctrine was transformed into a moral rejection of the strategic policy of deterrence designed to prevent any war from breaking out between the superpowers as a result of either nuclear or conventional aggression. Many pacifists, both nuclear and absolute, harbored a powerful dislike for the just war doctrine, and saw no use for it except as a platform for launching their attack against all nuclear weapons, any use of nuclear weapons, and the entire policy of nuclear deterrence. They did this by forging what appeared to be the interconnected links of an inexorably logical chain: Possession of nuclear weapons will inevitably lead to their use. Any use will inevitably become unlimited and lead to planetary cataclysm, a moral evil second only to the crucifixion of Christ, in Merton's words. Therefore, both their use and even possession are immoral, because deterrence will not work.

One of the pioneer Catholic nuclear pacifists in Britain, Canon F. H. Drinkwater, wrote a scathing denunciation of nuclear deterrence twenty-eight years ago which makes provocative reading today. Reflecting on what has happened in two world wars in this century, he said that there cannot be "the slightest confidence that our governments and generals would exercise any restraint in a real emergency." (It must be admitted that he was writing seven years before the Cuba Missile Crisis and therefore did not have the benefit of that experience.)

He called for a total renunciation, unilateral if necessary, of indiscriminate mass destruction *and all weapons which presuppose it.* Canon Drinkwater was willing to give up nuclear weapons but not conventional defense. In fact, he urged, we ought to keep ourselves armed with "ordinary" weapons and "fight, if need be, to the last ditch (with ordinary weapons) to resist aggression." What is the worst imaginable result if the West should dismantle its nuclear weapons? Communist divisions, he concedes, could roll at will.

> The whole world would be nominally under Moscow, but would not the task be too great for the Communist Party? Isn't even the present Communist empire too big for its own purposes? And all of this is assuming that Russia would take

advantage of the situation to make a military war, which is pure assumption.[12]

Not all English Catholic theologians were persuaded to accept the course of action advocated in Canon Drinkwater's eloquent prose. A few seemed to understand, with an intuition for the practical, that nuclear deterrence had served to stabilize a long-volatile Europe and, without elaborating a sophisticated theory of deterrence, they nevertheless defended it. L. I. McReavey, for example, asserted in 1959 that the NATO powers were not only morally entitled but even morally bound to adopt adequate measures for their defense.

> Since, at least in principle, there can be legitimate uses even for major nuclear explosives, the NATO powers break no moral law in constructing such weapons as deterrents and basing their defense policy on them, or in testing their efficiency (unless the genetic harm caused by such tests outweighs their utility), or in keeping them ready for instant use....[13]

Six years later, the English Jesuit Thomas Corbishley wrote about a moral problem which continues to trouble the American Catholic bishops much more than their European brethren:

> I think we need to give more time to the ethics of bluffing. It *sounds* logical to say "To *threaten* to do something which is immoral is itself immoral." Yet is this quite so certain? Here again perhaps life as we experience it cannot be fitted into the tidy categories of the logician. I personally see nothing *in principle* in the *possession* of immense reserves of power any more than in the possession of great wealth—*dangerous* as we know such possession to be.[14]

The Second Vatican Council came closer to the views of Corbishley than to those of Drinkwater.

The Debate on Nuclear Weapons at Vatican II

When the Second Vatican Council got under way in the fall of 1962, the issue of nuclear arms was not on its agenda; but many

Council Fathers insisted that the Church must come to grips, in the light of Gospel teaching, with this and other contemporary social problems. The debate over nuclear weapons took place at the Third Session in November 1964 and at the Fourth Session in October 1965 in connection with the Schema on the Church in the Modern World. Only about twenty of the two thousand Council Fathers spoke on the issues of war, nuclear weapons, the arms race, conscientious objection and disarmament, but several of them spoke on behalf of other bishops. A wide variety of views was presented, and most of them were couched in terms of just war, conscientious objection, and what may be appropriately called nuclear pacifism. A few of the Council Fathers, including Bernard Cardinal Alfrink, Bishop Jacques Guilhem of Laval, France, Patriarch Maximos IV Saigh of Antioch, Abbot of Downside Christopher Butler, Bishop Gordon Wheeler of Middlesbrough and Bishop Charles Grant of Northampton, wanted the Council to oppose the employment of nuclear weapons in all circumstances even in a just war. Some noted that it was appropriate to distinguish between possession and use of nuclear weapons, but others wished to eliminate any reference from the schema which appeared to condone the possession of nuclear weapons for deterrence. Several Council Fathers noted a contradiction between the tendency to pronounce an absolute ban on modern weapons and a tendency to hold their use lawful under certain circumstances. A few expressed dissatisfaction with the traditional just war doctrine as a mode of moral analysis in the nuclear age. Some called for the building of a more effective international organization to keep the peace and safeguard the rights and security of states, but conceded that this might take a long time, whereas the immediate goal is to avert war. Bishop Luigi Carli of Segni, Italy, reiterated Pius XII's argument that refusing to serve in a just war for reasons of conscience is illicit. He suggested that if Catholic pacifists demand recognition of the rights of conscience as an absolute Christian imperative, because they deem any application of force in political affairs to be evil, then they are serving notice that they will not participate in that aspect of building what Pope John XXIII had called an effective world public authority, because such an authority would require force to support law.

It is possible here to give only a flavor of the debate, not to summarize all of it adequately. Those who opposed and those who refused to condemn nuclear weapons outright for the most part based their stand on the just war doctrine and both groups disagreed on the question whether nuclear weapons could ever be used in a just war. No one questioned the modern papal pronouncements against the indiscriminate use of nuclear weapons upon urban targets, but doubt was expressed that all nuclear weapons are intrinsically indiscriminate. Philip M. Hannan, Auxiliary Bishop of Washington (later Archbishop of New Orleans), took strong exception to the notion in an early text of the schema that nuclear weapons necessarily produce effects greater than we can imagine and control and argued that nuclear weapons whose destructive force is narrowly circumscribed could be licitly used against military objectives in a just war.

The main point to be made here is that the conciliar debate was carried on almost exclusively in terms of just war and pacifism, at least nuclear pacifism. Only a few of the Fathers referred to the strategic policy of nuclear deterrence, and most of those who did criticized or condemned it. Dom Butler said: "No one thinks that the great powers merely *possess* such arms. The fact is that, on both sides of the curtain, there is a system of preparation for the use of these arms—and for their illegimate use in indiscriminate warfare." He wanted even a conditional intention of using them to be considered gravely immoral. The only prelate who had anything favorable to say about deterrence was George Andrew Beck, Archbishop of Liverpool, who spoke at the Third Session in the name of a number of bishops from England and Wales. Any academic theorist of international relations is likely to be impressed with the subtlety, honesty, and competence of what he had to say. He deserves to be quoted at length:

> The Council must, of course, maintain the traditional doctrine that indiscriminate destruction in which the direct killing of the innocent is sought and achieved must be condemned as murder and as something intrinsically evil.... The draft statement does in fact repeat the condemnation of Pope Pius XII and of Pope John XXIII of any weapon whose effect cannot be estimated and controlled. I would suggest, however, that it is important to make clear that this is not a universal condemnation of the use of nuclear weapons. There may well exist objects which in a just war of defense are legitimate targets of nuclear

weapons even of vast force .... If ... legitimate targets for
nuclear weapons may in fact exist, the Council should not
condemn the possession and use of these weapons as essentially and necessarily evil.

Archbishop Beck reminded his colleagues that responsibility for
all decisions concerning peace, war, and nuclear weapons rests with
the leaders of states.

The Council has a duty to express sympathy and consideration for those who carry the heavy burden of this responsibility .... The government of a country has a grave duty to
do everything in its power to promote justice and prevent
war. It must do this by peaceful means to the limit of its
power but it may be true that in certain circumstances peace
can be assured only by what has been called "the balance of
terror," by the threat of the use of nuclear weapons as a
deterrent against unjust aggression. Let us not too readily
condemn those governments which succeed and which
have succeeded in keeping peace, however, tentative, in the
world by the use of such means. Millions of people owe
them gratitude. Let the Council make clear, therefore, that
it does not demand of governments that they decide on a
unilateral abandonment of nuclear weapons because of the
very real and possibly proximate danger that these weapons
may be used in an unjust and immoral way. To turn the
other cheek is a counsel of perfection addressed to individuals, not to governments who have a grave duty to defend
the citizens entrusted to their authority.

At the Fourth Session, the Archbishop of Liverpool was the last
to speak on Chapter 5 of the schema. He began by noting that one of
the greatest obstacles to peace and the establishment of effective
international institutions is the "fragmentation of society" into so
many sovereign states. National sovereignty, class and race war, he
said, along with all forms of political and economic imperialism,
must give way to a wider acceptance of human solidarity. He praised
the schema for dealing with complex problems in a balanced way. It
called for the establishment of an international public authority.
Meanwhile, he added, we must live in the shadow of destruction, for

how long, no one can say. In the absence of international institutions capable of preventing war and insecurity, he thought that the possession of arms exclusively as a deterrent against an adversary equipped with the same weapons cannot be called in itself immoral.

> What must we say, however, of the morality of deterrence? How far may threats of reprisal go? May a state even threaten, by way of deterrence, that indiscriminate destruction of cities and whole regions which our Schema condemns as a crime against God and man? ... Have we yet, even among our experts, worked out the ethics of threat and counter-threat? .... It seems clear that a government which possesses nuclear weapons as a deterrent and threatens to use them as such is in a proximate occasion of grave sin. It may be argued that, until our international institutions become effective, so that a nation can sacrifice its deterrents without grave risks to its freedom and its cultural and spiritual values, this proximate occasion of sin is what moralists call a "necessary occasion" to be accepted as a compromise pending the creation of that balance of trust and discussion which must succeed to the present balance of terror.[15]

In the final text of *Gaudium et spes,* Vatican Council II reasserted the traditional Catholic teaching:

> As long as the danger of war remains and there is no competent and sufficiently powerful authority at the international level, governments cannot be denied the right to legitimate defense once every means of peaceful settlement has been exhausted.[16]

Weapons may not be used involving massive destruction far exceeding the bounds of legitimate defense. The Council reiterated the condemnations of total war and destruction of cities pronounced by Pius XII, John XXIII, and Paul VI; but it stopped short of condemning governmental policies of deterrence based on the possession and deployment of nuclear weapons, and refrained from proscribing every use of nuclear weapons despite the appeals of several bishops to do so. It recognized the possibility that states may amass such weapons with the intention not of carrying out but of dissuading a surprise attack through fear of retaliation.

The defensive strength of any nation is considered to be dependent upon its capacity for immediate retaliation against the adversary. Hence this accumulation of arms, which increases each year, also serves, in a way heretofore unknown, as a deterrent to possible enemy attack. Many regard this state of affairs as the most effective way by which peace of a sort can be maintained between nations at the present time. Whatever be the case with this method of deterrence, men should be convinced that the arms race in which so many countries are engaged is not a safe way to preserve a steady peace. Nor is the so-called balance resulting from this race a sure and authentic peace.[17]

The Council had condemned the arms race as an "utterly treacherous trap for humanity, one which injures the poor to an intolerable degree." The Holy See presented to the UN General Assembly on May 7, 1976, a statement on disarmament in which the nuclear arms race was condemned because there is already a surplus of what is needed for deterrence, and the race introduces elements of instability which could upset the balance of terror. In a passage that has since given rise to considerable controversy among economists, the Holy See linked the issue of nuclear weapons to the world poverty problem:

> Massive budgets allocated to the manufacture and stockpiling of weapons are tantamount to misappropriation of funds by the "managers" of the large nations or favored blocs.
>
> The obvious contradiction between the waste involved in the overproduction of military devices and the extent of unsatisfied vital needs is in itself an act of aggression against those who are the victims of it (in both developing countries and in the marginal and poor elements in rich societies). It is an act of aggression which amounts to a crime, for even when they are not used, by their cost alone, armaments kill the poor by causing them to starve.
>
> The condemnation by the Council, reiterated by the 1974 Synod, is understandable: "The armaments race is an extremely grave affliction for humanity and does intolerable harm to the poor."[18]

With regard to the Church's hope that resources now allocated to armaments could be redirected to the needs of the world's poor, economists have little doubt that the bulk of any budgetary savings to be realized from arms reduction, whether in the rich, industrialized countries or in the more impoverished countries of the Third World, would probably be diverted to other domestic uses rather than to long-range development purposes. In neither group of countries would most of the savings be likely to benefit the least advantaged segments of the population. This is due to the budget process in modern governments and the pent-up demands and claims of many organized groups upon resources which are deemed "scarce" even in the most affluent societies. The fact that the papacy realizes this makes it strive increasingly for reduced costs of international arms rivalry in the hope that at least a portion of the savings can be diverted to socio-economic development.

The Concept of Deterrence

The theory of nuclear deterrence is not understood best when attempts are made to fit it into the procrustean twin beds of just war and pacifism. Yet that is what most Catholics try to do. Deterrence cannot be completely divorced from the two older traditions of pacifist witness as a personal Christian option and the just use of military force for the defense of the state's common internal and external good. But, as noted earlier, deterrence presupposes a distinctive dimension of thought, one which Catholics simply have not elaborated very systematically. Deterrence theory is more congenial to just war theorists than to pacifists who react with considerable emotion against it. Many pacifists might admit grudgingly that deterrence can be said to have worked up to now, if we make the pessimistic assumption that the Soviet Union has ever really posed a threat of actual aggression. But they are unwilling to admit that it might succeed indefinitely and even less willing to favor efforts calculated to increase the rational probability of its continuing effectiveness. The sole response of which they seem capable is an emotional one—to condemn deterrence categorically out of hand. In this way some pacifists apparently prefer to achieve a sense of inner moral purification, while leaving nuclear weapon states to their own satanic works and pomps regardless of the political consequences. Virtually all pacifists—with no notable exceptions—do their best to persuade the public that deterrence cannot and will not continue to work. Their gratuitous thesis that it is bound to break down is exactly the same today—and just as unfounded—as it was twenty-five years ago, when the arsenals of nuclear deterrence were much smaller and less formidable than they are now.

Just war theorists, on the other hand, have a much better instinctive understanding of deterrence because they know much more about how the nation-state system actually works. They sincerely hope that deterrence will succeed indefinitely and that nuclear war will never occur. This is for them more than a purely spiritual hope based upon prayer, although prayer is helpful. Just war theorists would say that the continued effectiveness of deterrence into the indefinite future is feasible on the assumption of intelligent policymaking and diplomacy on the part of governments, particularly of the superpowers. Yet at the same time they insist, quite correctly, that a policy and posture based exclusively on deterrence through the threat of massive retaliation are not by themselves sufficient. There is a heavy moral obligation upon political leaders to make deterrence credible and to assure an operational readiness, in case deterrence breaks down, also to wage war (including nuclear war if aggression cannot be contained by conventional means) in as limited and discriminating manner as possible. Just war theorists are realistic enough to admit that a nuclear deterrent cannot be credible or effective unless the adversary believes that there is an ability and a will to employ nuclear weapons in case the deterrent collapses. They proceed from there to consider what uses of nuclear weapon against what kinds of targets and under what circumstances may be justifiable in light of the requirements of *ius ad bellum* and *ius in bello* proportionality.[19] This author is basically in sympathy with this approach and in full agreement with Paul Ramsey that the traditional moral doctrine of the just war "requires the avoidance of civilian damage as much as possible even while accepting this as in some measure an unavoidable indirect effect."[20] The author also agrees with John Courtney Murray, who insisted more than two decades ago that modern weapons technology cannot be allowed to dictate the entire gamut of military strategy on the basis of expecting a massive, retaliatory response; nuclear war might someday be forced upon us as an unavoidable necessity; we therefore must be ready to control it as fully as possible; the development of more limited, discriminating sets of capabilities, strategies, and operational doctrines, therefore, constitutes both a moral and political-military imperative of the highest order. In sum, if the tragedy of nuclear war, which it is possible for intelligent leadership to avoid, should be thrust upon us, we must be prepared to limit its effects. This requires planning, not thoughtless bombastic rhetoric, in advance.[21]

Murray's reasoning, quite valid within the framework of the traditional just war philosopy, compounds the dilemma which the United States Government and the Catholic Church have faced over nuclear weapons, for it represents an anguished effort by a penetrating Catholic intellect to bridge the chasm between the real political world and the spiritual realm of moral principles—between an irrational strategy which, if successful, would never have to be put to the test and a more rational, limited strategy which might some day have to be applied. Since the juncture of deterrence and just war is the crux of the dilemna, it bears close examination.

Deterrence is "simply the persuasion of one's opponent that the costs and/or risks of a given course of action he might take outweigh its benefits."[22] After World War II, as the effects of Hiroshima and Nagasaki gradually became known, a war fought with nuclear weapons came to be looked upon as the greatest of all possible humanly caused catastrophes. The fear of such a war became the most effective of all deterrents.

Prior to the nuclear age, there was an understanding that aggression could be deterred by making it appear futile, too costly in the expenditure of conventional forces needed to make a particular gain by imposing the aggressor's will upon the government and perhaps the population of the defeated state. War had always involved a threat of *punishment*, but never enough to deter its occurrence for very long. Historians have pointed to some instances in which conventional forces did succeed in deterring war.[23] But conventional deterrence also failed frequently, most notably with the outbreak of World War II, despite rising budgets for armies, tanks, battleships, submarines, carriers, long-range bombers, and a Maginot Line.

The atom bomb wrought a revolution in military thinking. The same technology which rendered nation-states and their populations more vulnerable to destruction than ever before also presented a hitherto unprecedented possibility of deterring war between nuclear weapon powers, not by the brutal use of violence but by posing the threat of it. Handled intelligently, nuclear weapons technology could make the more industrially advanced parts of the world safer from the scourge of war than they had ever been.[24] For the first time in history, the purpose of military force would be to prevent war rather than to fight and win it. In previous wars throughout history, populations had often faced the danger of having widespread pain and suffering inflicted upon them once the protective shield furnished by the state's military forces had been overcome. Nuclear weapons made it feasible to compress all the destructive fury of World War II, and much more, into a few hours. Moreover, whereas the expectation of early victory had often been a powerful motivating factor in the decisions of governments to go to war,[25] the existence of nuclear weapons would henceforth pose the specter of immediate, large-scale catastrophe for both parties, neither of which could expect a meaningful victory in any traditional sense.[26]

The theory of mutual superpower deterrence has often been described as a form of the classical balance of power in modern guise. In actuality, deterrence theory differs widely from the traditional theory, for the latter sometimes prescribed a war policy to preserve or restore a balance. The sole purpose of deterrence is to prevent both nuclear and conventional war among the superpowers and their alliance systems from breaking out. It is conceivable that a balance of power policy might succeed and survive a war designed to restore a disturbed balance (as the European system survived the Napoleonic Wars). But the *raison d'être* of deterrence is utterly destroyed if the kind of war which it is intended to prevent occurs. The only way in which deterrence theory can and should be compared with the balance of power theory is in the nuclear-age imperative. This moral, political, and strategic imperative requires that the superpowers pursue unilateral and bilateral policies of technological development, arms control and reduction negotiations, and political restraint which contribute to international stability in a framework of parity that is conducive to a mutual sense of confidence that their legitimate security interests are safeguarded and that deterrence will continue to work indefinitely until other fundamental changes occur within the international system to alter substantially the security problems of states.

The most urgent task of statesmanship today is to create a climate of international political rationality and to restore the kind of conviction that was beginning to emerge in the early 1970s—a conviction that neither side deems nuclear war thinkable and winnable, and that the two sides can move progressively toward security at lower levels of nuclear armaments than now exist. The worst and potentially most disastrous approach to the problems of war and peace at the present time is to arouse widespread hysterical fear that the world is tottering on the brink of nuclear war, and that deterrence can break down at any moment. The latter approach is not conducive to productive diplomacy.

The secular strategists do not deny that the concept of nuclear deterrence is fraught with paradoxes and perhaps contradictions; indeed, they are the first to admit it. Paradoxes are the inescapable inheritance of the nuclear age. All of the methods proposed for dealing with the frightful problems of nuclear weapons are bound to strike some people as absurd, irrational, or immoral, or all three. These methods include: limited conventional war, limited nuclear war, mutual stable deterrence based upon the maintenance of nuclear parity, anti-missile defense, finite or minimal deterrence at a low nuclear weapons level, general and complete negotiated disarmament, arms control measures to enhance the safety of a nuclear military environment, nuclear pacifism, conventional deterrence, unilateral nuclear disarmament or unilateral total disarmament, preparation for surrender and nonviolent resistance, and absolute and unqualified Christian pacifism. The governments of the superpowers do not have the luxury of abstractly optimal choice which minority groups of critics are free to entertain. Governments operate on the basis of experience and knowledge which they alone possess. Both Washington and Moscow choose to pursue policies of nuclear deterrence, to carry out such military modernization programs as they deem necessary to strengthen deterrence and prevent the other from gaining an exploitable advantage, and to engage in arms control negotiations for the purpose of regulating the costs and dangers of what might otherwise be an unlimited armaments competition. Many current intellectual critics of nuclear deterrence, who have flitted from one fashionable political and social cause to another during the last three decades and have only recently become experts on nuclear war, write as if they have no acquaintance with the thinking of those who originated the theory of nuclear deterrence and those who have subsequently elaborated upon it. Lesser minds with little comprehension of the complexity and subtlety of this theory have often been known to dismiss it out of hand as sheer nonsense.

But let us return to the acknowledged paradoxes of deterrence. Nuclear weapons may well represent the climactic achievement of a Western science and technology which in the seventeenth century became "value-free" so that they could be insulated from inhibiting religious pressures in a Christendom divided and at war with itself. Governments know that nuclear weapons exist. They cannot be uninvented. The nuclear genie unfortunately, despite all sorts of wishful rhetoric to the contrary, can never be put back into the bottle. Therefore governments perceive no choice but to live with nuclear deterrence. Governments instinctively understand, better than their critics, that politics is usually a bundle of paradoxes which seldom lends itself to neat, logical resolutions. Deterrence theory presupposes that the parties to be deterred from war are rational decision-makers. It also presupposes that the deterrent threat, if it is to be effective, must be believable to the other side. Henry Kissinger put it succinctly: "What the potential aggressor believes is more crucial than what is objectively true. Deterrence occurs above all in the minds of men."[27] Thus, the assumption of *rationality* on which a deterrence policy depends comes into conflict with the indispensable requirement of credibility.[28]

Many sensible people who hope that deterrence will succeed think that it would be the height of irrationality and immorality to carry out the threat of extreme nuclear punishment against an aggressor who violates the deterrent shield. In effect, each super-power says to the other: "I assume that you are sufficiently rational to wish to avoid nuclear war and therefore to be deterred by my threat. But if you believe that I am so rational as to fear nuclear war more than anything else, including your aggression against my fundamental interests (e.g., in Western Europe), then you might be tempted to undertake such aggression. I want you, therefore, to know that despite my own rationality which inhibits me from violating *your* deterrent in regard to *your* vital interests, I am sufficiently irrational where *my* vital interests are concerned to respond to your unjust aggression by initiating nuclear war if necessary, even though both you and I know that we cannot foresee the consequences of such a response. Ponder these things carefully and act with appropriate circumspection when I tell you that you are placing in jeopardy my vital and irreducible interests."

Strategic analysts have always recognized the tension that exists between deterrence and defense. More than two decades ago, Glenn Snyder clearly distinguished between a strategy of deterrence designed to dissuade the adversary from taking military action by confronting him with unacceptable risks and a defense strategy to be executed if the deterrent should fail. Snyder pointed out that the forces required for effective deterrence may not be the same as those required for effective defense. Deterrence, he said, is a peacetime objective, while defense is a matter of planning the way in which a war should be conducted. Government policymakers must simultaneously consider the best ways of reducing the probability of war and of limiting its scope if it should break out. These are two different sets of ends and they require different sets of means. Threatening a nuclear response against a major Soviet ground attack in Western Europe, therefore, may be a highly rational deterrent strategy for NATO, even if carrying out the threat might prove to be an irrational and undesirable defensive strategy:

> If we think the probability of attack is low enough, we may decide to continue relying on nuclear deterrence primarily, even though it does not provide a rational means of defense. In other words, we might count on the Soviet uncertainties about whether or not nuclear retaliation is rational for us, and about how rational we are, to inhibit the Soviets from attacking in the face of the possible damage they *know* they would suffer if they guessed wrong....Tactical nuclear weapons in the hands of NATO forces in Europe have considerable deterrent value because they increase the enemy's cost expectation beyond what it would be if these forces were equipped only with conventional weapons.[29]

When Snyder wrote those words in 1961, the strategic context was significantly different from what it is today, because at that time the United States possessed nuclear superiority. Yet his main point remains quite valid. The reasonable distinction between deterrence and defense has not been destroyed by the fact that the United States has lost nuclear superiority. Both Soviet and U.S. governments have engaged in rhetoric (either steadily in Soviet military literature since 1963 or in U.S. governmental pronouncements since the late 1970s) suggesting that nuclear war can be waged, limited, and won. It is highly doubtful, however, whether either government takes such rhetoric seriously or regards it as more than serving political and psychological purposes or that either expects the failure of the strategic policies of deterrence on which they have expended so significant a portion of their resources. Soviet military strategists, we might say, began "whistling their way past the nuclear graveyard" two decades ago. Their American counterparts have begun to emulate them only in recent years. The governments of the principal weapons states are profoundly committed to policies of deterrence. They have no doubt that each will do whatever it considers necessary to maintain a technologically up-to-date deterrent. In this respect they are both quite correct.

Antideterrent critics are so preoccupied with their own negative forensics that they are for all practical purposes incapable of appreciating deterrence as a political reality. They do not understand that the ability of the superpowers to dissuade a direct nuclear or conventional attack upon each other has become an "extended deterrent" to protect their alliances in Europe, thereby putting an end to that region's historical legacy of bloodshed. Virtually all twenty-two members of NATO and the Warsaw Pact had taken part in both world wars, suffering altogether scores of millions of casualties. Since 1945, there has been no international war in Europe, if we except the Soviet action in Hungary in 1956, the Warsaw Pact invasion of Czechoslovakia in 1968, and the Greek-Turkish dispute over Cyprus. Without the nuclear stabilizer, there is good reason to think that Europe would have experienced at least one more tragic world war since 1945, with millions of casualties, perhaps triggered by an uprising in Eastern Europe against Soviet oppression or uncontrollable tensions over the division of Germany.

Governments in modern states are conservative bureaucratic structures. Nuclear weapons technology has made the leaders of major power governments more cautious than ever before about resorting to the use of force, especially when it carries the danger of their becoming directly embroiled with each other. It cannot be denied that the military atom presents a frightful specter to people everywhere and induces a growing anxiety in thoughtful persons, while the great majority try to put it out of their mind in a psychological defense-avoidance reaction. Nevertheless, there are compelling reasons to think that none of the avowedly nuclear weapon powers wants nuclear war. Their policymakers "believe in" deterrence and do not look upon general disarmament as the only or necessarily the best alternative to nuclear war.[30] It is not possible for governmental policymakers to conceive of any rational political or military objective worth running the unpredictable risks of initiating a nuclear war. The motivation of either side to launch a surprise nuclear attack against the other—a possibility that has been the subject of frequent speculation in the public forum and the mass media in the last five years—remains in actuality infinitesimally low.

Military theoreticians and strategic analysts responsible for monitoring national security requirements are obliged to "think about the unthinkable" in order to keep it that way. That is what the society pays them to do: to worry about worst-case scenarios and then to work gradually, not frantically, to reduce the credibility of those scenarios by introducing posture modifications into the national defense designed to remove from the minds of their adversary counterparts any temptation to exploit a military vulnerability by stepping up intimidative political pressure.

It is clear from the foregoing discussion of deterrence that the concept is derived from a cost-gain analysis which presupposes a certain *homo oeconomicus* rationality. Many of the American strategists who elaborated the idea of deterrence in the 1950s were civilians with some background in economics. The theorists who developed the notion of deterrence were not inhuman monsters. They had seen and deeply abhorred the suffering, death, and destructiveness of World War II, undoubtedly the most just war of modern times in terms of the systemic values at stake. In some respects, deterrence theorists may be more humane than many rulers throughout history who waged what they sincerely believed to be just wars.

Deterrence theorists noted that the problem of war has never been solved throughout thousands of years of history. It has not been brought under control, much less eliminated, by religious conversion, homiletic exhortation, the conventional balance of power, education, social engineering by behavioral scientists, or utopian schemes for world government and complete disarmament. Deterrence strategists said, in effect, that since the international system could not create an effective Hobbesian sovereign to hold the world's governments in awe, perhaps the power of the atom would be able to serve as a substitute capable of imposing limits upon them and compelling them to exhibit restraint in dealing with one another, even to the point of becoming sensitive to the legitimate security apprehensions of other nuclear-armed states.

Granted, deterrence is a mechanistic and not a spiritual approach to the problem. It is designed to constrain war by posing a threat and causing fear in the lower part of human nature, not by appealing to the nobler, higher instincts in human beings. This concept is not inconsistent with the Petrine, Pauline, and patristic view of the purpose for which governing power was instituted. Fear is often irrational, especially fear of that which need not be feared. But some things ought to be feared, and the fear of those things is quite rational. Indeed, that fear is the beginning of wisdom. The peace movement is quite right to express fear over the possible consequences of nuclear war. This is a highly rational fear. But anti-nuclear demonstrators have only very recently become aware of data that were available to government policymakers, scientists, strategic analysts, and the military more than three decades ago. Governments have had to live with the facts of nuclear weapons for a long time. The strategy of deterrence has always rested on the assumption that the decision-making processes of modern bureaucratic governments, as analyzed by Max Weber and most contemporary political scientists, are essentially rational and conservative—both in free market and Marxist socialist systems, since both types place a premium upon cost-gain analysis. Those who believe that deterrence is bound to fail lean toward the view that political decision-making processes are basically irrational. Yet they apparently expect governments which are, in their view, incapable of acting rationally out of a combination of psychological fear and a cost-gain analysis of self-interest to act rationally out of altruistic, self-abnegating motives by renouncing power and pursuing goals which virtually all leading political scientists regard as quite impracticable in the present ideologically and politically divided international system.

A strategic policy of nuclear deterrence obviously cannot compel a state to do what it does not want to do, nor can it deter all or even most forms of undesirable international behavior. It was never intended to do so, and it would be ridiculous to expect it to.[31] Strategists realized in the 1950s that the Dulles doctrine of massive retaliation could not be counted upon for long to deter nonnuclear wars or insurgencies in Asia, Africa, and Latin America, nor could it alter the reality of Soviet control of Eastern Europe. Deterrence did not prevent the Soviet Union from exercising brutal repressive power in Hungary (1956), Czechoslovakia (1968), and Poland (1981–82); from building the Berlin Wall (1961); from turning Cuba into a satellite state (1962); from penetrating the Arab world with massive arms shipments since 1955; from employing Soviet arms and Cuban proxy forces to extend Soviet strategic influence into Angola, the Horn of Africa, and Southern Yemen since the mid-1970s; from invading Afghanistan in late 1979; or from acquiring leverage in Central America in recent years. It did not deter the Korean War, or the Vietnam War, or the recurring Arab-Israeli wars. Nor did it prevent the Iranians from seizing the American Embassy in Teheran in 1979. What good is deterrence, then? one may ask. The answer is simple: It has been a factor of major significance, and perhaps, as many knowledgeable analysts think though they cannot prove it, the decisive factor, in discouraging war between the superpowers and among the warprone Great Powers of Europe. That is no mean achievement.

Over the course of the last three or more decades, many skeptics have said that history shows no instance of an effective weapon ever having been invented which was not sooner or later used on a large scale in war. Frequent note has been taken of the fact that the United States did use two atomic bombs against Japanese cities near the end of World War II, and people often ask why it should not be expected to use them again. Deterrence strategists point out in rebuttal that the United States government might well have decided not to bomb Hiroshima and Nagasaki if it had known that Japan possessed an equivalent capability to deliver atomic bombs on San Francisco and Los Angeles. Japan lacked a deterrent force.* This author has pointed out elsewhere that, given the projected estimates of American and Japanese casualties that would result from a planned invasion of the islands, a case can perhaps be made for the atomic bombings on the grounds of proportionality; but they did constitute

---

* Deterrence theorists also note that Germany possessed large stores of chemical weapons which were never used in World War II, probably because President Roosevelt stated clearly that the United States would not resort to the use of such weapons unless they were first used by an enemy.[32]

a "gross violation of the principle of discrimination by any standard of allowable collateral damage."[33]

With the growth of nuclear arsenals first in the United States and soon afterwards in the Soviet Union, strategists became increasingly convinced of the effectiveness of mutual nuclear deterrence. Those strategists have been certain that the continued success of deterrence strategy depends upon a subtle and complex combination of political, military, and psychological factors referred to by the term "credibility." War is deterred by the fear that nuclear weapons will actually be employed, not by mutual assurances and beliefs that they will never be used if war breaks out. It is this requirement of making and keeping the nuclear deterrent credible and operational that has given rise to a paradox which baffles many strategists, no less than moral theologians and bishops.

For the better part of two decades, the official strategic philosophy which informed U.S. deterrence doctrine, force-posture planning, and arms control positions in negotiations with the Soviet Union had been based on the McNamara concept of Assured Destruction. This concept in turn rested on the premise that deterrence would succeed if the United States retained a survivable capability to inflict upon the adversary, following his nuclear first strike, an "unacceptable level of damage in retaliation"—originally defined as the destruction of 20 to 25 percent of the population and 50 percent of the industrial and economic capacity of the USSR.[34] This threat was thought to be quite sufficient to give an opponent "the strongest imaginable incentive" to refrain from launching a surprise attack on the United States with nuclear weapons. Europe was protected by the presence of thousands of U.S. tactical nuclear weapons assigned to NATO in the European region. If the Soviet Union tried to attack only Western Europe but not the United States, its forces were bound to encounter NATO nuclear capabilities. It was assumed that once the firebreak between conventional and nuclear hostilities had been crossed, there would be a great danger that the war would escalate to the strategic nuclear level. Realizing this, the Soviet leaders, who are generally regarded as extremely cautious about placing their homeland at risk, would not contemplate even limited aggression in Europe.

The Europeans were quite happy to live under the American nuclear umbrella as long as the United States enjoyed a reputation for possessing nuclear superiority. When the United States started stationing tactical nuclear weapons in Europe, the first people to welcome them were the Dutch, who originally looked upon them as a strengthener of deterrence, but who later took the lead in organizing the antinuclear movement in 1977, when the nuclear balance seemed to be tilting toward the USSR. On both sides of the Atlantic, voices roundly condemning the strategy of assured destruction could be heard from the mid-1950s until the late 1970s because a hypothetical future action was envisaged which appeared irrational, inhuman, absurd, and monstrous. Such action deserved to be rejected on moral, humanitarian, political, and military grounds. Such thoughts made many people uncomfortable in their consciences when they reflected on it, but they felt better when they remembered that as long as the strategy of deterrence kept nuclear war unthinkable, they really did not have to consider the consequences of its failure.

During the SALT process, U.S. policymakers sought to "educate" Soviet planners to accept the predominant American view concerning deterrence, strategic stability, and arms control, under which each side would refrain from deploying forces that seriously threaten the other's retaliatory capability. In contrast, Soviet military literature repudiated the assured destruction doctrine. That literature emphasized the crucial importance of a favorable "correlation of forces" (which may be taken to mean strategic superiority) and of the preemptive nuclear strike if nuclear war should ever appear to be inevitable and imminent. Soviet writers stressed the need to be prepared to wage, win, survive, and recover from such a war if it should occur. The notion of trying to keep a nuclear war limited has not loomed large in Soviet thinking, but there has been a preference for counterforce over countercity strategy. This is not to imply that the Soviet Union is any less interested in deterring nuclear war, or any more interested in starting one, than the United States. But the approaches of the two superpowers to deterrence—at least until a few years ago—have been quite different.[35]

The case can be made that Soviet strategic philosophy has produced a more pronounced effect upon the thinking of U.S. officials than vice versa. Military considerations more than moral ones led to the change. The steady accumulation of Soviet strategic forces raised at least the theoretical possibility that U.S. ICBMs, which constituted the most important leg of the strategic triad of land-based missiles, sea-based missiles and bombers, were becoming 80 or 90 percent vulnerable to a surprise first strike. Some analysts felt compelled to suggest "launch on warning" or "launch under attack/assessment."[36] Furthermore, there had long been a certain amount of uneasiness in high places over the strategies of massive retaliation and assured destruction. As early as 1961, President Kennedy had sought an alternative "between holocaust and surrender" and called for a "flexible response" strategy in NATO (much to the distress of West European, especially West German, defense planners who firmly believed in strategic and nuclear deterrence). The Joint Chiefs of Staff were always reluctant to make the assured-destruction doctrine the exclusive basis for U.S. operational planning. In 1974, Defense Secretary James Schlesinger called for a strategy of selective targeting and limited nuclear options. This tendency led to a fundamental review of U.S. targeting policy by the Carter administration in 1977 and culminated in the announcement of a strategic doctrine known as countervailing strategy, embodied in Presidential Directive 59 in August 1980.[37]

Walter Slocombe, former deputy undersecretary of defense for policy planning, has argued in his explanation of the countervailing strategy that the fundamental U.S. objective of deterring war has remained unchanged: Countervailing strategy is neither a new doctrine nor a radical departure from previous U.S. strategic doctrine, but only an evolutionary refinement and recodification of it. It is not assumed that the United States can either win a nuclear war or keep it limited. The strategy's sole purpose is to broaden the spectrum of U.S. capabilities (vis-a-vis the Soviet military buildup) in order to restrain a wider range of threats than could be restrained previously, including Soviet nuclear attacks on sets of targets smaller than a massive strategic strike would entail.[38] In a passage particularly relevant to a moral evaluation of the strategy, Slocombe wrote:

> The United States has never—at least since significant numbers of nuclear weapons became available—had a doctrine based simply and solely on reflexive, massive attacks on Soviet cities and population. Much of the current debate over our strategic nuclear forces has been distorted by the misconception that we have, in the past, been following such a doctrine. Though it is true that strategic forces programming was often discussed in terms of ability to destroy

urban/industrial targets, previous administrations, going back almost two decades, recognized the inadequacy of a strategic targeting doctrine—a plan for use of weapons if deterrence failed—that would give us too narrow a range of employment options.... The unquestioned attainment of strategic parity by the Soviet Union has underscored what was clear long before—that a policy based only on massive retaliation against Soviet cities is an inadequate deterrent for the full spectrum of potential Soviet aggressions.[39]

There can be little doubt that the increasingly strident rhetoric concerning the possibility of fighting, limiting, and winning nuclear war, whether short or protracted, has definitely frightened the moral critics of U.S. defense and deterrence policy, perhaps even more than it has frightened Soviet military and political leaders. That rhetoric began in the Carter administration and developed to a higher pitch in the Reagan administration, contributing on both sides of the Atlantic to the growth of an emotional reaction to all nuclear deterrence strategies and defense buildups or modernization programs of any kind. Catholic observers became filled with alarm over the "gradual acceptance of the possibility of war" and the slide "toward preparation for actual use of nuclear weapons."[40] Once again we were reminded that we have never developed a technology we have not used and that it is naive to hope that the horror of nuclear weapons has made nuclear war unthinkable. Weapons have been designed for accurate targeting and there is now serious talk of a winnable nuclear war, even though nothing can be gained or preserved commensurate with the expected loss. Weapons threaten but cannot defend. There are no military solutions. Not madmen but leaders who could pass any sanity test will press the button.[41] Whereas the older strategy had been condemned for envisaging an unlimited nuclear war which was immoral because unthinkable, the newer strategy is criticized for envisaging the possibility of a limited nuclear war which allegedly makes war more thinkable and thus more likely to occur.

Deterrence and Arms Control

Both superpowers are under a heavy obligation to seek a stable international strategic equilibrium and a political climate in which each can feel sufficiently secure to begin to move toward lower levels of nuclear arms, confident that such a move will itself increase the sense of security rather than exacerbate fears. Governments that signed the Nuclear Nonproliferation Treaty did so with the formal expectation embodied in Article VI of that treaty, that all parties would "pursue negotiations in good faith on effective measures relating to cessation of the nuclear arms race at an early date and to nuclear disarmament."[42] Equilibrium and arms control and reductions have been sought through unilateral arms procurement policies and through bilateral or multilateral arms agreements such as the Strategic Arms Limitation Talks (SALT), the Strategic Arms Reduction Talks (START), negotiations to limit Intermediate-range Nuclear Forces (INF) in Europe, the Mutual and Balance Force Reduction (MBFR) talks, and the United Nations Committee on Disarmament. Thus far in the nuclear age, a total of eighteen international agreements (of which fourteen pertain to nuclear weapons) have been negotiated. The most important of these have been the Limited Test Ban Treaty (1963), the Outer Space Treaty (1967), the Nonproliferation Treaty (1968), the SALT I Anti-Ballistic Missile (ABM) Treaty and Interim Agreement on Strategic Offensive Arms (1972), and the SALT II Treaty (1979). The latter was not ratified by the United States, but since early 1980, both the Carter and Reagan administrations have indicated that the United States would abide by its terms as long as the Soviet Union appeared to be exercising similar restraint.[43] Questions were being raised throughout 1983 as to whether the Soviet Union had recently departed from the provisions of the SALT II accords by testing two new intercontinental missiles (only one test is permitted) and by encoding test data in a way that impedes verification of compliance.[44]

Few will deny that the achievements of arms control negotiations to date have been modest indeed or even unimpressive. For years, critics have been contending that many of the agreements reached by the superpowers have been purely cosmetic, calculated to project only an illusion of progress. Some have charged that arms control negotiations have actually stimulated the arms race in certain respects while imposing no serious restrictions upon any type of new armaments which the superpowers were really determined to acquire. A minority of U.S. Catholic bishops opposed the SALT II accords because in their view it permitted the United States to build too many new nuclear weapons.[45]

All through the 1970s, the U.S. Catholic bishops had been moving gradually toward a stronger antinuclear stand. Their 1976 statement said that acts of war deliberately aimed against innocent noncombatants are gravely wrong, and no one may participate in such an act:

> No member of the armed forces, above all no Christians who bear arms as "agents of security and freedom," can rightfully carry out orders or policies requiring direct force against noncombatants.
>
> With respect to nuclear weapons, at least those with massive destructive capability, the first imperative is to prevent their use. As possessors of a vast nuclear arsenal, we must also be aware that not only is it wrong to attack civilian populations but it is also wrong to threaten to attack them as part of a strategy of deterrence.[46]

On September 9, 1979, John Cardinal Krol, speaking on behalf of the United States Catholic Conference in support of SALT II ratification, delivered a statement before the Senate Foreign Relations Committee which in its explicitness went considerably beyond the Vatican Council's *Gaudium et spes* by condemning *any* use of strategic nuclear weapons (not only use against population centers) and making the continued moral toleration of the possession of nuclear weapons for deterrence contingent upon progress in negotiations for nuclear arms reduction:

> The moral judgment of this statement is that not only the use of strategic nuclear weapons, but also the declared intent to use them involved in our deterrence policy is wrong. This explains the Catholic dissatisfaction with nuclear deterrence and the urgency of the Catholic demand that the nuclear arms race be reversed. It is of the utmost importance that negotiations proceed to meaningful and continuing reductions in nuclear stockpiles, and eventually, to the phasing out altogether of nuclear deterrence, and the threat of mutual-assured destruction.
>
> As long as there is hope of this occurring, Catholic moral teaching is willing, while negotiations proceed, to tolerate the possession of nuclear weapons for deterrence as the lesser of two evils. If that hope were to disappear, the

moral attitude of the Catholic Church would almost certainly have to shift to one of uncompromising condemnation of both use and possession of such weapons.[47]

Cardinal Krol, it should be noted, was speaking in the context of
SALT II, which pertained only to strategic nuclear weapons, not to
the entire range of nuclear weapons which includes intermediate
and medium-range weapons and tactical or battlefield weapons. His
statement must also be considered against the background of what
was then widely assumed to be U.S. strategy—the assured destruction of a substantial portion of an aggressor nation's population and
economic base. One cannot infer, therefore, that he was passing a
contingent moral judgment upon the use and possession of all
nuclear weapons. But so far as strategic weapons and the threat of
mutual-assured destruction were concerned, Krol definitely
appeared to be issuing a veritable ultimatum: "Make progress toward
disarmament or else the American Catholic bishops will withdraw
their moral approval of nuclear deterrence." It was not clear to whom
the ultimatum was being issued. Was it to the United States government only? Successful negotiation, of course, depends upon decisions taken by two sides, not just one, and cannot be subjected to
mandates or deadlines. Superpower negotiations in the area of
nuclear weapons are extremely complex. The problem was further
complicated within a few months of Cardinal Krol's testimony by the
Soviet invasion of Afghanistan and again two years later because of
the Soviet-backed crackdown on Solidarity in Poland, in December
1981.

Not all the Cardinals, however, were willing to emphasize the
negative aspects of nuclear deterrence. Terence Cardinal Cooke,
who before his death in October 1983 was the Military Vicar for
Catholics in the United States, issued a statement in December 1981
which stressed the right and duty of the government to protect its
people against unjust aggression:

> This means that it is legitimate to develop and maintain
> weapons systems to try to prevent war by "deterring"
> another nation from attacking.... Popes have also pointed
> out that a nation may have the obligation to protect other
> nations.... Although the church urges nations to design
> better ways—ideally, nonviolent ways—of maintaining

peace, it recognizes that as long as we have good reason to believe that another nation would be tempted to attack us if we could not retaliate, we have the right to *deter* attack by making it clear that we *could* retaliate. In very simple terms, this is the "strategy of deterrence" we hear so much about. It is not a desirable strategy. It can be terribly dangerous. Government leaders and peoples of all nations have a grave moral obligation to come up with alternatives. But as long as our nation is sincerely trying to work with other nations to find a better way, the church considers the strategy of nuclear deterrence morally tolerable; not satisfactory, but tolerable. As a matter of fact, millions of people may be alive in the world today precisely because government leaders in various nations know that if they attacked other nations, at least on a large scale, they, themselves, could suffer tremendous losses of human life or even be destroyed.[48]

When Pope John Paul II sent a message on disarmament to the United Nations in June 1982, his language seemed to constitute a judgment on the validity of deterrence that embodied elements of the views of both cardinals. However, where they regarded deterrence as "morally tolerable," the pope called it "morally acceptable":

In current conditions "deterrence" based on balance, certainly not as an end in itself but as a step on the way toward a progressive disarmament, may still be judged morally acceptable. Nonetheless in order to ensure peace, it is indispensable not to be satisfied with this minimum which is always susceptible to the real danger of explosion.[49]

Pope John Paul has frequently expressed abhorrence at the thought of nuclear war, condemned the wastefulness of the arms race, and called for nuclear disarmament at the United Nations, at Hiroshima, at Coventry Cathedral in England, and in his annual World Day of Peace messages. But following his predecessors and the Vatican Council, he has always insisted that the disarmament process be reciprocal and safeguarded. On New Year's Day 1983, he made some pointed remarks which appeared to be directed at the growing popular demand for arms restraint by the West alone:

Peace cannot be built by some without the others.... It

demands that all the parties work in common, to progress in common on the path of peace. It is therefore difficult to imagine how the problem of peace in the world can be resolved in a unilateral manner, without the participation and the concrete commitment of all .... In the search for peace, the problem of disarmament occupies as important position, and the desire to see the dialogue for this objective arrive at concrete results is more than legitimate. But like the dialogue the demand for the progressive reduction of armaments, nuclear or conventional, must be addressed simultaneously to all parties involved. The powers that confront each other must be able to proceed together through the various states of disarmament and commit themselves to each stage in equal measure.[50]

Neither the Second Vatican Concil nor any pope in the nuclear age ever said anything which would appear to commit the Catholic Church to unilateral nuclear disarmament, even if there should be no satisfactory progress in East-West arms negotiations. As John Cardinal Krol declared at an interfaith rally to express opposition to the arms race, held in Philadelphia in March 1982, "We advocate disarmament—not unilateral but reciprocal or collective disarmament, proceeding at an equal pace, according to agreement and backed up by authentic and workable safeguards."[51] So long as this remains the official teaching of the Church, it will not be possible for any Catholic to say that the Church regards the possession of nuclear deterrent forces by governments to be immoral.

4

Changing Bishops

in a

Changing American Catholic Church

In order to place the pastoral letter of the U.S. Catholic bishops on war, peace, and nuclear weapons in a proper historical perspective, one must say something about the problem of maintaining the continuity of Catholic doctrine and moral teaching in a changing environment. The Catholic Church has always believed that neither her inner spiritual essence nor her fundamental teachings in the areas of faith and morals can undergo change. Catholic popes, bishops, priests, theologians, historians, and others have long boasted that one of the splendors of the Roman Catholic Church through all the centuries has been the immutability and continuity of her fundamental religious message, even though her doctrine has undergone constant evolutionary development in the light of Christian experience.[1] The Church of unchanging doctrine and belief, however, exists in a world of cultural, social, and national environments which are in constant flux. Thus in its external appearances and in her teachings on the relations between itself and the temporal order, change is inevitable.

There is no need to belabor the obvious point that since the Second Vatican Council (1962–1965) the Catholic Church, which had seemed so fixed in its post-Council-of-Trent teaching and organizational form as to be almost oblivious to the passage of historical time, has undergone profound changes in liturgy, theological emphases, organizational style, and political-social outlook. Curiously enough, the experience of the Catholic Church in America produced a very significant impact upon the

Vatican Council. This is curious because the American Catholic Church had long been looked upon by many progressive European Catholics as extremely conservative in certain matters and by conservative European Catholics as dangerously liberal in others. Nevertheless, in several respects Vatican II witnessed the modernization of the Church according to an American model.

The Catholic Church in America

All churches in America were immigrant churches, but most of the early settlements were Protestant or dissident. Despite early Catholic settlements in Maryland, Florida, and elsewhere, the American colonial experiment was widely regarded in Catholic Europe as a Protestant enterprise. During the war for independence, Catholics in the colonies generally favored separation from Protestant England. In the early nineteenth century, especially in the 1840s, Irish Catholic immigrants in urban areas encountered nativist, "Know-Nothing" movements. Catholics who owed their loyalty to Rome had to go out of their way to prove that they were just as good citizens as others. Most conservative European Catholics, who lived under rather politically backward monarchical regimes, suspected the American democratic culture of being essentially Protestant and prayed that American Catholics might be able to preserve their faith against the threats posed by a hostile environment. Many American Catholics, especially in the midwestern German settlements and the Irish ghettos in Eastern cities, thought and prayed likewise.

The Americanist Heresy

To Europeans accustomed to the legal establishment of religion, the American notion of separation of Church and State seemed to be a dangerous principle, something to be grudgingly tolerated in a religiously pluralist country but never to be held forth as an ideal arrangement. Toward the latter part of the nineteenth century, Archbishop John Ireland of St. Paul became a leading exponent of the Americanist movement which sought to move the Catholic Church away from isolation and into a closer, more positive relationship with the political, social, and cultural climate of American democracy. Rome, of course, had long harbored misgivings over liberal political tendencies among Catholics, fearing—not without reason—a dilution of the orthodox theological tradition of the Church. In 1864, Pope Pius IX, declaring that the Successor of Peter neither "can nor should reconcile himself with progress, liberalism and modern civilization," had published a *Syllabus of Errors* concerning trends of thought unfavorable or hostile to Catholic faith. Some of its content, in spite of vague wording, could be interpreted as having been aimed at science, democracy and the idea of a "free Church in a free State." This was precisely what Archbishop Ireland later preached—a free, independent Church in a democratic state, not united with the state as it often was in Europe. Holding that the Church flourished best where it was politically unfettered and could rely solely on its inner spiritual power to grow in an atmosphere of freedom, he believed deeply in the separation of Church and State, and in the value of the Church as educator of law-abiding citizens, more valuable than armies and navies, courts and legislatures. As a child of the American Enlightenment, he also believed that the whole world was moving rapidly toward political and social conditions with which Americans had been blessed. Even after Pope Leo XIII condemned theological Americanism in 1899, in the letter *Testem benevolentiae*, warning against the notion that the Church, in order to attract dissenters, ought to relax its ancient vigor and show indulgence to modern theories in matters of both discipline and doctrines which are part of the deposit of faith, Ireland repudiated theological Americanism but continued to espouse the political brand.[2]

In the years before and after World War I, the American Catholic Church was determined to be loyal both to Rome and to the American political experiment. According to historian Edward R. Kantowicz, "a generation of American-born but Roman-trained bishops came to power in the largest urban dioceses of the United States," bishops who realized that the papal pronouncements mentioned above had left American Catholics in an awkward position—"too Roman for the native Protestants and too American for Rome." The bishops, said Kantowicz, charted a course between Scylla and Charybdis calculated to make their faithful followers feel fully Catholic and fully American. While avoiding theological and philosophical innovation, for which they were not particularly suited in any event, and reaffirming their loyal adherence to the doctrinal infallibility of the Bishop of Rome which had been authoritatively proclaimed by the Vatican Council of 1870, they "plunged headfirst into symbolic and emotional bursts of American patriotism on issues they knew would not irritate Rome."[3] The defeat of Al Smith, Catholic candidate for President in 1928, led many Catholics to conclude that they had not yet been fully integrated into the American political system, even though religion was not the only issue in that election. (Smith was a "wet," a big-city Tammany machine politician with an unmistakable "Brooklyn accent," and a liberal Democrat whose party depended heavily on the votes of the dry, rural, conservative South.) The anti-Catholic whispering campaign, however, lingered in the memory of Catholics, who thereafter adopted a low profile in national politics for many years. Not until the election of John F. Kennedy in 1960 did Catholics relax in the knowledge that they had "fully arrived" on the American political scene.

American Catholics and War

John Tracy Ellis has suggested that American Catholics throughout most of their history have compensated for their religious allegiance to the Holy Father (long a "foreign potentate" in the eyes of many Protestant fellow citizens down through the pontificate of Pope Pius XII) and have sought to demonstrate their domestic political loyalty by adopting super-patriotic positions of support for the United States in all of its wars. Archbishop John Carroll of Baltimore set the pattern for subsequent episcopal admonitions that Catholics should support the declarations of war by a legitimately constituted government even when their private views were at variance with them. In the war against Catholic Mexico in 1846 and against Catholic Spain in 1898, the bishops and their diocesan newspapers backed the United States, although James Cardinal Gibbons of New York and Archbishop Ireland of St. Paul were personally sympathetic toward Spain. Catholic support for the U.S. course was even stronger in World War I, except for Irish-Americans who did not want to fight on "the English side" and German-Americans who did not approve the war against the fatherland.[4]

In World War II there were very few American conscientious objectors during the course of a conflict which, in its anti-Hitler, anti-Nazi dimension was widely regarded by Catholics and other Americans not only as a just war, but almost as a kind of modern crusade. The number of Catholic C.O.s rose only slightly during the Korean War. The assumption endured that for all practical purposes, a Catholic could not be a conscientious objector.

The Vietnam War
and Selective Conscientious
Objection

In the post-Kennedy years, Catholics no longer had to be super-patriots. The number of Catholics inclined toward pacifism and con-scientious objection increased markedly during the Vietnam War, and the burgeoning debate which began at that time was instructive. Whenever the U.S. Congress has legislated military conscription, it has made provision for conscientious objectors. During the Civil War and World War I, it granted exemption to the historic "peace churches" such as the Quakers, Mennonites, and Brethren. The Catholic Church and the larger Protestant churches were never regarded as "peace churches" in the traditional sense. The Burke-Wadsworth Act of 1940 instituted universal military training, and the Selective Service Act of 1967 granted exemption to any person "who by reason of religious training and belief is conscientiously opposed to participation in war in any form." The term "religious training and belief" did not include "essentially political, sociological or philosophical views, or a merely personal code."

As domestic opposition to U.S. involvement in the Vietnam conflict mounted after the 1964 Gulf of Tonkin incident, a number of academicians and seminarians began to advocate the principle of selective con-scientious objection to particular wars. Within three years, the United Presbyterian Church, the American Baptist Church, the General Board of the National Council of Churches, the General Synod of the United Church of Christ, and the World Council of Churches had all gone on record in favor of selective objection, as did the Synagogue Council of America representing the Orthodox, Conservative, and Reform branches of Judaism in the United States.[5] While making it clear that they were asserting a moral rather than a legal right, they requested that the Congress amend the Selective Service Act to provide for alternative modes of service for selective objectors.

The question was whether the Catholic Church in the United States would pursue a similar path. As we have seen, in December 1956, Pope Pius XII, indignant over the brutal Soviet suppression of the Hungarian uprising, had seemed to place strict limits on the moral rights of the personal conscience of the Catholic in constitutional democratic states.[6] Nine years later, the Second Vatican Council said that "it seems right that laws make humane provision for the case of those who for reasons of conscience refuse to bear arms, provided, however, that they accept some form of service to the human community."[7] Since the Council made no specific reference to the issue of the selective conscientous objector (SCO), an issue just beginning to surface in public debate, it was taken for granted that the foregoing statement pertained to those who opposed all wars. But to the extent that the Council endorsed the idea that a Catholic could be a general conscientious objector, without appending Pope Pius XII's limiting condition, it appeared at first glance to be moving away from his position.

The Council, however, while calling for legal recognition of the rights of the individual conscience, did not put pacifism on a doctrinal par with the just war theory in Catholic teaching. It praised those who renounce the use of force in the vindication of their rights and who resort to nonviolent methods of defense which are available to weaker parties, provided that this can be done without injury to the rights and duties of the larger community. The Council also praised those who serve in the armed forces and who regard themselves as agents of security and freedom on behalf of their people. Such persons, declared the Council Fathers, make a genuine contribution to the establishment of peace.

The problem for U.S. Catholics was that they were no more agreed than other Americans over the politics of the war in Southeast Asia, despite the fact that many of them were sympathetic to the desire of South Vietnamese Catholics to resist a takeover by the Communist North. The decision as to whether a particular war is just or unjust presupposes several prior judgments which are essentially political. It is impossible to determine whether the conditions for a just war are present without going deeply into political analysis. With the passage of time, Americans came to differ vehemently over such political questions as these: Is it a civil war or an international one? Is the U.S. action being taken in fulfillment of solemn obligations to come to the requested aid of a victim of outside aggression, to help preserve the security of other treaty partner states in the region, or to establish a stable balance of power in Asia? Is it unwarranted intervention in a purely internal conflict that is not our business? Would any outcome seriously endanger the national interest of the United States? Do Americans have an obligation to help the South Vietnamese avoid having a detestable communist system being imposed upon them, with its usual aftermath of bloody purges, terror and suppression of human rights? Is there a realistic hope that more good than evil will result from a continuation of the struggle? Even though there may hae been an original *ius ad bellum* (reason for becoming involved in the war), has this been vitiated by violations of the *ius in bello* (right conduct of war) through the infliction of excessive collateral suffering upon civilians, the use of indiscriminate weapons and tactics, and even the commission, in some instances, of war crimes? The national Catholic Conference of Catholic Bishops (NCCB), no doubt concerned over the fate of Vietnamese Catholics, took up the question of the war at its annual Washington meeting in November 1966. The bishops issued a statement in which they expressed a general but cautious support for U.S. policy in Vietnam.[8]

John Courtney Murray on Selective Conscientious Objection

The bishops did not say anything about selective conscientious objection, but they left the door open to it. America's leading Catholic moral theologian and political philosopher on the subjects of war and Church-State relations in the modern democratic milieu, John Courtney Murray, S.J., entered the debate in 1967. Murray was a Jesuit priest who as professor of theology at Woodstock College and editor of *Theological Studies* had furnished a major intellectual input to the Catholic Association for International Peace and possessed a magisterial Catholic mind in matters of morality and politics. His thought, writings, and impressive personal presence had a significant influence at the Second Vatican Council. He was generally regarded as the finest modern American spokesman of that rich Scholastic theological-philosophical tradition derived from the works of St. Thomas Aquinas, Victoria, Suarez, Bellarmine, and Popes Leo XIII and Pius XII.

Murray fully realized that the SCO issue, raised in the midst of a war which many Americans rejected on political and military grounds, might very well be used, abused, and misused by some (as it undoubtedly was), and converted into a tactical weapon for politically thwarting the general course of U.S. foreign policy. He insisted, therefore, but largely in vain, that the general moral principle of SCO must be separated from the domestic politically controversial issue of the justice of the Vietnam War. He advocated SCO in the name of the traditional doctrine of the just war.

Father Murray added that he was prepared to make a moral case for the American miiltary presence and action in South Vietnam.

> But so it always is. The morality of war can never be more than marginal. The issue of war can never be portrayed in black and white. Moral judgment on the issue must be reached by a balance of many factors.... The issue about conscientious objection seems to have been drawn between the academic community and the political community....
>
> It has been observed that the commitment of the intellectual today is not simply to the search for truth, but also to the betterment of the world—to . . . peace. . . . The danger is lest the very strength of the moral commitment—to peace and against war—may foreclose inquiry into the military and political facts of the contemporary world—the naked facts of power situations and the requirements of law and order in an imperfect world, which may justify recourse to the arbitrament of arms.[9]

Murray readily admitted that the politician who must make the dreadful decisions of war and peace after trying to weigh the consequences of acting or not acting is not a prophet, and is not able to base his choices on what are, to the prophet, absolute certainties. Whereas for the prophet war is simply evil, the politician may feel compelled by conscience to choose it as the lesser evil under the circumstances; for he has a responsibility which the prophet does not know and he, after all, "creates the situation within which the prophetic voice may be safely heard."[10] Against those radical Catholic critics of the war who dismissed out of hand the argument that the citizen should defer to the government because it has superior sources of information at its disposal, Murray propounded the thesis that the government is entitled to a normal presumption in its favor. In his view, the argument that morally no one can decide for a free individual who would remain truly free was a position that had nothing in common with the traditional Catholic teaching on the person as a member of a moral and political community and no warrant in the just war doctrine. Murray demanded of SCOs that they try to achieve an exact understanding of that doctrine and a respect for what Socrates called "the conscience of the laws." When a government states its case for using military force, it is explaining a decision conscientiously arrived at in the interests of the international common good, and it submits that decision to the judgment of mankind.

> This is why in the just war theory it has always been maintained that the presumption stands for the decision of the community as officially declared. He who dissents from the decision must accept the burden of proof.... The citizen is to concede the justness of the common political decision, made in behalf of the nation, unless and until he is sure in his own mind that the decision is unjust, for reasons that he in turn must be ready convincingly to declare.... He does not and may not resign his conscience into the keeping of the State, but he must recognize that the State too has its conscience which informs its laws and decisions.[11]

In March 1971, the Supreme Court barred draft exemption to critics of a single war, holding that this did not unconstitutionally favor religious denominations that teach doctrines of absolute pacifism and did not abridge the freedom of religion of those who believe that only unjust wars should be opposed.[12] On several occasions from 1968 onward, the U.S. Catholic Bishops called upon the Congress to modify the Selective Service Act along the lines recommended in a two-person minority report, signed by John Courtney Murray and Kingman Brewster, Jr., President of Yale University and attached to the report which the National Commission on Selective Service submitted to President Johnson in March 1967, which requested an amendment providing for selective conscientious objectors. Congress, however, refused to provide for this, despite the argument that existing draft legislation incorporated the moral consensus of absolute pacifism which did not represent the moral consensus of the American people.[13] Many Congressmen regarded SCO as more of a political than a religious issue, and in the final analysis, the Congress was unwilling to turn over either to religious authorities or individual citizens the legal power to determine the justice or injustice of a war being waged by the government of the United States and to choose the wars in which individuals would fight. (One of the important domestic political aspects of the Vietnam War, of course, was the struggle between the executive and the legislative branches. But some of President Johnson's severest critics in the Senate and House were not at all eager to compound the military's manpower recruitment problems by making it easier for young men to exclude themselves from military service without having either to accept the legal penalties or to migrate to Canada, Sweden, or other foreign haven.)

Quite apart from the larger political considerations referred to above, there were other arguments lodged against SCO. Such a law would involve serious administrative difficulties: How would local draft boards be taught to judge SCOs, and what set of criteria would be used? A legal provision for SCO would discriminate in favor of better educated youth and against the disadvantaged. Legal recognition of the right of SCO might lead to the presumption that the individual citizen could engage in selective disobedience of the law (e.g., war tax resistance) or even choose selective conscientious violence on behalf of "just" socio-political causes not condoned by the government. In a more practical vein, given the size of the Catholic population, legal recognition of SCO might bring on a situation in which large numbers of young men would refuse to perform military service for reasons that would be as much political as moral. Moreover, if one of the bishops' requests were met—to allow SCOs to refuse to serve "in branches of services (e.g., the strategic nuclear forces) which would subject them to the performance of actions contrary to deeply held moral convictions about indiscriminate killing"—this could interfere with the maintenance of orderly command structures.[14] (It should be noted, however, that the military services for reasons of operational efficiency have long recognized the wisdom of allowing soldiers to transfer from specific functions which cause problems of conscience.) In any event, Congress never approved SCO, and it is reasonable to suppose that this fact contributed to the growth in the numbers of absolute Catholic pacifists, but this cannot be proved.

Although the entire moral-political debate about Vietnam pertained to the justice of counterinsurgency and conventional war and had nothing to do with nuclear weapons, it paved the way for the rise of nuclear pacifism in the U.S. Catholic Church. From 1968 onward, the American Catholic bishops became increasingly critical of U.S. defense policy, and especially nuclear policy once the Vietnam War was over. To understand why a hierarchy which had traditionally supported the defense and war policies of the government shifted toward the oppositon, we must look at two major factors that made for change.

Changes in the Church
Since Vietnam and Vatican II

The height of U.S. involvement in Vietnam, as well as its impact upon American society and the American Catholic Church, followed the Second Vatican Council by a few years, but it can be mentioned here first because, although it was an important external political precipitant of change in the thinking of the bishops, it was less important than the work of the Council as an internal spiritual source. The Vietnam War deeply divided the nation and the Catholic Church. In both dimensions, the causes of that division were more political than religious. The war produced effects the very opposite of those experienced in World War II. Democratic states, in virtue of their characteristic freedom of communication and policy debate, encounter almost insuperable difficulties in fighting apparently ambiguous, limited wars against unorthodox revolutionary insurgents who pursue a strategy of deliberate protraction and attrition. Guerrilla rebels are invariably portrayed in a romantic light, and their enemies, as oppressors, by religiously motivated idealists who seem to know little about the advanced politics and strategies of contemporary international conflict in the Third World. Older and more conservative clerics, both Catholic and Protestant, have for many years looked with suspicion upon the predilection of younger and more leftist clerics to support revolutionary movements in Latin America and Africa, not only with political arguments but also with direct support, including funds, arms, and, in a few cases, even personal participation as combatants.

The Vietnam War radicalized substantial segments of the American Catholic Church, especially among the younger clergy who were advising students in high schools and colleges on the Vietnam War draft. These students were confused by the heated national debate over the war and were unsure as to why they were being asked to go halfway around the world, fight, and die in a cause of whose justice the national leaders were unable to persuade them. Large numbers of priests became skeptical of U S. defense policy in those years. Some of them were radicalized in their political and social outlooks. Not a few of them are now bishops.

The overwhelming majority of the U.S. bishops were consecrated subsequently to January 1, 1968, the year in which domestic opposition to the Vietnam War became strong enough to force President Johnson to decide that he could not be a candidate for another term. At the beginning of 1982, there were in the United States 11 cardinals, 39 archbishops (of whom 8 were retired) and 324 bishops (of whom 54 were retired). All of the cardinals, 13 of the archbishops and 130 of the bishops had been consecrated prior to 1968. Out of a total of 286 active bishops (including cardinals and archbishops), 227 or 79 percent were consecrated from 1968 onward.[15] Another significant factor in the evolving sociology of the American Catholic episcopacy has been a fundamental change in the educational and experience background of the bishops.

Prior to the Second Vatican Council, there had been in the bishop-selection process an emphasis upon training in Rome as well as administrative experience in the ecclesiastical bureaucracy. After the Council, Pope Paul VI was determined to replace the hierarchical "old guard" with a younger episcopacy more attuned to "the signs of the times" and more willing to execute Vatican II reforms. He ordered bishops to retire at the age of seventy-five and shifted the emphasis in the selection process to pastoral experience. To carry out the policy in the United States he dispatched the progressive Belgian Archbishop Jean Jadot to Washington as the Apostolic Delegate of the Holy See during the period 1973–1980. Jadot played a key role in choosing more than a hundred new bishops. These were younger men, open to change, with pastoral experience not only in parishes but in various campus, social and other ministries, or in Third World missionary assignments. Some of them had been quite active in civil rights movements and peace organizations. There were also Black and Hispanic priests from inner city environments.[16]

The foregoing changes have been significant. Nearly four-fifths of those who voted on the pastoral letter in Chicago in May 1983 became bishops at the height of the Vietnam War or later. All of the bishops' formal statements on conscientious objection and war, peace, and nuclear weapons were issued after 1968. The post–Vatican Council emphasis on a different type of background and experience produced several consequences relevant to this study. It gave the mitre to men who are more sensitive to the problems of Catholic consciences on the issue of war. It increased the dependence of bishops upon clerics, religious and laity on their diocesan bureaucratic staffs for advice concerning the positions which bishops are expected to take in order to provide guidance on complex issues of public policy. Many of the newer bishops, having come from pastoral and social ministry environments, are particularly sensitive to cuts in federal welfare spending which affect the poor, the elderly, the disabled, the sick, youth and students, immigrants, and other ethnic minorities in their dioceses. They are readily persuaded that defense spending is the chief cause of these welfare reductions and deficits which have a depressing effect upon the economy and hold back the recovery that would ease the unemployment picutre. It is not surprising that domestic economic factors loom much larger in their thinking than considerations of national security. Thus were many bishops prepared to accept as natural the nexus that was about to be forged in the political forum between the opposition to the Vietnam War and opposition not only to U.S. nuclear policy but also to U.S. defense efforts in general.

The Vietnam War produced in the Church a generation gap no less wide and lasting than in any other segment of American society. But the impact of that war probably could not have transformed the thinking of the American Catholic bishops as profoundly as it did except in combination with a change in the whole world outlook of the Catholic Church that can only be called revolutionary.

The change had begun modestly and unostentatiously as early as the 1950s, while Pius XII was still pope. Like nearly all popes, he was theologically conservative. But his was the most comprehensive intellect to occupy the papal office for several centuries. He was interested in all phases of modern life and delivered allocutions on every subject imaginable. He was a thinker, not a doer. He initiated very few innovations himself, except in the Easter liturgy, which had remained substantially the same for a thousand years. Confucius once said that when ritual is altered, however slightly, it signals the beginning of a social revolution. What Pius XII began, John XXIII and Paul VI carried forward. The most important event of their pontificates was the Second Vatican Council (1962–1965), the most ecumenical, democratic and theologically progressive Council in Church history.

The Council laid the foundation for a new Catholic

Weltanschauung by restating traditional Catholic doctrine in a way which, while it remained essentially conservative in its basic theological substance, was idiomatically quite contemporary. So remarkable was the spirit generated throughout the universal Church that many, inside and outside, mistook renewal for the creation of something totally new, as if the Catholic Church had suddenly decided to accommodate itself so completely to the modern world that it became a different institution, henceforth to be known more for change than continuity, not only in organizational structure but also in matters of faith and morals. There was a naive expectation that all of the traditional doctrines and practices which gave rise to so much anguish in Catholic minds, or so much scandal in the minds of others, would be swept away like gossamer in the path of a broom. The Church, so it was thought by many, was about to put off its uncompromising otherworldliness and finally adjust to modern sociological reality in a world where the line between the sacred and the profane was being fast erased.

In the United States and throughout the world, especially in Europe and Latin America, some Catholic theologians were determined to press for changes in formulations of beliefs and ideas that went considerably beyond those which the Council Fathers were willing to approve, if they were even vaguely aware of them at the time. (Most of them—probably nearly all of them—were not.) Those who undertake to bring about a limited degree of modernization within a long-immutable institutional structure seldom realize that they will inevitably unleash revolutionary forces which moderate leaders find it difficult to control. Few of the Council Fathers doubted that the Catholic Church had to undergo certain modifications in "externals" in order to perform its mission more effectively in the contemporary world. They were well aware, however, that there are definite limits to the way in which doctrinal formulations can be changed.

Conservative Catholic bishops, pastors, theologians, and lay intellectuals, whose numbers are inevitably dwindling as a result of actuarial attrition, are often heard to remark that the moral and psychological tone of Catholicism has become noticeably different since the Council divested the Church of its medieval cultural adornment. While agreeing that something significant has been gained, they lament what has been lost: the sense of transcendental mystery, the silent awe with which the faithful once approached the Mass and the Eucharist, the otherworldly Gregorian chant (replaced by modern music), loyalty and obedience to a well-established hierarchical structure in a Church unified under one Holy Father in Rome, a stable certitude concerning permanence and universality in the teaching of faith and morals,[17] and a strong sense of sin, sacramental forgiveness, and salvation. The dogmatic unity and discipline which marked the pre-Vatican II Church and brooked no internal dissent in matters of faith and morals have given way to a de facto pluralism by which many Catholics who dissent from official Church teaching, especially on premarital sex, marriage, contaception, and abortion, nevertheless continue regular attendance at Mass and reception of the Eucharist.[18]

It is not correct, of course, to suggest that the sense of sin has disappeared. A more accurate statement is that the sense of sin has been undergoing a certain transformation. Particularly but not exclusively among the younger generational cohorts of clergy and laity, the emphasis has shifted from microcosm to macrocosm, from the individual to society, and from sexual morality to socio-economic ethics. The decline during the last two decades in the number of the faithful who go to confession to receive the sacrament of Penance (now called the sacrament of Reconciliation) is attributable in part to an undeniable loss of awareness of personal sinfulness deep within the spiritual psyche of the Christian, a phenomenon to which several psychologists have called attention. But it also reflects an increased emphasis in the teaching of several theologians on the contemporary dogma of social sin. Among many Christians throughout the world, the traditional hope of individual redemption, salvation, and fulfillment in the kingdom of God beyond history is being replaced by a neomillenarianist conviction that social salvation can and will inevitably be achieved in time when the senescent ideologies of imperialistic exploitation give way to a new order of world justice and peace. The church recognizes a close link between individual and social sin, and tries to inculcate a balanced sense of repentance for both. But growing numbers of Catholics feel less responsible for their own sins than previously and more responsible for the sins of institutions. They still admit the need for a personal *metanoia* (profound spiritual conversion), but now not so much to save themselves as to change the world for the better.

This phenomenon is one of the most remarkable results of the changes which have occurred in the Catholic Church since Vatican II. In all of human history, it is not possible to find a parallel case in which such a large, traditional religious organization has ever undergone a revolution in its doctrinal world-outlook as fundamental and far-reaching in implications as that which has occurred in the Catholic Church within the last quarter of a century, and nowhere more radically than in the United States. Indeed, it has been comparable in its effects to the Protestant Reformation, or the French liberal revolution, or the Russian Marxist revolution—perhaps to the three of them combined, but without the violence that usually accompanies revolutions.

Neither the popes, nor the Second Vatican Council, nor the College of Bishops in synod had carefully planned all the changes in the Church or in the thinking of Catholics. The American Catholic hierarchy can hardly be said to have presided with benign equanimity over all the theological and liturgical innovations which have occurred in this country. Christians who demand radical changes invariably claim to be acting on the inspiration of the Holy Spirit. According to Catholic doctrine, it is always the task of the popes and the bishops to exercise the final discerning judgment in this regard. The U.S. bishops are quite justified to ask that when we read their pastoral letter on war and peace we pay attention to what they are saying, and not worry about all the changes in the Church, some of which they may merely tolerate in a spirit of forbearance, rather than approve. But if we are to understand some of the difficulties and disagreements likely to arise in the course of Church efforts to implement the pastoral, it may be instructive to examine certain recent trends in Catholic and Christian ecumenical theology which probably give most bishops pause.

Political and Liberation Theology

Francis P. Fiorenza has noted that American Catholic theology has always had a derivative character influenced by such European thought trends as Puritanism, romanticism, the Social Gospel, and the "death of God" theology. More recently, he says, it has fallen under the sway of political theology from Germany and liberation theology from Latin America.

Political theology "seeks to overcome the relegation of faith to the private individualistic sphere by elaborating a new hermeneutic of the relationship between theory and praxis."[19] The "new hermeneutic" is one of the most recurring terms in recent theology. It simply means a new interpretation of faith. Political theology, associated with the German Reformed Calvinist Jürgen Moltmann and the Catholic Johannes Metz, proceeds from a conviction that the "God is dead" theology reflects the movement of history, philosophy, and science away from a divinized to a humanized and secularized world which no longer believes the truths of Christianity as expressed in traditional form. It holds that theology must be "deprivatized." Emphasis must be shifted from the quest for individual salvation and from the "I-Thou" relation of the existentialists to the quest for the transformation of society. It insists that every statement about God and salvation has full meaning only when made relevant to the human social and political condition and that the kingdom of God, long relegated exclusively to the metahistorical, supernatural realm of heaven, is to be approached in the order of time and invested as completely as possible with reality inside history. The kingdom of God becomes the standard by which all existing social and political institutions are to be judged. God does not reside in celestial aloofness, but summons us to cocreate the future of humankind. All Christians must work to build the new world and not shirk from engaging in a constant critique of all that exists, including the Church.[20] It is this aspect of the "new hermeneutic" which makes it possible for some of the more radical theologians of the Catholic Left to question the integrity of the Church's common teachings on the subject of war and peace for the last fifteen centuries by insinuating that it has been in complicity with the world for too long.[21]

Liberation theology may be looked upon either as a special manifestation of political theology designed for the Latin American region, or as a modification of it. The principal liberation theologians—Juan Luis Segundo, Gustavo Gutierrez, and Leonardo Boff—all postulate an intimate relationship between theology and politics; but they believe the European political theologians to be in error when they universalize the European secular situation. The

Catholic faith in God, Christ, and the Catholic Church, is still important in the life of Latin American societies and cultures. The Church
is not irrelevant to the social problem; it is central to it beccause it has
historically aligned itself with the oppressor class, which is much
more salient in Latin America than in a European region which has
its own long history of exploiting the peoples of the poorer and
erstwhile colonial areas. The "God is dead" theology is appropriate
for Europe but not for Latin America, where God is very much alive
and stirring revolutionary forces to life.[22]

Boff, a Brazilian Franciscan, emphasizes the historical Jesus
over the traditional Christ of faith as known from Bible and scholastic
theology. Faith is not something based on mere intellectual assent, an
internal "I believe," but rather it is the "historical *praxis* of liberation."
His Christology presents Jesus not so much as *Salvador* as *Liberatador*,
who does not explain reality but transforms it. He preached not
himself but the kingdom of God, "the realization of a utopia involving complete liberation."[23] Richard McBrien writes that Boff
"preaches a God to whom we have access not primarily through
prayer and religious observance but through service to the poor."[24]
The Word of God is heard only in the cries of the poor and the
oppressed. Gutierrez insists that only by participating in the struggles of the poor can Christians make the Gospel have an impact on
history, and Segundo argues that the "hermeneutic circle" requires
that the interpretation of the Bible be continually revised as individual and social reality changes. This, of course, is a far cry from
traditional theology and, as McBrien notes, the affinity of liberation
theology with the Marxist view of human existence is obvious.[25]
McBrien summarizes the main thrust of this school of thought as
follows: "The God of liberation theology (whether of the Latin American, black or feminist kind), is a God whose primary, if not sole,
passion is the freeing of the oppressed from the bondage of economic, racist or sexist exploitation."[26]

James V. Schall, S.J., a professor of government at Georgetown
University, has analyzed the attraction for the Catholic New Left of
the Social Gospel and the liberationists' flirtation with Marxism-
Leninism. Whereas Catholics had always believed that the priesthood
was an order set apart to perform a divinely instituted sacramental
function and which required no justification in political or
socioeconomic terms, many of the newer breed of clergy apparently

assume that unless a priest is engaged in politically and socially relevant causes, he is making no useful contribution to society. For warning them that they must not dilute their charism through an exaggerated interest in temporal problems, some of them regard Pope John Paul II as quaintly archaic, if not dangerously reactionary. Holding the old "Christendom of the Right" in contempt, they seek to establish a "Christendom of the Left" and relocate St. Augustine's City of God on earth. Schall wryly observes that the Enlightenment *philosophes* of the eighteenth century, of whom Carl Becker noted that they denied miracles but believed in the perfectibility of the human race, have evolved into the socialist Catholic clergy of the late twentieth century.[27]

The reader may well wonder what this excursion into modern currents of Catholic theology—some of them rather unorthodox and not at all representative of the doctrine preached by the Church in its magisterium—has to do with the present Catholic debate about nuclear weapons. In fact, the discussion is quite germane, because the "new hermeneutic" has had a significant influence upon the thinking of many bishops and theologians in general, including some conservative ones who reject outright the specific formualations of the political and liberation theologians. As early as 1971, an international Synod of Bishops in Rome issued an important statement containing the following passage:

> Action on behalf of justice and participation in the transformation of the world fully appear to us as a constitutive dimension of the preaching of the Gospel, or, in other words, of the Church's mission for the redemption of the human race and its liberation from every oppressive situation.[28]

The Synod was one of several innovations brought about in the Catholic Church by Pope Paul VI (1963–1978), who inherited from Pope John XXIII and the first session of the Second Vatican Council a Church in the ferment of early stages of change which would eventually become tumultuous. By the time it ended in 1965, the Council produced sixteen documents which reformulated, in modern spirit and idiom, the doctrine of the Church on such subjects as the liturgy, revelation, ecclesiology, priesthood, Christian ecumenism, non-Christian religions, religious freedom, the laity, and the role of the Church in the modern world. Within a very few years, Paul VI found himself confronted with serious challenges to traditional orthodox belief and practice, from the world at large and from elements within the Church, on a variety of fronts—a rising tide of sexual liberalism, calls for an end to the rule of priestly celibacy, accompanied by the laicization of large numbers of priests; demands for the revision of doctrine and law regarding marriage, contraception, divorce, and ecclesial rights of homosexuals, and the radical transformation of social structures. All of these demands and challenges were being presented during a period in which moderniz-ing changes perceived as necessary were taking place in the con-sultative and decision-making processes of the Church, the discipline and dress of religious orders, the cultural atmosphere of the liturgy, relations with Protestants, Jews, Muslims, Hindus and Buddhists, traditional fasting and abstinence practices, and canon law on marriage and annulment, the role of Mary in the Church, and other issues.[29]

Pope Paul VI, an experienced practitioner of international diplomacy and deeply trusted protégé and associate of Pope Pius XII, was the head of a Church which faced serious dangers of defection on the Catholic Left and schism on the Right (by those who joined Archbishop Marcel Lefebvre of France in his conviction that the Church by changing was abandoning the traditional deposit of faith entrusted to it). He chose to meet the crisis and hold the Church together by performing a skillful balancing act which combined a progressive approach in matters pertaining to international peace, justice, and socioeconomic development, especially in the Third World, with a conservative approach to doctrine, morals, and ques-tions of internal ecclesiastical organization.[30] In this respect he was by no means striking out on a new path. John Tracy Ellis has observed that papal documents in the modern era

> illustrate a repeatedly puzzling phenomenon in the history
> of the church, namely the often open and progressive
> approach of Churchmen on socioeconomic and political
> questions combined with the same Churchmen's highly
> conservative stance in matters theological.[31]

Pius XII, who was never required to assert a theological con-servatism, expressed enlightened and sophisticated views on a whole range of modern subjects: democracy, war and peace, nuclear weapons, technology, the mass media, medicine, psychiatry, among others. But as a strong antitotalitarian and inheritor of a long tradition of popes who never had to travel or address problems beyond the confines of Western civilization, Pius XII was concerned primariliy with the problems of the Christian West. Indeed, he was the last who could be thus preoccupied, given the changing global balance of power or what Soviet Marxists call the "changing world correlation of forces."

Paul VI, who was a disciple of the Thomistic thinker, Jacques Maritain, displayed his theological conservatism in the encyclicals *Mysterium Fidei* ("Mystery of Faith"—the Eucharist) in 1965, *Sacerdotalis Caelibatus* ("On Priestly Celibacy") in 1967 and *Humanae Vitae* ("On Human Life") in 1968. As the most widely-traveled pope in history up to his time, and the most international and universalist in outlook, he spoke dramatically on behalf of peace at the United Nations in 1965—"*Jamais plus la guerre!*"—and on behalf of social justice and economic development of the poor countries in the 1967 encyclical *Populorum Progressio*, in which he postulated the growing gap between rich and poor nations as a danger to world peace.[32] He criticized that system of unchecked liberalism "which considers profit as the key motive for economic progress, competition as the supreme law of economics, and private ownership of the means of production as an absolute right" without limits and social obligations.[33] In the view of Quentin Quade, *Populorum Progressio* constituted a "turning point at which the forces created by Vatican II moved from relatively traditional paths to more 'radically' politicized ones," contributed significantly to the development of political pretensions in the Church's name.[34] Without making any overt claim to a political capacity, it nevertheless asserts a specific competence in the realms of politics and economics, but fails to acknowledge that people of good will may honestly disagree over the diagnosis of and proposed solutions to the contemporary ills of the world.[35]

The Second Vatican Council and the encyclical *Populorum Progressio* led directly to the conference of 150 Latin American bishops at Medellin, Colombia, in September 1968, which produced a Document on Justice containing this passage:

It was God himself who sent his Son in the fulness of time.

He took on flesh to liberate mankind from all the shackles that weighed down on it because of sin, ignorance, hunger, poverty and oppression.[36]

That certainly sounded as if the bishops of Latin America were fully endorsing the theology of liberation. In November 1970 the Cardinal of Santiago said: "There are more evangelical values in socialism than there are in capitalism"[37] In the spring of 1971, as the government of Marxist Salvador Allende was growing stronger in Chile, the bishops of that country pointed out that the Church "is not tied to any political system." They said its mission is every age is to incarnate complete liberation for the human person and society. The Church is not competent to make political pronouncements on contingent solutions of a political or economic nature, but it does have authority to denounce whatever in these solutions might delude, enslave, or harm the dignity of the human person.[38]

An option for socialism of a Marxist cast poses legitimate questions. It is a system that already has concrete embodiments in history. In these concrete embodiments we find that fundamental rights of the human person have been trodden underfoot just as they have been in concrete embodiments of the capitalist system .... The Church, which has been sent by God to serve and liberate man, cannot remain indifferent to this fact.[39]

The bishops then addressed themselves to a declaration of eighty priests who called for a destruction of the prejudice existing between Christians and Marxists and a joint effort between those two groups "on behalf of the historic project that the country has set for itself": the emergence of the New Man once the lack of class consciousness among workers has been overcome and measures aimed at social appropriation of the means of production are taken. The Chilean bishops, taking their stand on the Vatican II mandate that "priests are never to put themselves at the service of any ideology or human faction," said that when priests become actively political, they threaten to disrupt the unity of the Christian people with their pastors; if they present their political position as a logical and inescapable consequence of their Christian faith, they implicitly condemn every other option and attack the liberty of Christians who follow other options.[40]

The Chilean bishops, however, were more circumspect than the drafters of the Medellin documents, who berated traditionalists because of a bourgeois mentality that showed little or no social consciousness and economic developmentalists with a technological mentality more interested in economic productivity than in social progress; and who attributed to the agricultural, industrial, social, cultural, and political structures a form of institutionalized violence which demands global, bold, urgent, and profoundly renovating transformations,[41] a euphemism for revolution that may have to assume violent forms.

Liberation theology was transmitted to segments of the Catholic Church in the United States during a week-long conference in Detroit, beginning August 17, 1975. Sergio Torres, Juan Luis Segundo, Gustavo Gutierrez, Leonard Boff, and twenty other Latin American liberation theologians lectured and listened to about one hundred and seventy-five North Americans, mostly social workers, parish priests, women, Blacks, Chicanos, Native Americans, Appalachians, and others. These outnumbered the few "white male professional theologians" who epitomized the "oppressive power structure" in the eyes of Latin Americans.[42] The week was filled with a mixture of Leftist Christian and Marxist analyses of global cultural revolution, institutionalized violence, the struggle against oppression, the tearing down of unjust structures and—above all—the need to recognize the "liberating praxis" as the norm of truth in theology. No participants quibbled with the proposition that the enlightened Christian Left must break away from the inherited theology of fixed positions drawn mainly from Roman sources and studied in universities. Theology henceforth must be seen as an open-ended, corporate and self-correcting process grounded in the experience of downtrodden communities. Catholics of the New Left were admonished to be concerned less about studying theology and much more about "doing theology," for truth is not a static thing to be known by conforming the mind to revealed knowledge, but a historic reality which is being fashioned dialectically in a world-building process.[43]

The degree to which the new emancipation theology was gaining influence, at least temporarily, among younger bishops, clergy, and laity who staffed many of the diocesan bureaucracies throughout the United States, became evident in October 1976, when the Bicentennial Catholic Call to Action Conference convened in Detroit. It was attended by some twelve hundred delegates and produced by overwhelming majorities more than one hundred and eighty resolutions, many of which favored a broadening of the base of Church power, the sharing of episcopal and clerical authority with the laity, a liberalization of attitudes toward sex and marriage (for example, the rights of homosexuals and of persons divorced and remarried), the rights of women and other minorities in the Church, and new programs on behalf of youth and minorities. The Conference also adopted positions strongly critical of nuclear deterrence, the arms race, and U.S. foreign policy, especially in Latin America and southern Africa.[44]

Catholic social theory, from Pope Leo XIII's Encyclical *Rerum Novarum* (1891) to John Paul II's *Laborem Exercens* (1981), has never been favorably disposed to liberal, laissez-faire capitalism. In papal teaching, unregulated capitalism exalts as an absolute dogmatic value the abstract economic liberty of the few at the expense of the misery of the many poor. It subjects weak, defenseless individuals to the callousness of the stronger and the hard-hearted greed of unchecked competition. It corrodes family life, organic community sentiment, and cooperation while it creates urban slums and conditions which not only foment class hatred but facilitate the emergence of the twin forms of the omnipotent totalitarian state, fascism and communism. Since the Gospel is much more important to the poor than to the rich, the Church has no choice but to uphold the dignity and rights of labor as having priority over the rights of capital to profit. But with equal vigor, Rome has always upheld the rights of private ownership of property and private enterprise, provided they be used responsibly for the common good, for the sake of which the state may intervene in the economic order. Papal teaching has invariably repudiated the Marxist concepts of class struggle and violent revolution. Catholic social doctrine, we might say, has gradually evolved toward a preference for a judicious mixture of socially responsible capitalism, democratic socialism on behalf of the less advantaged sectors of society, and moderate organic corporatism which promotes communication, understanding and cooperation among all occupational, professional, and socioeconomic groupings within the community.

American Catholics of the New Left have been shifting perceptibly during the past decade toward the Marxist side of Rome's balanced posture. A recent authoritative survey of theology professors in Christian seminaries and schools of religion (or theology) in the United States (as distinct from comparable departments in colleges and universities) indicates that Catholics, in comparison with teachers of other Christian denominations, are more critical of American institutions and values, more likely to consider the United States unfair in its treatment of the Third World, and more likely to look upon present levels of federal expenditures for social purposes (health, environment, and urban problems) to be insufficient, while criticizing U.S. defense expenditures as too high. Whereas Protestant teachers were extremely favorable toward laissez-faire capitalism (by percentages ranging from 86 to 100), 54 percent of the Catholics were of the opinion that a good Catholic could not adhere to this economic model, and 59 percent rejected the proposition that economic growth is a better way to improve the lot of the poor than redistributing existing wealth.[45]

It is likely that Catholic teachers of religion, theology and social ethics in Catholic colleges and universities are at least as critical of American capitalism as the Catholics in the sample just cited. Moreover, although reliable statistical data are not yet available, it seems reasonable to hypothesize that a correlation exists between those Catholics of the Left who adopt radical anticapitalist, pacifist, and anti-defense positions and those who favor more substantial and liberal changes in Church teaching on premarital sex, contraception, divorce and remarriage, an end to the celibacy rule for priests, the rights of homosexuals, the ordination of women as priests, and even—paradoxical as it may seem—violent revolution in certain Third World countries. J. Bryan Hehir, the Associate Secretary for International Justice and Peace of the United States Catholic Conference observed in 1981:

> The persistence of radically unjust socio-economic structures has led others, otherwise inclined to a non-violent witness, to find justification for the use of force as a last resort in situations like Somoza's Nicaragua, Ian Smith's Rhodesia and now El Salvador.[46]

Many American Catholic bishops, especially the older ones, were far from enthusiastic about either European political theology or Latin American liberation theology or—for that matter—any substantial revisions of traditional orthodox belief. Moreover, for a variety of administrative, political, intellectual, psychological, and theological reasons, they did not try to master the novel religious ideas underlying the esoteric terminology of the new theological trends. As practical administrators, they were no less interested than Paul VI in holding together a polarizing Church by trying to reach out to youth and the New Left without seriously alienating older and more conservative Catholics. They sought in several cases, therefore, to accommodate themselves to the specific recommendations of the liberationist Left without blessing the theoretical rationale for them. Those bishops, in effect, were acting out of a Christian humanist compassion in response to contemporary political movements within the Church whose basic theological tenets, if made explicit and fully understood, would probably have appalled them. Many Catholics of the New Left, of course, thoroughly appreciated the interconnectedness of liberationist issues with the new Christian-Marxist hermeneutic from which they flowed.

For several years, Pope Paul VI was favorably inclined toward a moderate liberation theology in Latin America. But, faced with the specter of a spreading international terrorism, he warned repeatedly against violent revolution.[47] Furthermore, since he was engaged in a delicate diplomatic effort to bring about an amelioration in the condition of the Church in Eastern Europe,[48] Paul was anxious to avoid the slightest appearance of espousing liberationist aims or arousing such hopes in the People's Democracies. Thus he was constrained to write: "In view of the varied situations in the world, it is difficult to give one teaching to cover them all or to offer a solution which has universal value."[49] What might be appropriate social teaching for Latin America was not appropriate for the Soviet bloc. Christians had to interpret the "signs of the times" in their own situations and their own regions.

Pope John Paul II has sought to clarify Catholic social doctrine and to reverse trends which in his view went too far under Paul VI. Critical of the dangerous tendencies inherent in liberation theology and "signs of the times" thinking, John Paul II neither equates a Christian prophetic stance with political involvement, nor does he regard widespread popular movements in an age of the mass media as enjoying the presumption of being manifestations of the Holy Spirit's working. Rejecting the Marxist concept of class struggle as the prime mover of history, the pope prefers to see the struggle for justice not as constitutive of the Church's mission as defined by the

1971 Synod of Bishops, but as another though not most important dimension of that mission. In contrast to Paul VI's willingness to decentralize the Church's social doctrine in order to distinguish East Europe from Latin America, John Paul II returned to the papal center the task of interpreting the "signs of the times" according to the mind and heart of the Catholic Church. His understanding of a centrist balance has brought him to caution the Latin American liberationists while expounding human rights in Eastern Europe more staunchly and more openly than did Paul VI. Perhaps his most consistent and characteristic teaching on the social order has been that temporal matters lie properly within the sphere of competence of the laity, not priests, nuns, and other religious, who should not dilute their spiritual charism by becoming excessively preoccupied with political, social, and economic problems in an effort to solve those problems.[50]

To sum up, the Catholic Church in the United States today is undergoing a theological upheaval. The radical Catholic New Left ignores traditional Augustinian-Thomistic theological orthodoxy and frequently criticizes Pope John Paul II as a reactionary for attempting to restrict the freedom won by the political and liberation theologians during the pontificate of Pope Paul VI. The Catholic Left now seeks to impose upon the entire American Catholic Church a curious dialectical mixture of absolute pacifism and opposition to defense programs on the one hand and justification of revolutionary violence in Latin America on the other. It is militant in its support of the nuclear freeze movement (regardless of the statistics of balance or imbalance in the East-West strategic and European equations) and can be expected to manifest increasing support for unilateral nuclear disarmament by the West. Although some Catholics of the Left occasionally suggest that emphasis should shift from nuclear to conventional capabilities, it is difficult if not impossible to cite instances in which they have actually supported specific new conventional weapons programs.

For the radical Catholic New Left, the just war theory continues to be relevant in a universal context, not for the defense of the "capitalist West" against Soviet-supported Marxist-Leninist forces, but only as an instrument of the class struggle against incumbent Third World governments alleged to be dominated by "oppressive capitalist-imperialist structures." In the thinking of the Catholic Left, the just war theory is now deemed applicable only to what Nikita Khrushchev in 1961 called "just wars of national liberation," while force is no longer available as a justifiable instrument in the hands of "capitalist" or "capitalist-oriented" governments. Every attempt on the part of the U.S. government to resort either to the use of military force or the granting of military assistance—for example, to Central America—is now strenuously resisted by the Catholic New Left and the NCCB itself.[51] Thus it would appear that a great many American Catholic pacifists have become highly selective, from a political standpoint, in condoning the use of military force. Yet in denying the option of force to the U.S. govenrment while supporting revolutionary insurgent guerrilla movements, they maintain a logical consistency within the framework of their own political and liberationist theology. What the Catholic bishops as a whole should be worried about is whether the current popularity of the antinuclear and antidefense movements will impel the National Conference of Catholic Bishops toward an absolute pacifist position, and whether the issue of war and peace in the nuclear age will be skillfully exploited as a weapon to discredit not only Pope John Paul II in his effort to moderate the liberation theologians and reestablish respect for the doctrinal authority of Rome with regard to social questions, but more generally to discredit or at least neutralize the doctrinal conservatism of the papacy over a whole range of other ecclesiastical and moral issues which have become controversial since the Second Vatican Council.

5

THE PASTORAL LETTER

AND THE

CATHOLIC DOCTRINAL TRADITION

The effort made by the American Catholic bishops from 1981 to 1983 to prepare a formal statement on the problems of war and peace should now be placed in perspective. First of all, the moral gravity of the challenge posed by the huge nuclear weapons stockpiles is beyond debate, as is the need for thoughtful ethical reflection upon it. The issues at stake cannot be analyzed exclusively in technical, political, and strategic terms as if they had no moral or religious dimension. It is unfair for some to charge that the bishops have no business leaping into a public debate over defense policy, or that they politicize the Gospel when they do so. The bishops clearly reject the argument that the Church should not become involved in politics. They have a perfect right, both as religious leaders and as American citizens, to do what other leaders of Christian churches have frequently done in the past. Throughout history, the Catholic Church has sought to exert influence on questions which arise in the social order by reason of sinfulness (*ratione peccati*) and present a case of conscience to the Christian, as this question certainly does.

Many bishops have apparently concluded that they bear a special obligation on this score, because the United States is the only superpower which permits the open questioning of public policy and the introduction of Christian (as distinct from Marxist-Leninist) morality into the debate over srategy. Many, including older conservative bishops who by no stretch of the imagination can be regarded as pacifist in sentiment, are sincerely convinced that if they are to be credible in their teaching on the sacredness of human life in regard to abortion, they must be equally zealous in their respect for life in face of the nuclear danger. Although it often appeared that the pacifist and nuclear pacifist bishops* were driving the debate on the pastoral, it was only with the support of other bishops, who remain staunch in their support of the just war tradition but who are concerned about the direction of U.S. nuclear policy in recent years, that it was possible to gain broad acceptance for a critique of nuclear deterrence strategies and specific nuclear weapons programs.[1] The bishops link their teaching on war to that on abortion and draw the appropriate distinctions toward the end of their letter.

Moral Authority and Technical Competence

Bishops, of course, can expect to encounter criticism and reasoned opposition when they go beyond the enunciation of general moral principles and guidelines on how these principles are to be applied to the analysis of contemporary real-life situations, and start to make recommendations as a religious body on specific issues of U.S. defense policy which require both technical or professional expertise not usually possessed by ecclesiastics and the kind of practical, prudential judgment which comes only from many years of political experience which—as Pope John Paul II has frequently reiterated—priests and bishops are not supposed to have if they perform conscientiously the duties of their spiritual office.

To make this assertion does not imply, as the more politically activist clerics often complain, that religious leaders are being told to confine their pronouncements to such harmless moralistic abstractions and homiletic appeals as to produce no impact on the body

---

* Those bishops generally recognized as the most outspoken nuclear pacifists include Raymond G. Hunthausen, Archbishop of Seattle; Thomas Gumbleton, Auxiliary Bishop of Detroit and President of Pax Christi-USA; Walter Sullivan, Bishop of Richmond; John R. Quinn, Archbishop of San Francisco; Leroy Matthiesen, Bishop of Amarillo; and Roger Mahony, Bishop of Stockton.

politic. But it is to say that several matters have to be sorted out. Above all, the moral teaching authority of the national episcopate, based upon an understanding of unchanging truths, has to be distinguished from the tentative political and strategic opinions and judgments of the bishops.[2] To their credit, it should be said that the bishops became increasingly aware of this imperative over a two-year period.

Only a small number of bishops would claim to have remained moderately well informed over several years on issues of nuclear weapons, deterrence strategy, and war, even though a great many, perhaps all, have had strong feelings on the subject for a long time. A few bishops have spent some time traveling around the country, attending conferences, lecturing on problems of war and peace, and explaining how they formed their views on war and deterrence in the nuclear age.[3] A larger number have written articles or pastoral letters on the subject.[4] There are probably very few who have never taken part in ecumenical services to protest the danger of nuclear war and pray for peace. The five bishops on the *ad hoc* drafting committee listened to several days of testimony in 1981–1982 from invited experts, including seven former government officials and four officials of the Reagan administration.[5] The great majority of the other 242 bishops who voted in Chicago had to rely heavily on the *ad hoc* committee and its staff, particularly Father J. Bryan Hehir,[6] and a relatively small number of other well-informed bishops, for guidance or leads on technical issues.

The members of the drafting committee were aware from the beginning of the problem of separating moral principles from tentative judgments, although the process of clarification took a long time. The first draft, for example, contained a denial of an intention on the part of the bishops "to make a technical judgment on the vast literature regarding the possible control of any use of nuclear weapons in regional conflicts"; but the obligation to follow the safest possible moral course led to a judgment against any initiation of the use of nuclear weapons in a war.[7] The first draft pointed out that "Christians and others of good will may differ as to whether nuclear weapons may be employed under any circumstances"—that is, even in retaliation—and added: "It is not easy to make a decision on this matter."[8]

The second draft, which ran to one hundred and ten pages,

compared to sixty-six pages in the first, incorporated many of the ideas received in seven hundred pages of comments from bishops and others, but it did not really do much to clarify the issue under discussion. At the Washington meeting of the NCCB in November 1982, Bishop Joseph A. Fiorenza of San Angelo, Texas raised a difficult but pertinent question:

> If the pastoral is the authoritative teaching of the American bishops on the morality of nuclear warfare, and if passed by our conference, does this mean that American Catholics are not morally free to form their conscience on the morality of this issue independent of our pastoral? Or does it mean that as only a guideline, Catholics are morally free to disregard our moral teaching?
>
> If the pastoral is passed and the Holy See finds no objection to it, I assume that it is to be received by Catholics as authoritative teaching. A basic question then, that the committee and the body of bishops should answer with clarity, is, in my opinion, the binding force of the moral teaching of our pastoral.[9]

Fundamental to the Catholic faith is the belief that the teaching and governing authority of the college of bishops as shepherds of the Church is derived from Christ and the Holy Spirit. The bishops are the successors of the apostles, through whom the apostolic tradition is manifested and preserved. For the sake of unity of faith and fellowship, their authority is to be exercised only in hierarchical communion with and subject to the primacy of the Roman Pontiff, the Successor of St. Peter and the Vicar of Christ, who has full, supreme, and universal power over the Church. Although individual bishops do not enjoy the prerogative of infallibility, they can, provided they maintain unity with Rome and among themselves, proclaim the doctrine of Christ infallibly when teaching authentically on matters of faith and morals.[10] Bishops belonging to the same nation or region are permitted to form an episcopal conference such as the National Conference of Catholic Bishops in the United States. Such a conference may not, of course, define a new moral doctrine which has not been assented to by the whole college of bishops in an ecumenical council acting with the roman Pontiff. Nor can it, which seems less likely but not impossible, define a new moral doctrine which has not received assent in a special mandate from the Apostolic See itself.[11] It is important to understand the limits of authority possessed by a national episcopal conference in the area of war and peace problems, where moral judgements are necessarily intermingled with political and strategic ones, where a national episcopal conference might seek to become more explicit in its teaching than an ecumenical council and/or the pope, or where two national episcopal conferences might not reach the same conclusions concerning what is politically and strategically prudent under certain circumstances, or even agree on how best to express the Church's traditionally held universal moral principles.

The fundamental tenets of traditional Catholic moral theology concerning the conscience of the individual and the teaching authority of the church may be summarized as follows: (1) Conscience is the final practical judgment of the reason (not the last feeling of the emotions) as to the moral rightness or wrongness of an act before it is placed, or a decision before it is taken. (2) The religious-moral conscience of the person is sacred and inviolable; it should not and cannot be coerced by any external power. (3) the Catholic has an obligation to form a "right conscience" not in accordance with his or her own predilections but rather in the light of the teaching of Christ as interpreted and preached by the Church. A "right conscience" is formed by adhering to the official teaching of the Pope and the whole College of Bishops rather than by following one's favorite moral theologians or priests as reported in the mass media. (4) The Catholic Christian cannot properly invoke his or her own conscience as a higher or more ultimate authority than that of the *magisterium* (or teaching authority) of the Church. (5) The opinions, beliefs, attitudes, and actual behavior of Catholics or Christians, however numerous they may be, cannot properly be cited as a refutation of the ecclesiastical *magisterium*. Christ did not entrust the Church's power to clarify good and evil for the guidance of the faithful to the democratic political principle of majority rule. (6) In the final analysis, every Christian is obliged to follow the honest promptings and dictates of a well-formed conscience. No one may pass judgment on the sincerity or moral culpability of the person who acts inconsistently with Church teaching, but those who know the teaching should point out the discrepancy with Christian charity.

The Rome Consultation

The Catholic bishops of the United States cannot issue a pastoral letter on war, peace, and nuclear weapons without producing waves that are bound to be felt by European Catholics, who are generally much more sensitive to subtle vibrations in the East-West psycho-political balance than are their more "isolated" transatlantic brethren. Within the last few years, since 1980, individual bishops and episcopal conferences in the United Kingdom, France, West Germany, Belgium, Netherlands, and Italy have exhibited a lively and nervous pluralism in regard to issues of nuclear strategies and weapons. One American observer has noted, with rather serene theological detachment,. that "a comparison of the official state-ments" of episcopal conferences in the countries of the Western alliance "reveals a posture which is variegated and constantly changing ... due to the renewed emphasis placed on episcopal collegiality by the Second Vatican Council," and has suggested that the current tension "is a result of the dynamics of a decentralized magisterium, which was one of the principal insights and achievements of Vatican II."[12]

There is undoubtedly a good deal of validity in the observation that Vatican II prepared the way for national conferences of bishops to strike out on their own much more than they have done in the past, especially on issues which pertain to "the world" and local national environments rather than to the received deposit of faith. But one must also recognize clearly that the recent discussion among Amer-ican and European bishops concerning the central issues of this study have been animated by differences precisely because the issues involved are not only moral, but every bit as much political, and in some specific respects more political than moral. The Europeans, however, have also been concerned on this matter, as on previous occasions in history, with American Catholic theology.

Copies of the first draft of the pastoral letter were sent to bishops in other parts of the world in June 1982, but foreign comments could

not be translated into English in time for the *ad hoc* drafting committee
to study them before the second draft was circulated in October prior to
the bishops' general meeting in Washington in mid-November
1982.[13] On January 18-19, 1983, representatives of the U.S. bishops'
conference and their counterparts from France, the Federal
Republic of Germany, England-Wales, Scotland, Belgium, Italy, and
Holland met at the Vatican with officials of the Holy See, under
whose auspices the consultation was organized. Archbishop John
Roach of St. Paul and Minneapolis, president of the NCCB, and
Cardinal-elect Joseph Bernardin of Chicago, chairman of the *ad hoc*
committee, explained the premise of the second draft: "that it is
necessary to build a barrier against the concept of nuclear war as a
viable strategy of defense and to draw a strong and clear line politically and morally against resort to nuclear weapons."[14] They
expressed a desire to make clear that the U.S. bishops cannot
approve of any policy of deterrence which involves an intention to do
what is morally evil, but they gave an assurance that the next draft
would state more explicitly that specific recommendations do not
carry the same moral authority as statements of moral principle.

Joseph Cardinal Ratzinger, prefect of the Sacred Congregation
for the Doctrine of the Faith, next raised a number of questions
regarding (1) the teaching mandate (*mandatum docendi*) which
belongs to individual bishops and the college of bishops with the
pope, but not to an episcopal conference as such; (2) the way fundamental moral principles are to be applied to the nuclear armaments
question; (3) whether the draft faithfully presents scriptural evidence; (4) whether in Church tradition nonviolence and the just war
doctrine are on the same level; and (5) how the morality of deterrence
is to be judged, taking into account the geopolitical context and
fundamental moral principles.[15] There followed a discussion of
these questions, which is of crucial significance for the point immediately at issue—moral authority and technical competence.

1. Should bishops' conferences limit their tasks to stating
   general principles or should they also apply these principles to concrete situations, strategies and policies and
   therefore propose certain practical choices as morally
   binding? . . . .
2. Granted that different practical options are possible, can

bishops in a pastoral letter propose one of these options as their own? Can it be presented as "the Christian option"? Can the contrary option be "condemned"?

3. Should a pastoral letter be limited to proposing only the teaching that is binding? Or should it also contribute elements to encourage a debate?

4. Can the same pastoral letter address itself to the Christian conscience and at the same time to the general public opinion, Catholics and nonCatholics alike? With what authority? Is it feasible for bishops in a pastoral letter to speak as *doctores fidei* and at the same time, as concerned citizens of their own country, address government policies and strategies?[16]

In a memorandum synthesizing the discussion and designed to serve as a point of reference and guide to the U.S. bishops in preparing their next draft, it was noted that the second draft

> mixes different levels of authority and it will be difficult for the reader to make the necessary distinctions. Hence grave questions of conscience will arise for Catholics. A clear line must be drawn between the statement of principles and practical choices based on prudential judgment. When bishops offer elements for reflection or when they wish to stimulate debate, something that for pastoral reasons they might be called upon to do in present-day situations, they must do it in such a way that they clearly differentiate this from what they are bound to propose as *doctores fidei*.

The same memorandum also left no doubt that the pastoral letter should be rewritten and the different levels of authority should be clarified for these reasons:

> First, in respect for the freedom of the Christian so that he or she be clearly informed about what is binding in conscience. Second, in respect for the integrity of the Catholic faith so that nothing be proposed as doctrine of the Church that pertains to prudential judgments or alternative choices. Third, for reasons of ecclesiology, that the teaching authority which belongs to each bishop not be wrongly applied and therefore obscure its credibility.[17]

These were strongly worded admonitions from European to American bishops, most of whom welcomed them and took them to heart. Without doubt some of the more radical pacifists, whether nuclear or general were not happy over the intervention which had been carried out by the European bishops with the obvious approval of Pope John Paul II. Subsequent references to the memorandum on the consultation at the Vatican will be necessary in the discussion of specific parts of the pastoral letter, especially those on pacifism and just war; counterpopulation warfare; no first use; limited nuclear war; nuclear deterrence; and the two evils to be avoided—nuclear warfare and the endangering of the independence and freedom of entire peoples.

The third draft and the final amended text went a long way toward complying with Rome's advice and spelling out the distinction between principles of moral teaching which have universally and permanently binding validity and the application of those principles to specific contemporary issues and circumstances which are, by their nature, transitory and subject to change. The bishops adopted the same rule of interpretation which had been laid down as a guideline at Vatican II in the Pastoral Constitution on the Church in the Modern World (*Gaudium et spes*), the basic document which has inspired all of the bishops' statements on war, peace, conscientious objection, and other social problems such as world hunger since the late 1960s. The passages in which the U.S. bishops clarify this matter are of critical importance, and bear quoting at length:

> In this pastoral letter too we address many concrete questions concerning the arms race, contemporary warfare, weapons systems and negotiating strategies. We do not intend that our treatment of each of these issues carry the same moral authority as our statement of universal moral principles and formal church teaching. Indeed, we stress here at the beginning that not every statement in this letter has the same moral authority. At times we reassert universally binding moral principles (e.g., non-combatant immunity and proportionality). At still other times, we reaffirm statements of recent popes and the teaching of Vatican II. Again, at other times we apply moral principles to specific cases.

When making applications of these principles we realize—and we wish readers to recognize—that prudential judgments are involved based on specific circumstances which can change or which can be interpreted differently by people of good will (e.g., the treatment of "no first use"). However, the moral judgments that we make in specific cases, while not binding in conscience, are to be given serious attention and consideration by Catholics as they determine whether their moral judgments are consistent with the Gospel.

We shall do our best to indicate, stylistically and substantively, whenever we make such applications. We believe such specific judgments are an important part of this letter, but they should be interpreted in light of another passage from the pastoral constitution:

"Often enough the Christian view of things will make itself suggest some specific solution in certain circumstances. Yet it happens rather frequently, and legitimately so, that with equal sincerity some of the faithful will disagree with others on a given matter. Even against the intention of their proponents, however, solutions proposed on one side or another may be easily confused by many people with the gospel message. Hence it is necessary for people to remember that no one is allowed in the aforementioned situations to appropriate the church's authority for his opinion. They should always try to enlighten one another through honest discussion, preserving mutual charity and caring above all for the common good."

This passage acknowledges that on some complex social questions the church expects a certain diversity of views even though all hold the same universal moral principles. The experience of preparing this pastoral letter has shown us the range of strongly held opinion in the Catholic Community on questions of war and peace. Obviously, as bishops we believe that such differences should be expressed within the framework of Catholic moral teaching. We urge mutual respect among different groups in the church as they analyze this letter and the issues it addresses.

Not only conviction and commitment are needed in the
church, but also civility and charity.[18]

The Jesuit theologian John Langan has pointed out that the
bishops had three options on how they might present their teaching:
(1) the traditional philosophical-legal approach inherited from the
medieval scholastics, based on just war theory and natural law reasoning and characterized by subtle distinctions regarding moral permissibility and impermissibility; (2) the prophetic word of salvation
approach which emphasizes Biblical precedents or themes and proceeds from reading the "signs of the times" (the favorite phrase of
Vatican II); and (3) a combination of the two. The first appeals to the
intellects of those who are right of center; the second to the wills and
hearts of those to the left of center. It was natural, therefore, that the
third option was adopted for this statement, just as it has been the
norm for modern encyclicals on social questions, even though "neither of the two modes are particularly good at capturing the irony
and paradox that are present in the theory and practice of deterrence."[19] One must add, however, that in the last decade or two, the
biblical and prophetic motif has grown stronger in formal Church
statements which have also tended to grow longer and more difficult
to comprehend and summarize in their basic thrust, inasmuch as
churchmen, not wishing to exclude anyone from their message, try
to communicate something for everybody.

In drafting their pastoral letter, the bishops went through a
process unprecedented in the history of the American Catholic
Church, despite its reputation in recent decades for responding to
the Vatican II summons for more democratic consultative procedures. (One can scarcely imagine German, French, or Italian
bishops developing a statement of social morality in quite the same
way.) Over a two year span, three drafts were produced. All were
discussed intensively by the bishops in conference. Comments
received on one draft were taken into account in the preparation of
the next. From first draft to final text, an interesting evolution of
thought can be traced. Michael Novak who, like the author of this
study, was critical of certain aspects of all the drafts and final text of
the pastoral letter, properly commended the bishops for giving an
example of "the open church" in practice and for listening to and

acting on the arguments of virtually all Catholics who took part in the debate.[20]

The Bishops on Peace and Pacifism

The first draft of the pastoral letter was entitled, somewhat oddly, "God's Hope in a Time of Fear." The title was no doubt selected during the period in 1981 when there was a great deal of frightening talk about limiting and winning a nuclear war. As the very opening paragraphs indicated, the "signs of the times" were ominous indeed. Presumably the title was intended to provide a counter to despair, but it was somewhat awkward inasmuch as it implied that God, like human beings, hopes for the best rather than being the source of the distinctive Christian virtue of hope. In any event, subsequent drafts carried a different designation. All of the scriptural texts chosen to introduce the theme appropriately stressed hope, reconciliation, a spirit of peace, love of neighbor, and forgiveness—ideas of which the world needed to be reminded.

The structure of the first seven pages of the first draft, however, including all of the New Testament passages quoted, conveyed a strong impression to the reader that the bishops were about to espouse doctrinal pacifism before they made any reference to wars and conflicts of interests and values in a sinful world. "Force has often been used to settle such conflicts and, at times, as a last resort this has been justified."[21] This seemed like a rather grudging and fleeting recognition of the just war doctrine which has been dominant in Church teaching on war and peace for more than fifteen centuries. The next two pages again stressed the commands to love, to offer no resistance to injury, to turn the other cheek, to walk the extra mile.

Although the Fathers of the Church and Church tradition regarded these as *counsels* of Christian perfection for individuals, the draft contained repeated references to them as *commands*, implying an obligatory posture of nonviolence as the proper public policy to be supported by Christians in today's world. "Many heroic persons now live by this precept, by renouncing all violence even in personal self-defense."[22] That was a startling statement, for according to traditional Catholic moral and political philosophy, it is precisely in the realm of personal defence that force should be renounced. According to Augustinian-Thomistic doctrine the use of force cannot be renounced where the common good of the community and the fundamental rights of many are at stake. The draft cited the examples of Francis of Assisi, Dorothy Day, Mohandas Gandhi, and Martin Luther King without making reference to the larger framework of social order, the rule of law, and the cultural environment which made their nonviolent approach possible and successful. In this connection it is interesting to note that Gandhi's non-violent resistance, based on *satyagraha,* proved effective against British imperialism, but no voices in India seriously suggested pursuing that tactic when the Peoples' Republic of China attacked the northeast frontier.

The third draft and the final text omitted the strong pacifist tone which marked the opening of the first draft and emphasized instead the motif that the Catholic Church has a long and complex tradition on war and peace reaching from the Sermon on the Mount to the statements of Pope John Paul II, and that the bishops wish to reiterate this teaching for two distinct but overlapping audiences and for two purposes—to help Catholics form their consciences and to contribute to the public policy debate about the morality of war: "It is not our intent to play on fears . . . but to speak words of hope and encouragement in time of fear . . . . Hope sustains one's capacity to live with danger without being overwhelmed by it."[23] As citizens of the first nation to produce atomic weapons, the only one to use them in war, and one of the few able to influence the course of the nuclear age, Americans have grave human, moral, and political responsibilities to see that a conscious choice is made to save humanity.

All drafts beyond the first carried the following passages:

> The Catholic social tradition as exemplified in the pastoral constitution and recent papal teachings is a mix of biblical, theological and philosophical elements which are brought to bear upon the concrete problems of the day. The biblical vision of the world, created and sustained by God, scarred by sin, redeemed in Christ and destined for the kingdom, is at the heart of our religious heritage. This vision requires elaboration, explanation and application in each age; the important task of theology is to penetrate ever

more adequately the nature of the biblical vision of peace and relate it to a world not yet at peace . . .

At the center of the church's teaching on peace and at the center of all Catholic social teaching, are the transcendence of God and the dignity of the human person. The human person is the clearest reflection of God's presence in the world; all of the church's work in pursuit of both justice and peace is designed to protect and promote the dignity of every person. For each person not only reflects God, but is the expression of God's creative work and the meaning of Christ's redemptive ministry. Christians approach the problem of war and peace with fear and reverence. God is the Lord of life, and so each human life is sacred; modern warfare threatens the obliteration of human life on a previously unimaginable scale. The sense of awe and "fear of the Lord" which former generations felt in approaching these issues weighs upon us with new urgency. In the words of the pastoral constitution: "Men of this generation should realize that they will have to render an account of their warlike behavior; the destiny of generations to come depends largely on the decisions they make today.[24]

The bishops propose to discuss "both the religious vision of peace among peoples and nations and the problems associated with realizing this vision in a world of sovereign states devoid of any central authority and divided by ideology, geography and competing claims."[25]

The church is called to be, in a unique way, the instrument of the kingdom of God in history. Since peace is one of the signs of the kingdom of God present in the world, the church fulfills part of her essential mission by making the peace of the kingdom more visible in our time.[26]

The bishops accept the challenge of Vatican II "to undertake a completely fresh reappraisal of war" based on a biblical vision and a theology of peace, without pretending that what they present is a final synthesis.

Whereas the first draft had made no reference to the experiences of the ancient Israelites, subsequent drafts devoted considerable attention to the ideas of war and peace in the Old Testament—peace as a gift from God, God as protector and leader in battle, the guarantor of victory,[27] and the relationship between genuine peace (not merely the absence of war) and the requirements of fidelity to the covenant established by God, including obedience, justice, compassion for the needy and helpless—requirements of which prophets repeatedly reminded the people. Those who proclaimed peace while idolatry and injustice flourished were condemned by Ezekiel as false prophets, and the leaders who depended on their own strength or alliances instead of trusting in God were similarly condemned by Jeremiah and Isaiah. The people knew from experience that war, injustice, and sin existed. But God is faithful even if the people are not, and His "promise of a final salvation involving all peoples and all creation and of an ultimate reign of peace became an integral part of the hope of the Old Testament."[28] The people longed constantly for that eschatological time when, in the words of the psalmist, justice and peace would embrace.

The New Testament, say the bishops, presents no notion of a warrior God who leads the people to victory over enemies, only the eschatological struggle in the Book of Revelation in which the Lamb triumphs over Satan. Swords appear as images of division, and the word of God itself brings division of soul and spirit. Jesus proclaims that the reign of God in which the beatitudes are fulfilled begins in him. The marks of this new way to which all are called are repentance, forgiveness, conversion, mercy, love, and righteousness. Peace is the fullness of salvation, the reconciliation of the world and God, the unity of all things achieved through the death and resurrection of Christ.[29] "Even a brief examination of war and peace in the scriptures makes it clear that they do not provide us with detailed answers to the specifics of the questions we face today," except that as Christians we are called to our own peace and to the making of peace in a world where, because of sin, "the realization of the peace of the kingdom is never permanent or total."[30]

The evolution in the tone of the pastoral letter from the prounounced pacifism of the first draft to a formal reaffirmation of the just war theory in the third draft resulted not only from debate and comments within the American Catholic community but also from the January 1983 consultation at the Vatican. The memorandum of synthesis which issued from that meeting called for greater caution in the use of scripture and a clear distinction between the Christian faith that the kingdom of God will come and our lack of certainty that true peace can be effectively achieved within history and this world. Some bishops at Rome faulted the second draft for seeming to propose a double Catholic tradition of nonviolence and just war theory, and of equating the two, whereas the former has never been seen as an alternative to the latter.

> The affirmation in the draft that "the witnesses to non-violence and to Christian pacifism run from some church fathers through Francis of Assisi to Dorothy Day and Martin Luther King" is factually incorrect and does not support the affirmation that there is a pacifist tradition which holds "that any use of military force is incompatible with the Christian vocation" nor that it is clear from the writings of leading theologians in the first four centuries that "there was a certain level of opposition to military service based upon particular gospel passages."
>
> It was further pointed out that affirming "that one characteristic of contemporary Catholic teaching on war and peace has been the re-emergence of support for a pacifist option in the teaching of Vatican II" goes beyond what *Gaudium et Spes* says . . .
>
> It is clearly affirmed that there is only one Catholic tradition: the just war theory, but that this tradition was subject to inner tensions coming from an ever present desire for peace.[31]

It was then up to the *ad hoc* committee to perform the virtually impossible task of reconciling the advice received in the Rome memorandum with the demands of the more than sixty American bishops who are members of Pax Christi for a resounding affirmation of the pacifist, nonviolent, and nonviolent resistance alternatives. As if walking a theological tightrope, the drafting committee did its best under the circumstances in the passages which follow:

> The Christian has no choice but to defend peace, properly

understood, against aggression. This is an inalienable obligation. It is the *how* of defending peace which offers moral options. We stress this principle again because we observe so much misunderstanding about both those who resist bearing arms and those who bear them. Great numbers from both traditions provide examples of exceptional courage, examples the world continues to need.

Of the millions of men and women who have served with integrity in the armed forces, many have laid down their lives. Many others serve today throughout the world in the difficult and demanding task of helping to preserve that "peace of a sort" of which the council speaks.

We see many deeply sincere individuals who, far from being indifferent or apathetic to world evils, believe strongly in conscience that they are best defending true peace by refusing to bear arms. In some cases they are motivated by their understanding of the Gospel and the life and death of Jesus as forbidding all violence. In others, their motivation is simply to give personal example of Christian forbearance as a positive, constructive approach toward loving reconciliation with enemies. In still other cases, they propose or engage in "active non-violence" as programmed resistance to thwart aggression or to render ineffective any oppression attempted by force of arms. No government, and certainly no Christian, may simply assume that such individuals are mere pawns of consiratorial forces or guilty of cowardice.

Catholic teaching sees these two distinct moral responses as having a complementary relationship in the sense that both seek to serve the common good. They differ in their perception of how the common good is to be defended most effectively, but both responses testify to the Christian conviction that peace must be pursued and rights defended within moral restraints and in the context of defining other basic human values.

The third draft and final text strongly assert that, although conscientious objection and nonviolence in response to aggression are alternatives available to Christians, pacifism cannot be urged as a basis for the public policy of the state as if this were a Gospel mandate.

In all of this discussion of distinct choices, of course, we are referring to options open to individuals. The council and popes have stated clearly that governments threatened by armed, unjust aggression *must* defend their people. This includes defense by armed force if necessary as a last resort. We shall discuss below the conditions and limits imposed on such defense. Even when speaking of individuals, however, the council is careful to preserve the fundamental *right* of defense. Some choose not to vindicate their rights by armed force and adopt other methods of defense, but they do not lose the right of defense nor may they renounce their obligations to others. They are praised by the council, as long as the rights and duties of others or of the community itself are not injured.[33]

Bishop Gumbleton is irrefutable when he says that "Jesus teaches us not how to kill, but how to die."[34] We must remember, however, that soldiers are also sometimes asked to die—not to save all humankind for life everlasting, but only a portion of it for the kind of human life it prefers to live. The bishops in their pastoral letter are reaffirming that the lesson of supreme self-abnegation to which Bishop Gumbleton refers is offered to individual persons as a way of evangelical witness. It is not necessarily to be considered a higher way than that chosen by the soldier who is willing, if necessary, to risk and sacrifice human life to defend the common good or the community. "Greater love than this no man has, than that he lays down his life for his friends." The Church has always taught that there are different ways to follow Christ. Which of the two options for individuals requires greater heroism may be a matter not only of purity of interior disposition but also of historical circumstances. When patriotic fervor runs high in wartime, objecting in conscience for the sake of the Christian message takes consummate courage. On the other hand, when objection to all things military becomes popular for political and economic reaons, one need scarcely have achieved the highest degree of sanctity to be a pacifist. But aside from this question, the two options are available only to the individual, not to the state. The state, as we have seen, cannot "turn the other cheek." It has an obligation to defend its citizens and their common good against unjust aggression in a world that lacks an effective international organization to safeguard the rights and security of all states and to guarantee the peaceful settlement of disputes between them. The individual may choose martyrdom, but no one may impose martyrdom on the whole community—or on another community which there may be an obligation to defend. *No Christian, therefore, may invoke either the commands or the counsels of the Gospel in order to justify a movement of political opposition to all national policies, programs, and expenditures for deterrence and defense.*

The Vatican Council, the popes, and the bishops of the United States have repeatedly upheld the rights and obligations of governments to maintain military forces for legitimate national self-defense. It would seem, therefore, that the Christian who goes beyond the espousal of pacifism as an option of evangelical witness and makes a career out of ridiculing and opposing every proposal for maintaining adequate military capabilities for a nation in a constantly changing technological environment does an injustice to the political community. This is not to suggest that the Christian citizen needs to support every new military program the Pentagon can dream up. Even the most defense-minded congressman would find that proposition absurd. But it is that abiding attitude of suspicion and hatred toward the entire military component of the U.S. government manifested by many pacifists, that is highly reprehensible from the standpoint of the Catholic tradition. More will be said about the call in the pastoral letter for the programmed development of nonviolent means of resisting aggresion, since this represents in the present context more of a political prescription than a moral teaching in accord with Catholic tradition.

The Just War

Whereas the first and second drafts appeared to equate pacifism and just war as authentic Christian responses to the political problem of war in Catholic social doctrine, the third draft and final text, as we have seen, distinguish between the renunciation of violence as an option for an individual and the necessity of the state to use force when necessary as a last resort to defend the common good and the lives of its citizens. This motif was strengthened following the Vatican meeting, which made the U.S. bishops more "conscious of the consequences our teaching will have not only for our own nation but for the lives of others."[35]

The pastoral letter reaffirms the essential Augustinian-Thomistic doctrine: States in an anarchic global system cannot be denied the right of self-defense. Given the nature of modern war, the decision to go to war, if it is to be morally permissible, "today requires extraordinarily strong reasons for overriding the presumption *in favor of peace* and *against* war."[36] It is absolutely clear that the West could not morally plan to launch a major war for the purpose of eliminating the communist government in Moscow.

> War is permissible only to confront "a real and certain danger," i.e., to protect innocent life, to preserve conditions necessary for decent human existence and to secure basic human rights.[37]

Earlier Church pronouncements in the nuclear age tended to ignore the criterion of just cause for which a nation could go to war, after Pope Pius II said in 1944 that the initiation of war for the purpose of redressing violated rights could no longer be justified. As indicated earlier, the right of a nation to defend itself against aggression was never at issue. In the nuclear age the Church became more concerned about the *ius in bello* than the *ius ad bellum*—about the rightful conduct of war than about the reasons why a nation might be justified in undertaking a defensive war on a large scale for the purpose of preserving its values, its way of life, and about the degree and modes of force it might use to prevent its own destruction as a juridically organized community capable of being the master of its own political destiny. As the political, social, cultural, human, and religious value stakes grow higher for the nation, does the amount of justifiable defensive force increase commensurately?

Unfortunately, the Church has not given a clear answer to this and related questions, preferring only to warn against the potentially cataclysmic consequences of modern warfare, particularly nuclear warfare. In 1982, when only the first drafts of the pastoral letter had been completed, William V. O'Brien wrote as follows on the moral dilemma of deterrence in official ecclesiastical statements:

The church pronouncements simply neglect *ius ad bellum* .... Indeed, since no concrete threat of aggression and its consequences for freedom and human rights is even mentioned, much less evaluated, it is hard to see how this moral dilemma of nuclear deterrence arises. Is there a specific threat of aggression against the United States and/ or other states? What would successful aggresssion mean for the defeated? Apparently there is some kind of threat since an awkward deterrence posture is tolerated. But there is no clear "just cause" to which just deterrence and defense can be related in recent church pronouncements.[38]

The final text is not really much more helpful except for the sentence quoted on the permissibility of war. The difficulty with that sentence is that it probably constitutes too broad a warrant in the minds of some. Might it, for example, justify an intervention by NATO military forces in Poland if in some future crisis involving the activity of Solidarity the Soviet Union should invade Poland with military force? Quite apart from wondering whether the United State and its allies should respond with force to secure the basic human rights of the Poles, if the Polish people, under overt Soviet military invasion and suppression, should appeal desperately for Western aid, the more germane question is whether the U.S. Catholic bishops gave any thought to this problem and its implications for their teaching before approving that single sentence quoted above, which can be interpreted to encompass a military intervention by Western powers in Eastern Europe under certain circumstances—something that the NATO governments, mindful of the security apprehensions of the Soviet Union, did not contemplate at the time of the Hungarian uprising in 1956, the Warsaw Pact invasion of Czechoslovakia in 1968, or the Polish crisis from mid-1980 onward.

Archbishop Hannan's criticism of the first two drafts for completely ignoring the nature of the Soviet system and threat was mentioned earlier (see p. 8). At the Vatican meeting of January 1983, Agostino Casaroli, papal secretary of state, offered a personal commentary on the two dangers of (1) nuclear war and (2) loss of freedom and independence by entire peoples. He declined to indicate whether these two dangers were equal or whether one was greater

than the other, but concluded that there is "a clear moral responsibility to do everything possible with total commitment and good will
to prevent both" dangers by political means (e.g., negotiations) and
deterrence, in spite of its risks.[39] The third draft and final text of the
pastoral letter corrects the deficiency of earlier drafts by recognizing
the political, philosophical, and ideological differences between the
two superpowers, their alliances—one imposed, the other freely
chosen—and the threat of Soviet military expansionism, however
difficult that may be to evaluate.

> The fact of a Soviet threat, as well as the existence of a
> Soviet imperial drive for hegemony, at least in regions of
> major strategic interest, cannot be denied, The history of
> the Cold War has produced varying interpretations of
> which side caused which conflict, but whatever the details of
> history illustrate, the plain fact is that the memories of
> Soviet policies in Eastern Europe and recent events in
> Afghanistan and Poland have left their mark in the Amer-
> ican political debate. Many peoples are forcibly kept under
> communist domination despite their manifest wishes to be
> free. Soviet power is very great. Whether the Soviet Union's
> pursuit of military might is motivated primarily by defen-
> sive or aggressive aims might be debated, but the effect is
> nevertheless to leave profoundly insecure those who must
> live in the shadow of that might.
> Americans need have no illusions about the Soviet
> system of repression and the lack of respect in that system
> for human rights or about Soviet covert operations and pro-
> revolutionary activities.[40]

The bishops by no means idealize the American system which,
they point out, has its flaws, for it sometimes supports repressive
governments, carries out repugnant covert operations, and fails to
ensure equal rights for all at home. Nevertheless, having said this,
they feel compelled to confront reality:

> The facts simply do not support the invidious com-
> parisons made at times even in our own society between our
> way of life, in which most basic human rights are at least

recognized even if they are not always adequately supported, and those totalitarian and tyrannical regimes in which such rights are either denied or systematically suppressed. Insofar as this is true, however, it makes the promotion of human rights in our foreign policy, as well as our domestic policy, all the more important. It is the acid test of our commitment to our democratic values. In this light, any attempts to justify, for reasons of state, support for regimes that continue to violate human rights is all the more morally reprehensible in its hypocrisy.[41]

The bishops also acknowledge their political freedom to publish a pastoral letter critical of the government—a freedom which could not be exercised in the Soviet bloc. "Free people must always pay a proportionate price and run some risks—responsibly—to preserve their freedom."[42]

The bishops, then, do delineate the contrast between the two systems, and express a strong preference for Western constitutional democracy over Marxist-Leninist tyranny; but they refrain from drawing any linkage between this comparison and the criterion of just cause for undertaking even defensive war, probably because they fear that drawing such a linkage might stimulate sentiment for an anti-Soviet crusade, whereas they wish to emphasize the importance of political dialogue and negotiation based on a common interest in avoiding nuclear war. They do not even call for Western political initiatives aimed at producing greater freedom for citizens of the Soviet Union and the People's Democracies of Eastern Europe. In this respect, without realizing it, they appear to share the prudence of Henry Kissinger's *Realpolitik*.

Under the heading of "comparative justice" as a criterion for the right to go to war, the bishops stress the presumption against war which stands at the beginning of just war teaching and ask whether the values at stake are "critical enough to override the presumption against war" and justify the killing, suffering, and destruction involved in war, especially since it is incumbent upon states to refrain from assuming that absolute justice is on their side. The test of comparative justice may be extremely difficult to apply, although it may be clear in some instances. "Blatant aggression from without and subversion from within are often readily enough identifiable by all reasonably fair-minded people."[43] The bishops also reaffirm the *ius ad bellum* criteria of right intention, last resort, (including the resources of a possibly reformed and more effective United Nations), probability of success, and proportionality (i.e., an evaluation of "the good expected" from the war in the light of the likely total cost of the war, measured in deaths, damages, and effects not only upon the warring parties but also on the international community).[44]

One other criterion for the *ius ad bellum* must be mentioned— declaration of war by competent authority responsible for public order, not by private groups or individuals. In the Middle Ages, this was a necessary prerequisite to curb the penchant of petty feudal lords to resort to warfare for reasons of personal power aggrandizement. In the modern nation-state period, it was all but forgotten because only well-established governments could embark upon international war. But it has regained significance as a result of the rise of revolutionary insurgency movements throughout the Third World (the erstwhile colonial world) in recent decades.

St. Thomas Aquinas had put forth a moderate theory of just revolution against a government which had become intolerably oppressive, but he issued a strong warning against individuals who would take it upon themselves to employ lethal force against tyrants and their regimes. He insisted that such rulers be deposed only by the natural leaders of the people, persons who already had considerable political experience within the community, not malcontents driven by an inner voice of mission or power drive that had nothing to do with the common good of the people.[45] The bishops allude to the problem:

> Insufficient analytical attention has been given to the moral issues of revolutionary warfare. The mere possession of sufficient weaponry, for example, does not legitimize the initiation of war by "insurgents" against an established government any more than the government's systematic oppression of its people can be carried out under the doctrine of "national security."
>
> While the legitimacy of revolution in some circumstances cannot be denied, just-war teachings must be applied as rigorously to revolutionary-counter-revolutionary conflicts as to others. The issue of who constitutes

competent authority and how such authority is exercised is essential.[46]

It is regrettable that the following passage which appeared in the third draft was deleted from the final text at the insistence of radical "pacifists," whose liberation theology condones resort to violence against socioeconomic structures that are deemed unjust.

> Some who normally argue that *no* war can ever be justified seem to exempt certain "wars of liberation" from this prohibition, and even praise and support wars waged by revolutionary forces, while denying established governments the right to wage wars against revolutionaries. Such a position is clearly unacceptable.[47]

The remainder of the treatment of just war is devoted largely to a discussion of the principles of proportionality and discrimination, as applied to both the *ius ad bellum* and the *ius in bello*. The bishops set the tone for this discussion when they say that:

> Today it becomes increasingly difficult to make a decision to use any kind of armed force, however limited initially in intention and in the destructive power of the weapons employed, without facing at least the possibility of escalation to broader, or even total, war and to the use of weapons of horrendous destructive potential.[48]

This thought is controlling in the bishops' treatment of nuclear war, although they recognize that modern "conventional war" (including incendiary bombing, the use of gas, and other forms of chemical warfare) brings horrors of its own.

Following the Vatican Council and all the popes of the nuclear age, the bishops condemn war waged on a catastrophic scale which would wipe out a large part of civilization, endanger its very survival, and trigger major and irreversible ecological and genetic changes whose limits cannot be predicted.[49] They repeat the Church's earlier unequivocal condemnations of "any act of war aimed indiscriminately at the destruction of entire cities or of extensive areas along with their population."[50]

Prior to the August 1980 announcement of the countervailing strategy in Presidential Directive 59, it had been widely taken for granted on both sides of the Atlantic that the McNamara Doctrine had strongly implied a threat of retaliation against Soviet urban centers. One remarkable result of the debate over the bishops' views, particularly their condemnation of any strategy which aimed at annihilation of cities was that it elicited from former National Security Adviser William P. Clark and Secretary of Defense Caspar Weinberger the first unambiguous assurance ever given by high-ranking U.S. government officials that this country is not committed to a strategy of leveling cities. Clark wrote to Cardinal Bernardin on January 15, 1983 as follows:

> For moral, political and military reasons, the United States does not target the Soviet civilian population as such. There is no deliberately opaque meaning conveyed in the last two words. We do not threaten the existence of Soviet civilization by threatening Soviet cities. Rather, we hold at risk the war-making capability of the Soviet Union—its armed forces, and the industrial capacity to sustain war. It would be irresponsible for us to issue policy statements which might suggest to the Soviets that it would be to their advantage to establish privileged sanctuaries within heavily populated areas, thus inducing them to locate much of their warfighting capability within those urban sanctuaries.[51]

The bishops appreciated Mr. Clark's statement, but they were not entirely satisfied with the assurance given by him and Secretary of Defense Caspar Weinberger. The principle of proportionality requires that an answer be given to this question: Once we take into account not only the military advantages that will be achieved by using this means, but also the harms reasonably expected to follow from using it, can its use still be justified?[52]

Closely related to this issue is the principle of discrimination, which prohibits directly intended attacks on noncombatants and nonmilitary targets. In a later section of the document dealing with "Reverence for Life," where they condemn the direct attack on innocent human life in abortion, the bishops acknowledge the traditional just war doctrine and state that "justifiable defense against aggression may result in the indirect or unintended loss of innocent human lives."[53] But here, in attempting to apply the principle of discrimination, they admit that the concepts "intentional," "noncombatant," and "military" are difficult to define with precision. Who are non-combatants in modern warfare?

> Mobilization of forces in modern war includes not only the
> military, but to a significant degree the political, economic
> and social sectors. It is not always easy to determine who is
> directly involved in a "war effort" or to what degree. Plainly,
> though, not even by the broadest definition can one
> rationally consider combatants entire classes of human
> beings such as schoolchildren, hospital patients, the elderly,
> the ill, the average industrial worker producing goods not
> directly related to military purposes, farmers and many
> others. They may never be directly attacked.[54]

What targets are military? If a munitions factory has been placed
in the heart of a city or if guerrilla revolutionaries use the people of a
village as a shield, who is directly responsible for the deaths of
noncombatants if these targets are attacked? How many indirect,
unintended deaths of noncombatants are "tolerable" in attacks on
otherwise legitimate military targets? The bishops raise these questions, but instead of answering them, they shift the focus of their
attention to "The Value of Nonviolence," a discussion much more
helpful to Christian pacifists than to just war theorists. Perhaps this is
a subtle episcopal way of saying that the answers to these hard
questions cannot be given in advance by religious leaders but only
found in the crucible of war by those who bear the responsibility for
political decisions. The bishops, in sum, employing the just war
criteria of proportionality and discrimination, condemn all counterpopulation warfare, whether in the form of nuclear countercity or
counterforce attacks which would cause such widespread collateral
annihilation in populated areas (with casualties numbering in millions or tens of millions) as to be for all practical purposes indis-
tinguishable from the destructive effects of a countercity targeting
strategy, except that they would be indirect and unintended.

Any strategist with a shred of moral or humanitarian sensibility
must insist that, if the time ever comes when nuclear weapons are
used, they must be used in the most limited and discriminating
manner possible against military targets with minimum collateral
damage to populations.[55] (The United States, which has historically
preferred "miniaturization," i.e., lower yield warheads and optimal

accuracy, is in a much better position than the Soviet Union to comtemplate such a strategy.)

The memorandum resulting from the Vatican consultation had stipulated that the pastoral letter should "state more clearly what is meant by condemnation of counterpopulation warfare, taking into account the contingency of judgment."[56] The final text of the letter, however, remains obscure and unhelpful on this point. It condemns, as it must, a strategy which aims at the deliberate killing of noncombatants, but it furnishes no guidance regarding the number of casualties that might be justified unintentionally and indirectly in a limited counterfore attack. Counterpopulation warfare, the bishops declare, is no less immoral in retaliation than in a first strike.

> Retaliatory action, whether nuclear or conventional, which would indiscriminately take many wholly innocent lives, lives of people who are in no way responsible for reckless actions of their government, must also be condemned. This condemnation, in our judgment, applies even to the retaliatory use of weapons striking enemy cities after our own have already been struck. No Christian can rightfully carry out orders or policies deliberately aimed at killing noncombatants.
>
> We make this judgment at the beginning of our treatment of nuclear strategy precisely because the defense of the principle of noncombatant immunity is so important for an ethic or war and because the nuclear age has posed such extreme problems for the principle.[57]

Throughout the nuclear age, some prominent Catholic just war theorists such as John Courtney Murray and William V. O'Brien, following lines of analysis laid down by Pope Pius XII, have insisted that it is possible and might someday be unavoidably necessary, to consider a limited and discriminatory use of nuclear weapons that would not be disproportionate in the face of massive totalitarian aggression against a democratic society. Neither the popes nor Vatican II went so far as to proscribe the use of nuclear weapons under all circumstances, even though some Catholic pacifists, in their zeal for the cause, have exaggerated the degree to which the Catholic Church has formally condemned every use of nuclear weapons.[58] If the Church condemned every use of such weapons, the approval given nuclear deterrence by the popes, the Vatican council, and the bishops would make no sense. In fact, Pope Pius XII and several Catholic moralists have cited the example of an encounter between fleets at sea, in which nuclear weapons could be used without jeopardizing civilian populations and structures. Their use in a mountain pass, ravine, gorge, or highway through a forested area to interdict the passage of massed armor is also conceivable with minimal civilian casualties. With regard even to these hypothetical uses, however, the bishops would point to the risk of escalation.

At the Vatican meeting with European bishops, the U.S. representatives explained the American bishops' rationale for their stand on the two closely related questions of limited nuclear war and no first use of nuclear weapons. They wanted to stress the qualitative differences between conventional and nuclear war and react against tendencies in the United States to present nuclear war as more likely and more acceptable. Some European bishops agreed that the Americans have a duty to warn those in authority about possible consequences. It was thought, however, in regard to the problem of limiting nuclear war and the danger of escalation, "that the text should clearly state to what extent the episcopal teaching authority can be committed when the draft itself states that 'technical opinion on this question and the writings of moralists remain divided' and . . . 'the policy debate on this question is inconclusive'."[59] On the subject of first use, the Vatican memorandum said:

> Some were of the opinion . . . that the draft contains an apodictic moral judgment rejecting first use of nuclear weapons, although the affirmation in the same text 'that serious debate is under way' does not seem to warrant such a statement, which remains highly contingent. Others saw the possibility of first use as still necessary at this stage within the context of deterrence.[60]

The American bishops, going beyond the statements of the Popes and Vatican II and guidance from the Rome Consultation, take a clear stand against any first use of nuclear weapons and come very close to opposing *any* use of such weapons, even in retaliation and against military targets. While stopping short of branding every use immoral, they remain profoundly skeptical.

We do not perceive any situation in which the deliberate initiation of nuclear warfare on however restricted scale can be morally justified. Non-nuclear attacks by another state must be resisted by other than nuclear means. Therefore, a serious moral obligation exists to develop non-nuclear defensive strategies as rapidly as possible.[61]

The bishops recognize that their opposition to any initiation of nuclear war and their call for a modification of strategic policy have serious implications for NATO. They take this stand because of what they conceive to be unacceptable risks in light of the danger of uncontrollable escalation. They acknowledge that this stand represents their own empirical and prudential judgment, based on their evaluation of expert views, and hence is not a morally binding conclusion, but one which Catholics must ponder carefully.

Nuclear Deterrence

At this point a central thesis of the present study can be restated: Compared to the traditional Catholic just war doctrine and the concept of individual conscientious vocation to give witness to the Gospel spirit of peace, there was no well-developed corpus of Catholic thought on the subject of deterrence to which the bishops could turn in writing their pastoral letter. Although a small number of Catholic moral theologians and political scientists have begun to pay more attention to the concept of deterrence in the last few years, and to take seriously the ideas of strategic theorists instead of ignoring or dismissing them out of hand the bishops cannot be said to have formulated any systematic theory of deterrence, even though the question of whether the nuclear deterrence is "morally acceptable," "marginally tolerable," or "immoral and wicked" has been a critical one throughout their two years of deliberations. Most of the bishops would be candid enough to acknowledge this fact.

It is clear from the tone of their letter that the bishops fear an almost imminent breakdown of the deterrence which has helped to keep "peace of a sort" for nearly four decades. "We live today . . . in the midst of a cosmic drama" in which nuclear weapons threaten civilization and "even the created order itself." The world has arrived at "a new moment" when a prominent "sign of the times" is "a sharply increased awareness of the danger of the nuclear arms race," and when "opposition to the arms race is no longer selective or sporadic, [but] . . . is widespread and sustained," thanks apparently "in large measure to the work of scientists and physicians."[62] One is moved here more by the emotional eloquence of the rhetoric than by the substantive content of the analysis, in which there is lacking a comprehensive approach to the philosophical, psychological, and changing political-military-strategic factors in the international environment which have produced the new antinuclear and "peace" movements in the West. It is unfair, however, to fault the bishops for not having discoursed at length on that subject.

In their understandable determination to say a resounding "no" to nuclear war, the bishops exhibit only a marginal and conditional tolerance of deterrence. "What previously had been defined as a safe and stable system of deterrence is today viewed with political and moral skepticism."[63] By whom? The bishops do not say, but it is so viewed by antinuclear and absolute pacifists—not by governments, defense-knowledgeable elites, strategic analysts, and most legislative representatives and executive decisionmakers in the dozen Atlantic Alliance member nations that make significant contributions to Western defense. The bishops assure us that they understand how in "a world of sovereign states devoid of central authority and possessing the knowledge to possess nuclear weapons many choices were made, some clearly objectionable, others well-intentioned with mixed results," and how we have been brought to our present precarious situation.[64] This is an honest assessment of the situation, one to which it is not easy to take exception.

Throughout their discussion of nuclear deterrence the bishops oscillate between contradictory positions which they never really reconcile or synthesize coherently. This is due partly to the fact that the strategy of deterrence involves a profound paradox which, they readily admit, has strained their moral conception to the utmost. The dilemmas which inhere in deterrence are not of the bishops' making. But the deficiencies and ambiguities in their teaching arise partly from the inescapable nature of the problem and partly from the fact that they appointed for the drafting of their letter a committee sufficiently representative of a broad spectrum of opinion to include something for everyone: absolute pacifists, nuclear pacifists, nonviolent resisters, just war theorists, and advocates of deterrence. They then voted for or against scores of amendments to the text, much like a legislative body putting together an omnibus bill to placate various constituencies, demonstrating along the way the danger inherent in any effort to define universally binding moral precepts through the methods of parliamentary rule-making.[65] As a result, the letter does not present a single logically consistent approach to the problem of war and peace, but at times moves simultaneously in different directions. This is probably unavoidable because of the nature of the subject. The dilemmas of nuclear deterrence cannot be easily resolved with logically neat formulas.

In a paragraph of particularly sophisticated analysis, the bishops note that "strategies have been developed which previous generations would have found unintelligible," for the declared purpose of never having to use the weapons produced. But "threats are made which would be suicidal to implement," and these strategies depend on perceptions of what is rational and how convincing one side's threat is to the other. "May a nation threaten what it may never do? May it possess what it may never use?"[66] Thus do they formulate the moral dilemmas, while reiterating that the main problem is how to prevent nuclear war, recognizing the distinction between "declaratory policy" and "action policy," and hastening to add that "there has been substantial continuity in U.S. action policy in spite of real changes in declaratory policy."[67] In a thinly veiled criticism of written assurances from administration officials that it not U.S. policy to target civilian populations, the bishops deny that the assertion of an intention not to strike civilians directly, however honest, by itself constitutes a moral policy for the use of nuclear weapons.[68]

In the final analysis, the bishops appear to be more concerned with the ethics of consequences than with the ethics of intention, and their focus is almost exclusively on the potential consequences of nuclear war. These would indeed be frightful. But political leaders also have to fear other consequences of taking positions which weaken deterrence, consequences which may be no less frightful, but which could be avoided if an adequate posture of deterrence can be maintained to support intelligent diplomacy. The letter does not deal as comprehensively as it might have with the fuller range of potentially adverse consequences. Even though the pastoral letter is quite long, this author wishes it were longer in some respects and shorter in others—longer in probing the meaning of traditional moral principles for today's international political-strategic environment and shorter on specific policy prescriptions.

The Bishops as Shepherds

The bishops display their pastoral understanding best in Section 4 which opens with a moving reminder that the Church is a community of conscience, prayer, and penance. This is as it ought to be. There are here many thoughts which merit deep pondering—what it means to be a Christian, a disciple of Jesus, in a world of deadly nuclear missiles. The section is well worth a thoughtful reading. It is not, any more than the whole letter, designed to give comfort. In fact, it is bound to generate cognitive dissonance in the minds of Catholics of left, center, and right, who are strongly urged by the bishops to read and meditate upon the whole letter, not only those passages to which they are favorably disposed.

The bishops urge "balanced and objective educational programs" in every diocese and parish to help people at all age levels to understand better the issues of war and peace, with the pastoral letter in its entirety and complexity to be used as a guide. The fact that these issues are political "is no excuse for denying the Church's obligation" to help form consciences. "We are called to move from discussion to witness and action."[69] Some Catholics involved in the educational process will probably take "witness and action" as an implied exhortation to move toward pacifist and antimilitary positions. (One does not usually speak of "witness" in connection with the Church's official just war doctrine, although there is no reason why one cannot.) The NCCB had no intention here of endorsing pacifism as a basis for a Catholic public policy. Indeed, it could not do so without flouting the Vatican guidelines and raising the specter of a new Americanist heresy.

The bishops reiterate the crucial distinction between the Church's teaching authority with respect to moral principles and to the proposal of particular technical solutions to questions over which people of goodwill may disagree.

The church's educational programs must explain

clearly those principles or teachings about which there is little question. Those teachings, which seek to make explicit the gospel call to peace and the tradition of the church, should then be applied to concrete situations. They must indicate what the possible legitimate options are and what the consequences of those options may be. While this approach should be self-evident, it needs to be emphasized. Some people who have entered the public debate on nuclear warfare, at all points of the spectrum of opinion, appear not to understand or accept some of the clear teachings of the church as contained in papal or conciliar documents. For example, some would place almost no limits on the use of nuclear weapons if they are needed for "self-defense." Some on the other side of the debate insist on conclusions which may be legitimate options but cannot be made obligatory on the basis of actual church teaching.[70]

The bishops speak of the threat of violence in various forms to the dignity of the human person. It is here that they relate war to abortion. Any Catholic well grounded in the traditional theological and philosophical teaching of the Church is bound to react instinctively with sympathy to the effort to draw an analogy on behalf of the sacredness of human life between both abortion and war—not only nuclear war, but any war in which innocent lives may be lost, as they invariably are. The bishops do not draw such an analogy for the purpose of arousing a visceral Catholic pro-life response. They understand very well the significant difference between the morality of abortion and the morality of war; to confuse them would distort the Catholic theological tradition. The bishops recognize that "even justifiable defense against aggression may result in the indirect or unintended loss of innocent human lives" and this, although tragic, "may conceivably be proportionate to the values defended"; however, nothing can justify direct attack on innocent human life, as in abortion or in the course of warfare.[71] Thus there can be no proper analogy between a decision to abort a fetus and the just use of force by a legitimate government for the necessary defense of the common good. The principal fear of the bishops is that a nation which readily tolerates more than a million abortions a year as a constitutional right of individuals may have no qualms of conscience when it comes to killing innocent populations in wartime. No Catholic, however, is entitled to employ loose emotional rhetoric in which every war or act of war, regardless of justice, is equated to "abortion writ large."

It is not possible to review and comment upon the pastoral advice which the bishops offer to specific classes of persons: priests, educators, parents, youth; men and women in military service, or in defense industries, science, the media, and public office; and Catholics as citizens. "To teach the ways of peace," say the bishops, is not 'to weaken the nation's will,' but to be concerned for the nation's soul."[72] It is not their intention to create problems for Catholics in the armed forces, except to remind them of the special challenge which their letter poses to the military profession. They remind all in authority and in the chain of command that their training and field manuals prohibit certain actions in the conduct of war, especially those which inflict harm on innocent civilians. "The purpose of defense policy is to defend the peace; military professionals should understand their vocation this way. We believe they do, and we support this view."[73] This might be interpreted as a summons to Catholics in the armed services to approach their tasks with the intention of strengthening deterrence and prolonging its effectiveness rather than of actually waging nuclear war, even though plans and preparations may be necessary to maintain the credibility of the deterrence.

Deterrence, however, is not explicitly mentioned in Section 4. The bishops missed an opportunity to relate one of the central theses of their letter—that deterrence remains morally acceptable under the circumstances prevailing in the world—to the constructive role that could be urged upon Catholics in academic, scientific, military, and public life to participate with a spirit of Christian witness in the intelligent analysis, planning, development, and management of deterrent forces, strategies, and policies for the purpose of increasing the probability that those forces will never have to be used before enlightened statesmanship, diplomacy, arms negotiations, and changes in the institutional structures and operational processes of international systems can substantially alter the security apprehensions of nation-states. One derives from the language of Section 4 and of the letter as a whole an impression—which may be mistaken—that even though the bishops grudgingly grant a conditional moral acceptance to nuclear deterrence, many of them expect Catholics who reflect prayerfully upon their teachings gradually to have less and less tolerance for deterrence and eventually wash their hands of it entirely. If so, that might be not a prudential judgment on the part of bishops but, in the longer view, a case of serious episcopal imprudence, fraught with potentially undesirable, even disastrous, consequences, which the bishops certainly do not intend. Most of the bishops would probably agree that the cause of morality is hardly well served by moving from a situation in which a war between the superpowers is deterred to one in which it is not.

6

MORALITY AND STRATEGY
IN THE PASTORAL LETTER
IMPLICATIONS FOR DETERRENCE

No one today denies that a city-annihilation strategy is immoral and irrational. For a traditional Thomist, those two terms are virtually interchangeable. The bishops have not been criticized, but rather, applauded, for condemning such a strategy, thereby adding the powerful voice of the American Catholic Church to earlier similar condemnations by the popes and Vatican II. Some of the specific recommendations on policy contained in the pastoral letter, however, have aroused concern among certain strategic analysts of deterrence and arms control, including this author, who are otherwise in complete sympathy with the bishops' effort to undertake a fresh appraisal of the problem of war and to make us aware, as Catholics and American citizens, of our grave human, moral, and political responsibilities to see that a deliberate and conscious choice is made to save humanity.[1]

There are two dangers facing humanity today: nuclear war and totalitarian tyranny. Cardinal Casaroli, the papal secretary of state, has seen no need to assign such a priority to either one of these dangers that we risk lapsing into the other; for the real challenge confronting us is to save humanity—not just the West, but ultimately all humankind—from both. Many of the bishops are undoubtedly as aware as Casaroli of the profound dilemma confronting the Church, that twin specter of nuclear self-extermination and totalitarian domination of which the German philosopher Karl Jaspers said more than a quarter of a century ago: "By one, we lose life; by the other, a life that is worth living."[2] The bishops, of course, are not concerned about mere biological survival. They seek to avoid a moral evil. The first two drafts of their letter were focused almost exclusively upon avoiding one evil, the potential consequences of nuclear war. The pastoral letter finally incorporated a recognition that Soviet expansionism poses a threat to the West and to other parts of the world, but this is certainly not portrayed as a danger equally to be dreaded.

One might even assign a higher priority to avoiding large-scale nuclear war yet still deem it extremely imprudent to adopt positions which would have the effect of increasing, in however small a measure, the onset of the opposite evil. This, unfortunately, did not appear to be an overarching concern of the bishops in proposing their specific policy recommendations. The letter contains only sparse indications that they worry about the potential consequences of weakening Western deterrence, which would cause some erosion of the West's bargaining position in arms control negotiations with a tough-minded Soviet government, increase the risk of political intimidation of Western Europe by Moscow, produce asymmetrical, unilateral effects within a delicate system of mutual deterrence, and thereby contribute toward a political and military destabilization that could conceivably raise the probability of war breaking out by political miscalculation. Certainly the bishops do not want their letter to have any such adverse effects. One is entitled, therefore, to comment on the possible implications of some of their specific political, technical, and strategic policy recommendations which contain their prudential and contingent judgments rather than morally binding principles. This is done for the purpose of continuing the dialogue which has now begun among bishops, theologians, strategists, government policymakers, political scientists, and others by offering critical commentary and posing questions which are bound to arise during the course of the American Catholic Church's efforts to carry out its educational program in elucidation of the pastoral letter.

Nonviolent Resistance

In all drafts and the final text of their pastoral letter, the bishops deny that armed force constitutes the only defense against aggression, especially in view of the horror and perversity of war waged with scientific weapons. Hence they call for the development of non-violent means of resisting aggression:

There must be serious and continuing study and efforts to develop programmed methods for both individuals and nations to defend against unjust aggression without using violence.

We believe work to develop nonviolent means of fending off aggression and resolving conflict best reflects the call of Jesus both to love and to justice.[3]

At this point the bishops are not clear as to what they mean. Later on, they insist that means must be found to defend peoples without threatening annihilation, and they become more specific:

The Second Vatican Council praised "those who renounce the use of violence in the vindication of their rights and who resort to methods of defense which are otherwise available to weaker parties, provided that this can be done without injury to the rights and duties of others or of the community itself." To make such renunciation effective and still defend what must be defended, the arts of diplomacy, negotiation and compromise must be developed and fully exercised. Non-violent means of resistance to evil deserve much more study and consideration than they have thus far received. There have been significant instances in which people have successfully resisted oppression without recourse to arms. Non-violence is not the way of the weak, the cowardly or the impatient. Such movements have seldom gained headlines even though they have left their mark on history. The heroic Danes who would not turn Jews over to the Nazis and the Norwegians who would not teach Nazi propaganda in schools serve as inspiring examples in the history of non-violence.

Non-violent resistance, like war, can take many forms depending upon the demands of a given situation. There is, for instance, organized popular defense instituted by government as part of its contingency planning. Citizens would be trained in the techniques of peaceable non-compliance and non-cooperation as a means of hindering an invading force or non-democratic government from imposing its

will. Effective non-violent resistance requires the united will
of a people and may demand as much patience and sacrifice
from those who practice it as is now demanded by war and
preparation for war. It may not always succeed. Nevertheless, before the possibility is dismissed as impractical or
unrealistic, we urge that it be measured against the almost
certain effects of a major war.[4]

The bishops then appear to be endorsing the Gandhian doctrine of nonviolent resistance (NVR) when they say that popular
defense would go beyond conflict resolution and compromise to a
"basic synthesis of beliefs and values." The object is not only to avoid
injuring another, but to seek the other's good; not only to blunt
aggression, but to make the adversary a friend. This sounds like a
combination of Christian-Marxist dialogue and Gandhi's *satyagraha*
or "truth force." Quite apart from the proposition that the roots of
the theory of political nonviolence can be traced to Scripture and
Tradition, the Church Fathers, and the martyrs—a proposition
which derives more from Gandhi than from Rome—the Bishops' call
for the development of "programmed methods" of NVR is bound to
give rise to many thorny questions. Although commentators on the
letter have generally ignored it, this idea could eventually turn out to
be one of its most controversial recommendations.

No Christian and no civilized government can but prefer the
nonviolent resolution of conflicts that arise inevitably between
nations. Diplomatic negotiation, mediation, conciliation, arbitration,
ajudication, and other peaceful methods of settling international
disputes should always be the norm. But an appeal for nonviolent
resolution of differences and preparations for nonviolent defense
against military aggression are two very different things. The stress
on developing methods of nonviolent resistance was inserted into the
pastoral letter largely at the behest of approximately sixty bishops
who are members of the American branch of Pax Christi. The
literature of this organization is generally critical of all arms expenditures. It is also highly favorable to unilateral disarmament by the
United States. A Pax Christi educational publication in the early
1980s deprecates the fear that unilateral disarmament would lead to
a nuclear strike by the Soviet Union, because the principal motive for
a first strike is fear of an enemy's first strike, and the United States
would then no longer pose a military nuclear or conventional threat

to the USSR. If the Soviet Union were still to carry out conventional aggression to occupy the industrial West in order to exploit its economic potential, Christians in Europe and the United States should meet that threat by nonviolent means of resistance.[5]

As a theorist of international relations, the author of this study can only regard the Pax Christi analysis of the problem of U.S. national security in the nuclear age as a harmless imaginary excursion into a never-never land far removed from political reality,[6] an analysis which could become a recipe for a potential disaster of considerable magnitude if taken seriously by a sizable portion of the American Catholic community. NVR might be appropriate for a post-surrender situation in circumstances of vast power differential between two states, where the weaker party realizes the utter futility of any resistance, as did Holland after four days of fighting against an overwhelming Nazi invasion force in 1940. It should not be forgotten that the heroic resistance (not entirely nonviolent!) carried on by Danes, Norwegians, and Dutch during the period of Nazi occupation was sustained by a credible political expectation of eventual liberation with outside Anglo-American military help. If Europe and the United States were ever to be overrun and occupied by foreign foes, it is difficult to see how there could be such an expectation. Without it there could only be resignation to the grim choice of submission to tyranny or martyrdom.*

Actually this scenario is quite bizarre. One simply cannot imagine large numbers of Catholics or other citizens in member countries of the Atlantic Alliance opting in advance for NVR in case of a Soviet attack and pursuing that option if war should really break out. In the event of war it might make strategic sense, especially in Western Europe (which would be invaded long before the United States), for governments and civilian groups to supplement the defensive operations of regular military forces by organizing both passive non-cooperation efforts and underground resistance (which can involve a great deal of violence such as sabotage, ambush, assassination, and

---

* It should be noted that nonviolent resistance differs from the response of Christ. He offered no resistance, nor did He want His disciples to do so. The Evangelical witness chooses death in preference not only to violent resistance but to any resistance. NVR is essentially a Gandhian rather than a distinctively Christian response. This, however, is a theological, not a political-strategic question.

other normal techniques of insurgency). Governments might find it useful to do this for the purpose of obstructing the advance of invading armed forces or of preventing them from consolidating their control over territory. It is extremely doubtful that this is what the members of Pax Christi have in mind. They are talking about preparation for martyrdom, and they do not hesitate to use that term.

Inasmuch as proposals for nonviolent resistance have been invariably linked in recent decades with proposals for unilateral disarmament, NATO governments can hardly be expected to take them seriously, much less to cooperate with the Church in their development.* The U.S. government in general (perhaps apart from a few members of Congress in desperate search for an issue which might bring extra votes in a closely contested election) will certainly want to know much more about this proposal. Do the bishops envisage the development of such "programmed methods" as an alternative to regular military service, particularly in a future situation in which it might become necessary to reinstitute conscription? Who would be responsible for conducting the training in such a program—the government, the Church, or some other organization? Would NVR training be separated and insulated from or integrated with "the organized popular defense instituted by government as part of its contingency planning" to which the bishops make reference? One can readily see that a considerable amount of clarification of the bishops meaning will be required during the years ahead.

For the bishops to urge nonviolent resistance training upon American Catholics as a feasible alternative to military defense under present circumstances will be considered politically irresponsible by many. If such a recommendation were to be taken up by substantial numbers of American Catholic citizens in the years ahead, it would signal their unwillingness to bear arms even in a just conventional war, for example, in fulfillment of the U.S. commitment to help

---

* In recent decades, nonviolent resistance and/or unilateral disarmament have/has been advocated by the Quakers and by such figures as Victor Gollancz, Lewis Mumford, Bertrand Russell, C. Wright Mills, Erich Fromm, Jerome Frank, Gene Sharp, and Mulford Q. Sibley, but by no Catholic thinker of any prominence.[7]

defend the NATO allies. The development of "programmed methods" of nonviolent resistance will be taken to mean that many Catholics are embracing not only nuclear pacifism but a qualified form of general, not absolute, pacifism à la Gandhi and Martin Luther King.

As we shall see below, the pastoral letter hedges the U.S. nuclear deterrent about with reservations and restrictions which could have the effect of eroding its psychological and political effectiveness. A growing advocacy of nonviolent resistance by Catholics can have the further effect of undermining the conventional deterrence in Europe to which the bishops seem partial. The simultaneous weakening of both nuclear and conventional deterrence by a withdrawal of public support for both forms by sizable numbers of Catholics could offer to a future aggressor a powerful temptation, almost an invitation, to test the Atlantic allies' will to resist intimidation by creating a crisis and presenting a carefully calibrated political and military challenge. If hostilities were to erupt in such a situation, the first victims would not be American Catholic advocates of NVR, but Europeans and U.S. troops serving in Europe with their families. Jean-Marie Cardinal Lustiger, the archbishop of Paris, commenting on the growing attraction of unilateral disarmament for some U.S. bishops, said that "American pacifism is the pacifism of people who believe that nothing will happen to them anyway."[8] Pacifists and proponents of nonviolent resistance are fond of pointing optimistically to how well their proposed methods will work in the future, but they cannot point to a single historic instance in which either pacifism or the prospect of nonviolent resistance ever succeeded in deterring international aggression. They do not even bother to try. But we know of at least one case in recent history, in the 1930s, when the spread of pacifism, defeatism and moral degeneracy in the Western democracies was a significant factor spurring on Hitler's preparations for aggressive war.[9]

Deterrence: From Counterpopulation to Counterforce

Given the prevailing tone of the document, one could plausibly argue that the bishops have sought to fashion a sort of "ethical pincers" with which to squeeze the U.S. government. They rightfully condemn a countercity strategy. They concede that nuclear deterrence is still morally acceptable under the circumstances, but hedge any counterforce strategy about with several reservations, including strictures against any first use, any "limited nuclear exchange," the acquisition of "war capabilities," "retaliatory action which would take many wholly innocent lives" (even in a counterforce instead of a countercity strike with no guidelines on how "many" would be disproportionate), and against a "hardtarget kill" capability[10] (although such a capability would be necessary in the calculus of deterrence as usable in a second strike against nuclear weapons held in reserve or in a residual force). If the United States government were formally to modify its policies in keeping with the bishops' advice, most strategic analysts would fear a substantial, destabilizing erosion of deterrence credibility. There is no such thing as an effective nuclear deterrent force without an operational doctrine to govern its use. Yet what the bishops seem to be calling for is a morally acceptable deterrent without a militarily credible doctrine to support it.

In their attempt to analyze the morality of nuclear deterrence, Catholic writers have had great difficulty deciding whether to focus on the ethic of intention or on the ethic of potential consequences. Some contend that the primary intention in possessing nuclear weapons is not to use them but to pose an implicit threat for the worthy purpose of deterring war. Such an intention may be seen as morally permissible and even good. The bishops, however, remind us that one cannot threaten to do that which it would be immoral to do. James Finn questions that traditional moral principle:

> The security of that reasoning crumbles when it is applied
> to nuclear weapons. We threaten to do what it would be
> immoral to execute—in order to deter the execution.[11]

"The overriding moral imperative is to deter the use of nuclear weapons," says Michael Novak, who concludes that it is immoral to weaken the required public will to sustain the social sacrifices needed for deterrence.[12] As we shall see, the French bishops disagree with the American bishops on this point.

Other Catholic writers argue that the intention is not the good one of deterring war but the evil one of using nuclear weapons for the purpose of punishing with inescapably large-scale death and destruction (even in a counterforce strategy) in case deterrence fails, and is therefore immoral. Germain Grisez, a professor of Christian ethics, argues that what he calls "the precise intent to kill" makes it impossible to call the nuclear deterrent tolerable or justifiable as a lesser evil pending progress in arms control or disarmament. Even maintaining the deterrent is immoral in his eyes, for it means either that a moral evil may be done to avoid some other evil, or the killing of millions of innocent persons may be morally acceptable on the grounds of proportionality.[13] This is, of course, similar to the rationale of the radical pacifist bishops who condemn deterrence outright.

Presumably it would be difficult to formulate any single statement on the morality of nuclear deterrence with which all bishops could agree, or with which some would not find themselves in disagreement—even Pope John Paul's statement of June 1982 to the United Nations. The government of a philosophically and religiously pluralistic society like our own cannot enter any meaningful public debate over such concepts as the morality of threat and intention. These are reserved to bishops and ethicians, who cannot agree among themselves.

A political scientist is compelled to conclude that we appear to be faced with a moral and political anomaly—which neither bishops nor strategists can resolve—of a deterrent policy which is good as long as it succeeds and evil if it breaks down. For the sake of averting war, can a government threaten to take retaliatory action which might become immoral in its magnitude regardless of the intention to avoid killing innocent people and to minimize civilian collateral damage to the fullest possible extent? The assessment of intention has always been a tricky area in moral theology as in law, for it pertains to what is in the minds of individuals. It becomes even murkier and more questionable when we try to transfer a concept from the realm of individual moral action to the very different plane of governmental bureaucratic policy-making structures. What do we mean when we say that the government *intends* to do something? Where is the repository of this intention? The people? Their elected leaders and representatives? The President? The Administration? The Secretary of Defense? The Joint Chiefs? The Commanding General of Strategic Air Command? Is there any way of knowing whether all these and others in political and military authority positions all intend the same thing?

It would seem that much more thought must be given to the

morality of individual intentions and the morality of such public policy declarations as they relate to nuclear deterrence. This is not to suggest that the state exists beyond the moral code, as Machiavelli held, but rather that the state, in view of its obligations, cannot be subjected to the rational moral law according to the same modality as the individual.

The state and the individual are essentially different beings. That was clear to traditional scholastic thinkers in the tradition of St. Augustine and St. Thomas Aquinas. Merely because some contemporary theologians move beyond the tradition, know little of Augustine, Thomas, and Murray, and shift their moral focus from individual to social sin, social scientists cannot let them escape with the methodological sloppiness of attributing to modern governments the concepts of intention and threat as if such complex bureaucratic structures were perfectly analogous to individual persons or medieval monarchical sovereigns. This is no less misleading than long discredited efforts to explain the causes of macrocosmic war between nation-states by referring to the microcosmic inner psychic conditions of individuals.[14] Traditional Catholic moral theology is based upon a profound experiential knowledge of the individual human being. The new Catholic socio-political morality will be no better than the degree to which it is founded on a comparable understanding of socio-political reality and the way contemporary governments make policy, as well as the policy environment.

The state takes its decisions on the basis of a great variety of internal and external pressures. In a world of power balancing, where there is no effective international authority capable of protecting the security and rights of all states and of guaranteeing the peaceful settlement of disputes, no state can seek security for its people by adopting the moral posture of turning the other cheek. Whereas the individual citizen is required to abjure any resort to force to obtain justice (except in extreme cases of self-defense), the state is required to use force as an instrument of justice, and to use the threat of force to keep peace. A state which acts with a moral public "conscience" should not, in its declaratory policy, explicitly threaten to do anything that would be clearly immoral—e.g., destroying cities in a retaliatory strike. But the state is under no moral obligation to reveal to an adversary exactly what strategic course it will pursue if deterrence should fail, or to repudiate every implicit threat that might involve immoral consequences if executed.

The United States, in sum, cannot be expected to publish detailed information about its targeting doctrine.

Within the real international environment in which the U.S. government must shape its deterrence/defense policy, the overriding imperative is political, not moral in purely theological terms: it is to prevent the outbreak of a war that might escalate to the nuclear level. Politics can often be more subtle and complex in its demands than moral theology. The government of the United States, it its effort to maintain a stable, credible, and effective deterrent, must sometimes make more difficult decisions than those involved in the moral analysis of countercity and counterforce doctrines. Governments may strike moral postures for political purposes, but they do not seek security by that route. The Harvard Nuclear Study Group, commenting on the bishop's letter, recently summed it up this way:

> The issue is whether our strategy and arsenal can reduce the prospect of war in a time of crisis. Since the moral claims for deterrence rest on averting large-scale nuclear war, the truly immoral behavior is to have nuclear forces and doctrines that invite preemptive attack by one's opponent or by oneself . . . Morality is not just about choices at a time of crisis; it can also be about averting terrible choices at a time of crisis.[15]

The essence of a credible deterrent is a threat and a known capacity to carry out the threat. To divest the nuclear deterrent of either its threat or its capability is to deprive it of its effectiveness as a barrier to nuclear or conventional war between the superpowers and their allies. Every Catholic, indeed every sensible human being, must lament the present paradox of mutual deterrence confronting the industrialized world, of which James Finn has said succinctly: "One must currently choose between the unsatisfactory and the still more unsatisfactory. Anyone who thinks otherwise has not grasped the strange and desperate quality of our situation."[16]

Arms Control:
Weapons Modernization or Nuclear Halt

The bishops declare themselves strongly in favor of several specific unilateral, bilateral, and multilateral arms control measures which in their view would improve the international climate and reduce the risks of war. Some of these are not likely to provoke much debate within the U.S. arms control community, e.g., negotiated deep cuts in the arsenals of both superpowers, such as the proposals on the table in the Geneva START and INF talks, especially if they would lead to reductions in destabilizing weapons, and the strengthening of command and control over nuclear weapons to prevent inadvertent and unauthorized use.[17] Their proposals for removal by all parties of short-range nuclear weapons and nuclear weapons likely to be overrun in the early stages of war would probably be supported by American arms controllers, assuming consultation with and approval by allies, as well as adequate verification procedures. Similarly, their opposition to proposals "which have the effect of lowering the nuclear threshold and blurring the difference between nuclear and conventional weapons" makes a good deal of sense.[18]

The bishops' call for the conclusion of a comprehensive test ban treaty is a more complicated matter, as both superpowers are well aware, in a world where some nuclear weapon states (e.g., France and China) are not at all ready to subscribe to a total or even a partial test ban; where verification still constitutes a problem; where prooftesting of nuclear stockpiles will occasionally be necessary by states whose security still depends on nuclear forces; and where technological modernization for the maintenance of strategic stability will remain necessary in a world of nuclear armed powers. The superpowers have been involved intermittently in negotiations for a comprehensive test ban (CTB) ever since 1958. Although some analysts argue that a CTB will be a barrier to nuclear weapons proliferation and an important step toward disarmament, it does not seem likely that the superpowers will permenently renounce underground testing except as an integral part of a comprehensive arms limitation and reduction program to which all nuclear weapons states adhere. If we depend on nuclear weapons, we must test them.

The bishops warn against the acquisition of a "prompt hard-target kill" capability which would threaten to make the other side's retaliatory forces vulnerable. Such weapons, they say, "may seem to be useful primarily in a first strike," and in a footnote they point out that several experts place the MX and Pershing-2 missiles in this category. Lest they be accused of being lopsided in resisting U.S.

weapons programs, they also express opposition to "Soviet deployment of such weapons which generate fear of a first strike against
U.S. forces."[19] The difficulty is that more than six hundred Soviet
heavy missiles (SS-17, SS-18, and SS-19) and more than three hundred fifty SS20s—to which the MX and the Pershing-2, respectively,
are responses—are already in place, whereas the counterbalancing
U.S. missiles were planned for deployment during the five years after
the pastoral letter was issued. When they make their recommendations on MX, the bishops enter a quagmire of strategic analysis
concerning the vulnerability of land-based missiles. The *sine qua non*
in a relationship of strategic parity requires that the United States
possess as effective, secure, and survivable a countersilo capability as
the Soviet Union in order to reduce destabilizing asymmetries in the
ability of the superpowers to destroy hardened strategic forces in the
initial stages of nuclear war. Other strategic problems involve
residual or reserve strategic forces, damage limitation, and the deterrence of anti-city strikes. The bishops make no reference to the fact
that several experts deny that the MX would decrease crisis stability
by heightening Soviet fears of a U.S. first strike beyond the level
which the United States has had to tolerate for several years.[20] All
these questions are closely intertwined with the basic issue of
whether deterrence will be strengthened or weakened by a shift of
policy emphasis from assured countervalue (population and economic base) destruction to the countervailing strategy which
envisages the possibility of limited and selective counterforce attacks.
At the present time, neither bishops nor strategists can give a satisfactory answer to this question, since it requires a prudential judgment
on the basis of empirical evidence of which none is available.

The issue of Pershing-2 missiles is more complex than that of
MX, because during the last decade the problem of nuclear balance
(imbalance) at the European regional level has become even more
serious and acute than the intercontinental strategic balance
(imbalance) between the superpowers. Prior to late 1983, the United
States had deployed in the NATO European area no land-based
missiles comparable to the 350 Soviet SS-20s, about two-thirds of
which were targeted on Western Europe. Thus there was no symmetry of vulnerability between the territory of Western Europe and that
of the Soviet Union. It is interesting to note that in the mid-1970s,
Moscow insisted that there was a balance of forces in Europe. After

deploying 250 SS-20s by 1983 (each with three nuclear warheads), Moscow continued to insist that there was a balance of forces in Europe. It is understandable that knowledgeable defense elites in Western Europe were apprehensive concerning what the Soviet Union means by "balance," and what the deployment trends portended for the future ability of the USSR to project a shadow of nuclear power that would increase pressures for what the Europeans themselves called "Finlandization." The Soviet Union pointed to U.S. planes in the NATO area, but planes are not missiles. It was the West Germans who called attention to the danger of the growing imbalance and demanded that it had to be redressed through a combination of new NATO deployments and U.S.-Soviet arms negotiations. Later, the Soviet Union offered to balance its Eurostrategic missiles against 162 Anglo-French missiles (which it had earlier insisted on including in the calculus of the superpower strategic balance in SALT I). Had the United States accepted the Soviet offer to that effect in late 1982, it would have been signaling to its NATO allies that henceforth the nuclear balance in Europe was a matter to be negotiated between France and Britain on the one hand and the USSR on the other. Both the French and the British have always made it quite clear that their nuclear weapons are intended solely to deter a Soviet attack on their own national territory if the U.S. deterrent should break down. No one in Europe, least of all in Germany, expects either France or Britain to place itself at risk to defend the West German Federal Republic. The West Germans know that there is only one power capable of guaranteeing them against aggression, and that is the United States. It is to be hoped that the superpowers can arrive at some mutually satisfactory or dissatisfactory compromise regarding the deployment of intermediate-range missiles, combining partial NATO deployments with partial Soviet dismantling—a compromise in which each side demonstrates a readiness to understand and accommodate the legitimate security apprehensions and political-diplomatic interests of the other. NATO, for example, should take adequate account of Soviet expressed fears that the Pershing-2s, given their short delivery times, might upset the central strategic balance by threatening command, control, and communications capabilities. Conversely, the Soviet Union must recognize the U.S. requirement for a restoration of allied confidence in the credibility of the deterrent. One cannot fairly expect bishops to take into account all of the subtleties in the contemporary texture of international politics. This is precisely why they should not be too detailed in their policy recommendations.

The bishops say they cannot approve of every weapons system, strategic doctrine or policy initiative advanced in the name of strengthening deterrence. But after reading the letter carefully and plotting the course of the general thrust, one wonders whether a majority of the bishops would approve any new program or whether they are disposed to regard every U.S. nuclear modernization program with suspicion regardless of the fact that the Soviet Union has continued to test, produce, and deploy new or modernized nuclear weapons at a steady pace since 1972, when SALT I was supposed to "codify parity" between the superpowers. Both SALT I and SALT II, of course, permitted modernization. The Soviet Union has taken full advantage of the provisions of these agreements. The United States had not tested, produced, or deployed any new strategic land-based missiles during the fifteen years up to 1983 and had reduced its total nuclear throw-weight by at least half within that period. In fact, the United States had adhered to a unilaterally imposed freeze on the number of strategic delivery vehicles since 1968. As Defense Secretary Harold Brown once said, "When we build, they build. When we stop building, they build." The insinuation, detectable in the first two draft letters, that the United States is chiefly responsible for the arms race has been corrected in the final text; but there lingers a disposition to look askance at virtually every new U.S. military program as fueling an unlimited acceleration of the arms race and bringing nuclear war closer. Yet it seems inevitable that some modernization of obsolescent U.S. systems will be necessary in the years ahead, even if it should prove possible to negotiate a more stable international strategic situation through symmetrical and equitable arms control and/or arms reduction agreements. At the very least, a credible expectation of U.S. modernization will be a prerequisite incentive to serious negotiations on the Soviet side. Bishops who understand very well the arts of bargaining with teachers and other employees in their own dioceses ought to be sensitive to the U.S. reluctance to make unilateral and unreciprocated concessions of leverage in advance to improve the climate of negotiations.

What is missing from the pastoral letter, no doubt because of a strong emotional bias on the part of many bishops against any suggestion that nuclear weapons can serve a useful purpose as a sheathed sword in this world, is an appreciation of the fact that the superpowers, far from being engaged in a frantic arms race, continually monitor their security requirements in light of the geostrategic situation, the international political climate (e.g., tension or detente), and the perception of emerging military threats in an everchanging technological environment. When all other sectors of society—industries, farms, banks, universities, airlines, the media, hospitals, the vendors of games and fast food, and even ecclesiastical bureaucracies point with pride to their modern planning methods and computerized equipment—it is scarcely realistic to expect the military sector, historically always on the cuttingedge of technological change, to become unique by announcing that it has "enough" and will henceforth abstain from modernization. "Enough," said Schelling, "depends on how much the opponent has."[21] The superpowers assess their deterrence and defence needs and move to fill them as they see fit by making the appropriate adjustments and by acquiring the capabilities which they require.

This does not always involve an action-reaction process on the part of the superpowers. Much of the time it does not, because their security commitments and requirements are far from being mirror images of each other. The Soviet Union keeps accumulating strategic and Eurostrategic nuclear capabilities at a steady, plodding pace regardless of what the United States does; the latter's defense efforts over time exhibit a much more pronounced cyclical character, its curve reflecting the intermittent peaks and valleys of international tension, conflict, and detente. It would be desirable for the United States to put long-term defense planning and procurement on an even keel instead of going through alternate periods of optimism and pessimism, relaxation and anxiety; but the nature of the democratic system, its electoral politics, the ideological polarization of "hawks" and "doves," and the pendular swings of public mood, seems to make a steady course hard to maintain.

It is a gross exaggeration to postulate a mad and unbridled arms race between the superpowers. The United States certainly has not been racing. We should not forget that the U.S. strategic community of deterrence and arms control analysts began debating the merits and demerits of antiballistic missiles in 1960–61, not long before the Soviet Union started to deploy an ABM system around Moscow. Not until 1967 did the Johnson-McNamara administration decide to deploy a "thin" Sentinel ABM system; this was renamed Safeguard, modified and slightly enlarged by Nixon in 1969, just a few months prior to the opening of SALT negotiations which culminated in the ABM Treaty of 1972. Today the United States has no ABM deployed, although the Soviet Union has its system around Moscow. This record scarcely indicates "an acceleration of the arms race," although anyone who so much as favorably mentioned ABM in the 1960s was accused of trying to accelerate the arms race.

Similarly, NATO began in 1977 to discuss the need for intermediate-range missiles (INF) in Europe to counterbalance the threat of Soviet SS-20s, not by targeting them (since they are mobile) but by creating a symmetry of vulnerability. NATO decided to pursue a "two-track" approach to deployment and negotiation in December 1979, although deployment was not scheduled to begin until four years later. When negotiations got under way in November 1981, President Reagan offered a "zero option"[22]—no NATO deployment in return for the dismantling of the SS-20s—but the Soviet leaders were not willing to bargain existing missiles for planned ones. The failure of the bishops to take these subtler aspects of international arms competition into account, glossing over them vaguely and ambiguously while belaboring the dangers of the "arms race," makes it difficult at times to accord their penetrating moral analysis of the dilemmas of nuclear deterrence the thoughtful reflection it deserves.

In support of the concept of "sufficiency" as an adequate deterrent, the bishops recommend "support for immediate, bilateral, verifiable agreements to halt the testing, production and deployment of new nuclear weapons systems."[23] This was a controversial part of the letter. By the spring of 1983, nearly one hundred and fifty bishops (or about half the number of actives) had already formally endorsed the nuclear weapons freeze. The second draft had called for a "halt" to "new strategic weapons systems." Several bishops thought that this language could be interpreted as taking a public stand on a currently controversial political issue with partisan overtones, inasmuch as the freeze resolution in Congress was strongly supported by Democrats and opposed by the Reagan administration, which favored a freeze *after*, not *before*, negotiated arms cuts. The third draft, therefore, carried the word "curb" rather than "halt," but also the broader term "new nuclear weapons' systems," thereby emcompassing all substrategic systems.[24] Just prior to the Chicago meeting, the *ad hoc* committee, responding to numerous proposed amendments by bishops after the third draft was circulated, changed "curb" back to "halt," but retained the broader category to which it applied—"new nuclear weapons systems."[25] In a footnote, the bishops said that "we have chosen our own language in this paragraph, not wanting either to be identified with one specific political initiative or to have our words used against specific political measures."[26] Nevertheless, the change was generally interpreted as a shift of stance toward endorsement of a nuclear freeze. In fact, Bishop James W. Malone of Youngstown, Ohio, who favored the change to "halt," said the tougher language was needed because its "content and symbolism set the tone for the rest of the pastoral letter," and that "'curb' indicates no support for nuclear freeze," whereas "'halt' does indicate support."[27]

The difficulty with the nuclear freeze approach is that it cavalierly sweeps off the board more than a decade of SALT-type analysis of the arms problem, which presupposes strategic parity and the need for modernization to maintain a stable equilibrium between the superpowers.[28] The bishops, moreover, do not seem to realize or care that the nuclear freeze movement, if successful, would lock the United States into the strategic posture of deterrence which they properly condemn as patently immoral, a posture which poses the threat of retaliation primarily against population centers.[29]

Under existing circumstances, a nuclear freeze would not contribute to international stability, but might lead to a prolongation of the present unstable situation in which there is a real danger of nuclear war. Andrei Sakharov, the Soviet nuclear physicist who won the Nobel Peace Prize in 1975, has sent a warning to this effect from his exile in Gorki. Long an ardent advocate of substantial arms cuts and an opponent of new weapons systems, Sakharov has come reluctantly to the view that the most urgent task at present is to restore, between the East and the West, a balance of nuclear and conventional armaments through a combination of new Western arms deployments and diplomatic negotiations for arms reductions. This, in his view, is necessary because of the Soviet military buildup. If the main danger of slipping into an all-out nuclear war is to be averted, says Sakharov, then the deployment of MX and of intermediate-range missiles for NATO may unfortunately prove necessary in order to reduce the chance that the Soviet Union might be tempted to exploit the imbalance and blunder into war. In order to keep the peace, the West may have no choice but to pay the price of continuing the arms race for another ten or fifteen years. While expressing deep sympathy for the yearning for peace of peoples in the Western and socialist worlds, Sakharov contends that the aspiration for peace is not enough: it is imperative to keep in mind the prevailing political, military, and strategic realities, including the ability of pro-Soviet propagandists to take advantage of pacifist public opinion in Western countries to perpetuate the present highly dangerous imbalance.[30]

The great virtue of the freeze proposal, declare its advocates, is its utter simplicity. Albert Einstein once said that we should try to make things as simple as possible, but no simpler. The freeze oversimplifies. The author hopes the freeze movement will be replaced by the "build-down" concept, combined with the smaller missile recommended by the Scowcroft Commission as a successor to MX. Such a development would simultaneously serve the purposes of deterrence and arms control. It would permit stabilizing modernization without duly arousing fears of a U.S. first strike against Soviet ICBMs. It would also guarantee that for every new land-based nuclear warhead produced, two older ones would be eliminated.[31]

Limited Nuclear War and No First Use

Those passages of the pastoral letter dealing with these problems are among the most controversial in the eyes of political-military strategists. The bishops are aware of the argument that nuclear warfighting strategies enhance the credibility of deterrence, particularly extended deterrence in Europe. While they recognize that the policy debate over the issue of the *real* versus the *theoretical* possibility of a limited nuclear exchange is inconclusive, strong doubts on this score lead them to reject all strategies for not merely deterring but actually fighting and trying to limit and win a nuclear war. They ask whether leaders would have sufficient information to know what is happening, whether under conditions of great stress and confusion they could make the extraordinarily precise decisions needed to keep the exchange limited, whether military commanders could maintain a policy of discriminate targeting, whether we have assurances that computer errors could be avoided, whether the casualties would run into the millions, and how limited the effects of radiation, famine, and socioeconomic disruption would be.

Strategists have been asking these questions for decades, and disagreeing in their assessments. Since definitive, assuring answers cannot be given, the bishops remain skeptical.

> A number of expert witnesses advise us that commanders operating under conditions of battle probably would not be able to exercise strict control; the number of weapons used would rapidly increase, the targets would be expanded beyond the military and the level of civilian casualties would rise enormously. No one can be certain that this escalation would not occur even in the face of political efforts to keep such an exchange "limited." The chances of keeping use limited seem remote, and the consequences of escalation to mass destruction would be appalling. Former public officials have testified that it is improbable that any nuclear war could actually be kept limited. Their testimony and the consequences involved in this problem lead us to conclude that the danger of escalation is so great that it would be morally unjustifiable to initiate nuclear war in any form. The danger is rooted not only in the technology of our weapons systems, but in the weakness and sinfulness of human communities. We find the moral responsibility of beginning nuclear war not justified by rational political objectives.[32]

Anyone who has pondered the problems and uncertainties of limited nuclear war and uncontrollable escalation can appreciate the bishops' concern. Prediction in the social sciences is very uncertain, and the forecasting record of social scientists is by no means impressive. Broad aggregate trends may lend themselves to probability forecasting under carefully prescribed conditions and on the basis of a solid and comprehensive empirical data base extending with sufficient depth backward time, and with additional insightful knowledge of new factors and forces likely to exert influence on future events. Unique events, however, especially those which depend upon the choices of individuals or small groups of decision-makers, are virtually unpredictable.[33] Albert Wohlstetter writes:

> The bishops cite experts as authority for their judgment that any use whatever of nuclear weapons would with an overwhelming probability lead to unlimited destruction. And some of their experts do seem to say just that. But some they cite appear only to say that we cannot be quite sure ... that any use of nuclear weapons would stay limited.[34]

None of the experts to whom the bishops listened or whose writings they cited can judge with any reliable degree of accuracy or certitude the probability either that nuclear war will or will not occur, or that it can or cannot be limited. Donald M. Snow is correct when he says that

> ... since nuclear weapons represent an unprecedented phenomenon in military experience, there is essentially no experiential, empirical base on which to build theory about nuclear consequences. For example, it is either true or false that nuclear war would inevitably escalate to general exchange, but since there has never been a nuclear war in which both combatants possessed these weapons, what would happen remains speculative.[35]

A bishop is as entitled as anyone to arrive at a prudential and contingent judgment that nuclear war cannot be limited. Bishops and strategists are also entitled to come to an opposite conclusion. The world will probably be better off if the most influential policymakers in the United States and Soviet Union (as well as other nuclear weapon states) assume in advance of the outbreak of war that a nuclear exchange could not be limited. Such a conviction, if shared on a widespread basis by both superpowers, would tend to strengthen deterrence against the outbreak of any war containing a built-in escalation potential. But if deterrence should fail and nuclear war should break out—either a war that begins as nuclear or a conventional war in which the nuclear firebreak is crossed—it will then be of the utmost urgency for the leading political and military officials on both sides to become convinced quickly that it can and must be limited, that city destruction must be avoided, that the command, control, and communications (C^3) networks of the adversary must be kept intact for the sake of controllability. The use of nuclear weapons against military targets must be as discriminating as possible, with minimal collateral damage inflicted upon innocent populations, until both sides can terminate the conflict as quickly as possible on terms no more disadvantageous to each other than a continuation of even limited nuclear war would be for each other and for the international community.

Democratic governments should listen carefully to the warnings of bishops and strategists concerning the escalation danger and conduct themselves with commensurate caution in time of crisis. But responsible governments, unlike their critics, cannot be content with this. They must also be prepared for the possibility, however low the probability may be, that deterrence might fail. They must be ready to do whatever they can to compensate with rational decision making *after* the fact for a collapse of rational decision making *before* the fact. To accomplish this, discreet planning ahead of time is essential, even though it may be highly desirable to mute public rhetoric about strategies for fighting nuclear war. Part of the discreet planning upon which John Courtney Murray insisted as a moral imperative might even include letting the adversary know about a firm intention to limit a nuclear war as much as possible, since it is very much in his interest to reciprocate. Soviet military literature has reflected practically no interest in the subject of limited nuclear war in recent decades. But just as Soviet theoreticians believe that their strategy of the preemptive strike (if nuclear war should appear inevitable and imminent) strengthens deterrence,[36] an American strategic doctrine of selective targeting and limited nuclear options in retaliation, rather than an unrestrained assured destruction strike, can, if handled properly, also be viewed as a strengthener of deterrence on the Western side.

The political objective is always to strengthen deterrence rather than to make nuclear war more likely, and at the same time to improve the prospects for successful East-West arms negotiations. In the final analysis, only a responsible, intelligent government, fully aware of developments in the international strategic, technological, political, and diplomatic environment, knows how to devise the proper mix of policies best calculated to achieve the desired results.

It is the bishops' fear of human inability (flowing from the ineradicable fault of sinfulness) to keep nuclear war limited (since this would require both a high degree of rationality and highly efficient C³ under conditions of chaos) which leads them to the "no first use" position. In their judgment, even though the use of nuclear weapons might be theoretically justifiable in certain situations for self-defense, the risk of uncontrolled escalation is so great that the deliberate initiation of nuclear warfare against conventional aggression, for example, in the NATO area, would not be morally justified. In their first draft, the bishops saw an obligation to pursue the safest possible course, and said that the first use of nuclear weapons would not meet that test. The second draft seemed even more strongly opposed to first use:

> We do not perceive any situation in which the deliberate initiation of nuclear warfare, on however restricted a scale, can be morally justified. Non-nuclear attacks by another state must be resisted by other than nuclear means.[37]

The second draft contained a recognition that "it had long been American and NATO policy that nuclear weapons, especially so-called tactical nuclear weapons, would likely be used if NATO forces in Europe seemed in danger of losing a conflict that until then had been restricted to conventional weapons," and a warning that the employment of very many such weapons would totally devastate the densely populated countries of Western and Central Europe.[38]

The second draft went no further than that in expressing any appreciation of the dilemmas confronting NATO in its efforts to maintain continued successful deterrence of war in Europe. The bishops were obviously impressed by an article in *Foreign Affairs*,[39] written by four former government officials who had played a key role in earlier administrations in the formulation of U.S. deterrence and arms control policies. They warned against uncontrollable escalation and advocated a policy of "no first use" for NATO—policies which they were never known to espouse during their period in office. The bishops were apparently less moved by a response to that article written by four West German analysts—two from each of the major political parties—who cautioned against selected ideas which cater to current widespread anxieties in an environment in which there exists much confusion between a strategic, offensive "first strike" against the adversary's homeland and a purely defensive "first use" of nuclear weapons on the territory of the victim of aggression. "What matters most," they said, "is to concentrate not only on the prevention of nuclear war, but on how to prevent *any* war, conventional war as well" in Europe.[40] Effective deterrence in Europe throughout the history of NATO has always depended upon the possibility that an overwhelming Soviet conventional assault would be met with a NATO nuclear response at some extreme point.

During the writing of the third draft, "nuancing" became a favorite term to describe what the *ad hoc* committee was doing. Since the recommendation for a "no first use" policy in the NATO context had been one of the most controversial features of the pastoral letter, the bishops "nuanced" their position on this point, probably as a result of the Rome consultation and comments received from within the American Catholic community of professisonal experts. The final text, instead of categorically denouncing any first use as immoral, refers to the bishops' quest to reinforce the barrier against any use of nuclear weapons, especially any risk of quick and easy resort to nuclear weapons, as J. Bryan Hehir put it in a debate with the author in Boston early in 1983.[41] The nuanced passages in the final text follow:

> At the same time we recognize the responsibility the United States has had and continues to have in assisting allied nations in their defense against either a conventional or a nuclear attack. Especially in the European theater, the deterrence of a *nuclear* attack may require nuclear weapons for a time, even though their possession and deployment must be subject to rigid restrictions.
>
> The need to defend against a conventional attack in Europe imposes the political and moral burden of developing adequate, alternative modes of defense to present reliance on nuclear weapons. Even with the best coordinated effort—hardly likely in view of contemporary political division on this question—development of an alternative defense position will still take time.
>
> In the interim, deterrence against a conventional attack relies upon two factors: the not inconsiderable conventional forces at the disposal of NATO and the recognition by a potential attacker that the outbreak of large-scale

conventional war could escalate to the nuclear level through accident or miscalculation by either side. We are aware that NATO's refusal to adopt a "no first use" pledge is to some extent linked to the deterrent effect of this inherent ambiguity. Nonetheless, in light of the probable effects of initiating nuclear war, we urge NATO to move rapidly toward the adoption of a "no first use" policy, but doing so in tandem with development of an adequate alternative defense posture.[42]

Much of what the bishops say here makes logical sense, but whether their prescription will prove politically and economically feasible for the NATO nations raises other questions to which we must turn before passing any final judgment on the viability of a "no first use" policy for NATO.

The Economics of Nuclear and Conventional Deterrence

Ever since Vatican II, papal teaching has frequently addressed the issue of the arms race as "an act of aggression against the poor." The U.S. bishops reiterate this formula of criticism. Such a moral judgment, however, depends on questions of fact over which many economists strongly disagree, except perhaps in the sense that one can regard expenditures for education, highways, space research, or most items in government budgets as allocations which divert resources from the poor. Church leaders and others hope that resources now allocated to armaments could be redirected to the needs of the world's poor. It must be remembered, however, that defense programs in many countries make a contribution toward GNP, industrial growth, technological know-how, employment, foreign exchange, and other factors which help in a positive way to generate economic wealth. A portion of defense resources is simply not reallocable to programs that would alleviate poverty. The bulk of any budgetary savings to be realized from arms reductions, whether in the rich, industrialized countries or in the more impoverished countries of the Third World, will probably be diverted to other domestic uses rather than to socioeconomic development purposes.

In neither group of countries are most of the savings likely to benefit the least advantaged segments of the population. This is because of the nature of the budget process in modern governments and the pent-up demands and claims of many organized groups upon resources which are deemed scarce even in the most affluent societies.

Popes, the Council, and bishops have frequently reiterated the legitimacy of national defense efforts in a world which lacks an effective international authority to enforce peaceful settlement of disputes, protect the rights of states, and guarantee their security. National defense always costs something. Much more precise analysis than has yet been performed will be needed before the bishops can properly conclude that a particular level of defense spending is excessive. The bishops only fleetingly recognize that their letter contains a contradiction insofar as it endorses the proposition that the arms race is an act of aggression against the poor while at the same time acknowledging that their own recommendations may require even higher military expenditures.

> Many analysts conclude that in the absence of nuclear deterrent threats more troops and conventional (non-nuclear) weapons would be required to protect our allies. Rejection of some forms of nuclear deterrence could therefore conceivably require a willingness to pay higher costs to develop conventional forces. Leaders and peoples of other nations might also have to accept higher costs for their own defense, particularly in Western Europe, if the threat to use nuclear weapons first were withdrawn. We cannot judge the strength of these arguments in particular cases. It may well be that some strengthening of conventional defense would be a proportional price to pay, if this will reduce the possibility of a nuclear war. We acknowledge this reluctantly, aware as we are of the vast amount of scarce resources expended annually on instruments of defense in a world filled with other urgent, unmet human needs.[43]

It is a curious fact that the bishops do not excoriate higher expenditures for conventional defense either as "an acceleration of the arms race" or as "an act of aggression against the poor," although in their own terms it is difficult to see why such expenditures should not be regarded as both. If the NATO allies were to agree to adopt a strategy of "no first use" of nuclear weapons and to proceed to acquire the conventional capabilities that would be required to make such a strategy credible both to the West Europeans and to the Soviet Union, this would mark a fundamental shift in the basis of the U.S. extended deterrence policy inaugurated in the 1950s. The bishops have simply not given this aspect of the problem the attention it deserves. If they had, they might well have had second thoughts about their call to revise fundamentally a NATO strategy which has preserved political and military equilibrium in Europe for three decades.

Anyone who undertakes to make pronouncements on the economics of defense, the degree to which military spending burdens the poor, and the relative costs and effectiveness of conventional and nuclear deterrence should take into account the following factors:

1. U.S. defense spending, which dropped to 5 percent of the gross national product (GNP) after World War II, rose to nearly 14 percent during the Korean War, leveled off in the range of 8 to 9 percent during the Eisenhower years, increased to 10.3 percent under President Kennedy, dropped to 8 percent after the Cuba Missile Crisis, went up again to about 10 percent at the height of the Vietnam War, and then steadily declined during the years of Nixon, Ford and Carter to slightly over 5 percent in 1980. President Carter's last defense budget called for a reversal of the downward trend to 5.5 percent and this has continued under President Reagan from 6.1 percent to a projected 6.8 percent in 1984.[44]

2. During the last decade, the European nonnuclear weapons members of NATO have devoted considerably smaller percentages of their GNP to defense budgets, which have averaged between 2.5 percent and 3.5 percent for Belgium, Denmark, Italy, the Netherlands, Norway, Portugal, and West Germany.[45]

3. Soviet military expenditures have usually been estimated at anywhere from 11 percent to 15 percent of GNP, measured on an economic base about half that of the United States. Soviet military forces have much lower manpower costs, however, and can devote a substantially larger part of their budget to weapons and equipment. A roughly similar comparison can be drawn between the Warsaw Pact countries of Eastern Europe and the NATO countries of Western Europe. Soviet and Eastern bloc economies suffer

much more serious problems and deficiencies than those of the Western alliance. Yet neither Eastern nor Western economists blame those problems on defense budgets. In contrast, it is now highly fashionable to blame nearly all of the West's economic problems—unemployment, inflation, budget deficits, and dissatisfaction with social and human welfare spending levels—on defense.

4. During the last three decades, defense spending in the United States and the NATO countries as a proportion of GNP has shown a long term decline, apart from the years when the United States was emphasizing the buildup of conventional forces. During the same three decades, U.S. and NATO country expenditures for education, health, and human welfare services of all kinds have risen steadily as a proportion of GNP. For the decade up to the late 1970s, U.S. defense spending as a percentage of combined federal health and education expenditures went down from 95 percent to about 60 percent; while the comparable figures for the Soviet Union held fairly steady in the range of 160 to 170 percent.[46] During 1982, the percentage of the U.S. federal budget spent on health and welfare programs was 51 percent compared to 26 percent for defense.[47]

5. Michael Novak points out that the foregoing figures do not include the cost of human welfare services provided by state and local governments and by private institutions such as corporations, churches, foundations, and a wide variety of charitable, philanthropic, and humanitarian organizations at all levels. Novak offers the following startling estimate:

> Since the United States bears the world's heaviest defense burden, comparisons of percentages of human services expenditures to military expenditures in West Germany, the United Kingdom, and other nations are even more favorable. In the free nations, moneys from all sources spent on health, education, welfare and other human purposes exceed moneys spent on weapons by a factor of about 20 to 1.[48]

6. The relative decline in U.S. and West European defense spending as a percentage of GNP and of total welfare services has been due

in large measure to defense economies made possible by nuclear weapons and nuclear deterrence. The total annual cost of the nuclear weapons systems on which the deterrent depends amounts to less than 10 percent of the U.S. military budget and less than 0.6 percent of GNP. Thus, concludes Novak after citing these statistics,

> . . . when in 1976 the Holy See condemned the arms race as a danger, an act of aggression against the poor, and a folly which does not provide the security it promises, the Holy See could not reasonably be interpreted as asking the Western allies to apend much less than they are. The reason for poverty in the world is not adequate defense. Furthermore, efforts to supplant reliance on nuclear weaponry with reliance on conventional weaponry are bound to raise military costs dramatically, since conventional weapons are far more expensive.[49]

The bishops are by no means alone in urging a fundamental revision of NATO strategy, nor is the idea new. It has surfaced on several occasions in the past. The debate over nuclear versus conventional deterrence is almost as old as NATO itself, dating back to the "New Look" in strategy adopted by the Eisenhower administration once it was realized that NATO could not achieve its original goals because the effort to match Soviet conventional strength over the long haul was deemed prohibitive in cost and poltically unacceptable to the allies.[50] The ensuing years heard endless arguments about raising or lowering the nuclear threshold, developing for NATO a capability to enforce a "conventional pause" and the ability of a populous and prosperous Western Europe to parry Warsaw Pact conventional strength, especially given the possibility that East European armed forces, because of the political reliability problem, might have to be subtracted from rather than added to those of the Soviet Union.[51]

Ever since the first year of the Kennedy administration, the United States, in an effort to reduce reliance upon the need for an early NATO nuclear response to an otherwise uncontainable Soviet conventional aggression in Europe, has sought to persuade its allies to bring about a substantial increase in NATO's conventional capabilities. This effort has been in vain, for the simple reason that the West Europeans have always preferred deterrence to defense, and maintaining a nuclear strategy to planning for actual conventional war. No matter how assiduously the Kennedy administration sought to pursue a "flexible response" strategy as an alternative between holocaust and surrender, it was never able to retreat very far from the deterrent threat of a possible first use of nuclear weapons by NATO.[52] The Carter administration also tried, with extremely limited success, to persuade NATO member governments to commit themselves to substantial conventional force improvements. During the late 1970s, those governments, faced with the severe economic problems of unemployment and inflation brought on by the energy crisis, preferred to concentrate on East-West trade to keep alive the flickering embers of detente rather than incur the displeasure of both Moscow and their own electorates by raising defense budgets.

The past decade has witnessed several appeals for a NATO shift to greater emphasis on conventional capabilities. Those who have studied the question carefully realize that a conventional arms race might get out of hand more readily than a nuclear one. Moreover, as the Soviet military buildup has continued unabated, the nuclear and conventional balance in Europe has tilted eastward, and the credibility of the U.S. deterrent has eroded in European perception, most analysts have been compelled to realize that NATO deterrence operates within certain limits: The alliance can neither swing so far toward the nuclear side as to reduce its conventional forces, nor can it go so far in the opposite direction that it would renounce its option of using nuclear weapons first, if necessary. Both conventional force improvement and nuclear modernization are necessary to preserve stable equilibrium.[53] Those who have proposed a renunciation of the first use option are in the minority, and even they do so only on the highly dubious supposition that it can be replaced by adequate conventional deterrence. The more usual prescription is for a conventional force effort which will make it possible for NATO to adopt a policy of "no early use" or use only in extreme circumstances. NATO still needs, in the words of Laurence Martin, "sufficient defensive potential at each line to discourage attack by promising enough resistance at each level to raise the spectre of escalation to the next."[54] The bishops' fear of the danger of escalation is a healthy, rational fear. Strategists assume that this fear is an indispensable component of extended deterrence.[55]

The West Europeans have become more concerned about security since the Soviet invasion of Afghanistan, growing turmoil in the energy-critical area of the Persian Gulf which may entail the redeployment of some U.S. conventional forces from Western Europe in a future crisis, and the suppression of the Solidarity movement in Poland. New technologies now emerging—including communications-jamming equipment, precision-guided missiles and pilotless aircraft, miniature land mines dropped by jet planes before advancing tanks, etc.—hold promise for enhancing NATO's conventional defense capabilities; but it will be several years before they become available in operational quantities, and they will be expensive. Conventional deterrence is considerably more costly than nuclear deterrence.[56]

It is chastening to recall that in 1940 Belgium maintained an army of 600,000, devoted 25 percent of its national budget to defense, and felt very insecure, with good reason. The comparable figures in 1980 were only 60,000 and 6 percent, yet Belgians, though nervous at times, were much less fearful of war. The bishops probably have no conception of what it would cost to shift over completely from the present nuclear-conventional strategy to a conventional one. Even in the unlikely event that the nonnuclear NATO allies should double their military budgets, it is highly doubtful that this would furnish an adequate substitute for the loss of deterrence which is implicit in the first use option.

The bishops insist that they do not wish to make the world or Europe "safe for conventional war" whose horrors might well be scarcely distinguishable from those of a war waged with low-yield nuclear weapons in a discriminating manner. Yet many strategists fear that this might be the unintended consequence of advocating an absolute, unconditional "no first use" policy. The strategists, moreover, are apprehensive over any proposed change in a strategy which has kept Europe at peace for more than three decades, especially a change which might make conventional attack appear the least bit more attractive to Soviet leaders. A conventional war in Euope, launched on a miscalculation, would probably become nuclear, sooner rather than later, regardless of declared policies . The bishops, discomfited by the nuclear-conventional contradiction in their statement, seek to escape from their dilemma by expressing a hope, which we can all share, that nuclear and conventional arms levels will go down together, despite the lack of progress after ten years of Vienna MBFR negotiations on reduction of conventional forces.

Certainly NATO should do whatever it can, including the enhancement of conventional forces, to reduce to an absolute minimum the possibility of being forced *in extremis* to resort to even the most discriminating first use of nuclear weapons to halt an otherwise overpowering aggressive force. Irving Kristol, who favors a "no first use" policy, criticizes NATO for clinging to a nuclear strategy as cheaper by far, and for being unwilling to make the great sacrifices in money and manpower needed to steer away from it.[57] For several years to come, however, it will be impossible for NATO to think in terms of "no first use." The problem is not only one of defense budgets. In the Federal Republic of Germany, where the birth rate declined by 50 percent between 1965 and 1978, the *Bundeswehr* now faces a period of critical manpower shortage.[58]

As long as the Soviet Union presents both a conventional and a nuclear threat to Western Europe, NATO cannot renounce the first use option. We can be reasonably sure of two things:

1. Except for the Netherlands, the West European allies will continue to be wary of any rapid shift of emphasis to a conventional strategy, because they regard it as economically wasteful, politically unwise, and militarily less effective as a deterrent and therefore more dangerous as increasing the probability of war.

2. If the shift is nearly as pronounced as the bishops would like, we can expect it to provoke a reaction both from Soviet spokesmen and Western pacifists who will accuse NATO of being interested not in deterring war but in heightening European tensions by actually preparing to wage conventional war. Conventional warmaking strategies are more credible than nuclear ones. Unfortunately, there are no simple solutions to the West's security dilemmas in the nuclear age.

One can readily imagine that the President of the United States, after consulting the leaders of the Atlantic allies, might decide, on the basis of the dictum that "no war is just if it does more harm than good to the state,"[59] that it would be disproportionate, counterproductive, and unjustifiable to invoke nuclear weapons in a concrete war situation. Yet in the present international political-strategic real world, it could be irresponsible for NATO to announce in advance that it will renounce the initial use of nuclear weapons under all future contingencies. If this were not merely a sham, but could be taken seriously by the other side, it would be bound to reduce in the other side's calculations what up to now has operated as an inhibiting element of uncertainty which makes a westward thrust by the Warsaw Pact a leap into the unknown and unpredictable.[60] The removal of that uncertainty would inevitably weaken deterrence more than could be compensated for by any shift to conventional emphasis within the realm of realistic expectation.

Cynics have been heard to say that a "no first use" declaration now would not really weaken the NATO deterrent because Soviet planners would not be able to take it seriously as long as NATO deploys nuclear weapons in Europe. There is a certain Machiavellian cleverness in this position, but in the long run it would be too clever by half, for it would be bound eventually to produce a noticeable effect on NATO doctrine, deployments, and planning. The Soviet Union would be able to exploit, at least politically if not militarily, NATO's lack of an operational doctrine to back up its facade of deterrence. A real danger is that the Soviet leaders might be emboldened to engage in imprudent risk-taking in a future critical confrontation in Europe on the expectation that the West, paralyzed by fear of a massive conventional attack, might feel compelled to back down. But in that situation, the West, with its back to the wall, may very well decide it can retreat no further. Thus NATO must be extremely careful concerning the public declaration of its policy, which democratic peoples should take very seriously if they expect their adversaries to do so. Quite aside from this consequential consideration, the argument of the Machiavellian cynic hardly enhances the integrity of the moral case which the bishops sincerely wish to make.

American Bishops, European Bishops

West European Catholic episcopal conferences, generally speaking, have been more cautious than their American counterpart when it comes to going beyond the pronouncements of Vatican II and the popes with statements condemning deterrence and all uses of nuclear weapons. In late 1980, the Bishops' Conference of England and Wales issued a statement which read in part:

> We are frequently asked to make a statement on the morality or otherwise of the nuclear deterrent . . . As a Conference of Bishops we have to say frankly that we are not yet able to give a comprehensive and authoritative judgment on every aspect of this difficult matter.
>
> It is often supposed that the Church can provide an immediate answer to every moral question, however complex. This is not the case. Sometimes the passage of time and much prayerful consideration are required before the mind of the Church can be clarified and a pronouncement made.[61]

Basil Cardinal Hume of Westminster, the most prominent Catholic voice in England, has appeared at times to be personally inclined toward a nuclear pacifist stance and to insist upon the fulfillment of conditions for justified counterforce use of nuclear weapons which would be extremely difficult to meet: no widespread collateral killing of innocent civilians and no escalation. Nevertheless, he has not condemned outright either the possession of nuclear arms directed at military targets or all uses of nuclear weapons. He has also kept a watchful eye on the increasing politicization of the Campaign for Nuclear Disarmament (CND) whose secretary is the Catholic Monsignor Bruce Kent, an active advocate of the view that unilateral disarmament would have a contagious effect.[62]

Hume's position has been portrayed as midway between the more radical pacifist bishops of International Pax Christi who categorically condemn the possession of nuclear weapons as immoral and favor unilateral disarmament, and the "mainstream" bishops who support the NATO strategy of deterrence as essential for stability and the preservation of a civil order of freedom in which Christians can profess their faith. The latter group includes Joseph Cardinal Hoeffner of Cologne, Bishop Jean Vilnet, president of the French episcopal conference, Monsignor R.P. Bar, Auxiliary Bishop of Rotterdam, and other bishops who took part in the Rome Consultation of January 1983.[63] The Pax Christi bishops are actively involved in the European peace and antinuclear movements, which are unalterably opposed to the deployment of new NATO missiles; the Christian Democratic parties that are politically dominant in West Germany, Italy, the Netherlands, and Belgium have been publicly committed in recent years to the need for missile modernization. Thus the issue of nuclear deterrence, in Europe as in the United States, contains a potential for dividing the Catholic Church deeply, not only politically but doctrinally as well. The Netherlands branch of Pax Christi prepared the initial draft of a pastoral letter for the Dutch bishops recommending support for unilateral disarmament. Monsignor Bar argued that the Dutch hierarchy could not issue a binding statement of a political nature on the subject of deterrence which went beyond the teaching of Vatican II, because Catholic teaching on moral issues must be universal. In other words, the general notion of nuclear deterrence cannot be morally acceptable in one country and sinful in another. In August 1982 the Dutch bishops announced that the publication of their pastoral letter would be postponed. When it was released in mid-June 1983, it was similar to that of the American bishops in rejecting unilateral disarmament and condoning possession for the sake of deterrence as a temporary strategy; but it condemned "virtually any conceivable actual use of nuclear weapons."[64]

Whereas some of the severest critics of nuclear weapons and deterrence at the Second Vatican Council were French, the bishops of France have been more muted in their criticism in recent years. The last two decades have seen a remarkable reversal in the positions of the American and French hierarchies. During the debate on *Gaudium et spes* at Rome in 1964–65, it was Archbishop Beck of Liverpool and a group of Americans headed by Philip Hannan (then Auxiliary Bishop of Washington), who led the effort to tone down the Council's treatment of deterrence and to produce a statement that would reflect an appreciation of the dilemmas facing Western governments. At that time, too, political relations between the United States and France were marked by a certain acrimony resulting from divergent national attitudes toward the Alliance and nuclear weapons. There exists in France today a high degree of consensus over the need for an independent national nuclear deterrent. The socialist government of President Francois Mitterrand, concerned over the adversely tilting balance in Europe, displays a much more favorable attitude toward the U.S. "nuclear umbrella" than one would have thought possible during the de Gaulle era, and supports both NATO missile deployment and a shift of emphasis from conventional to nuclear capabilities.

The French bishops, by a vote of 93 to 2 with 8 abstentions, approved a pastoral letter entitled "Win the Peace" in November 1983. In that document, they held nuclear deterrence to be a legitimate defense against the threat posed by a Marxist-Leninist system with an aggressive and dominating ideology and a tendency to use everything, even the popular aspiration for peace, in its desire for world conquest. In the choices between nonwar and slavery, between the *gulag* and Finlandization, nuclear deterrence is better than nothing, better than the risks involved in unilateral disarmament. The French clearly disagree with the U.S. bishops on whether one may ever morally threaten what one may not morally do:

> The threat of violence does not constitute violence. That . . . is something we often forget when we attribute the same moral status to the threat as to the use of violence.[65]

Throughout the postwar period, the West German bishops have been supportive of the philosophy of the Christian Democrats (CDU/CSU), somewhat as the weightier part of the U.S. Catholic hierarchy in this century has been favorably disposed toward the Democratic Party for its socioeconomic stands. The German bishops were under pressure from Pax Christi and other Catholic pacifists to join the Protestants with a pronouncement on nuclear weapons. The demand intensified once the initiative of the U.S. episcopal conference became known. The German bishops, however, did not want their pastoral letter to become an issue in the campaign for the March 1983 national election. The newly incumbent Chancellor Helmut Kohl was a Christian Democrat; the Green Party and the left wing of the Social Democratic Party (SPD) did their utmost to make the NATO deployment of cruise and Pershing-2 missiles a major campaign issue. Consequently the West German bishops kept secret their pastoral letter, which was not published until late April 1983.[66]

Of all the Catholics in the world, it is the Germans who understand with the deepest intuition the subtle political and psychological factors involved in the maintenance of a credible and effective deterrent. It is they who are situated in the zone of initial encounter.

If war should come to Europe as the result of a failure of deterrence, the Germans will be the first ones—some of them are afraid they might be the only ones—to feel its full destructive effects. They have the strongest reason to fear and loathe war, and to bend their intelligence most strenuously to the task of avoiding it, lest their country become a nuclear battlefield. The Germans and the French, who by reason of geographical location and historical experience have an intimate knowledge of how European powers behave, have long been the staunchest advocates of a strategy of deterrence. American Catholics would do well to pay attention to what West European Catholics have been saying in the last few years.

In sharp contrast to the former, the latter exhibit a keen appreciation of the fact that weapons have not only a military but also a political function as well, and that in the case of nuclear weapons the political function is decisive. Since the Soviet Union knows very well how to use nuclear weapons for psychopolitical purposes to bring pressure to bear on other states, the Western alliance must equip itself with comparable weapons to defend itself against political coercion. Thus concluded the Central Committee of German Catholics in November 1981, in a sophisticated statement on the delicate interface between morality and the international politics of deterrence.[67] The German bishops in their pastoral letter walked the following fine line:

> From the standpoint of war avoidance, there are certain criteria which deterrence must satisfy if it is still to be ethically acceptable: military means already existing or planned may make war neither fightable nor more probable.
>
> It is clear to us that with this demand we are thrust into an almost insoluble contradiction, because weapons are effective as means of deterrence only when their use can also be credibly threatened. But from the standpoint of war prevention, the mutual threat of unacceptable damage and all of its corresponding risks are the principal elements of a deterrent strategy. It is precisely the thought that conventional and nuclear war cannot be limited, and conceals an incalculable risk for an opponent, that should provide a guarantee against war, indeed any war.
>
> To threaten a mass destruction that one may never

carry out—a morally unacceptable conception—is seen as particularly effective for the purpose of war prevention. This horrible tension is to be tolerated only if the total security policy is geared toward the goal of war prevention and military measures remain incorporated into the primary concept of securing the peace by political means. Only such and so many military means may be developed as are required for the purpose of war-prevention-oriented deterrence. Military means should be aimed not at gaining superiority but much more to the goal of a stability that exists when neither side can derive political or military uses from its weapons systems.[68]

They said nothing about "no first use," whether a nuclear exchange can actually be limited, counterforce strategies, specific weapons systems, a nuclear freeze, or the development of programmed methods of nonviolent resistance.[69] They limited themselves to the enunciation of general moral, political, and strategic principles; yet one cannot call their statement platitudinous merely because they refrain from offering recommendations on specific policies. This work they leave to governments.

The German bishops echo Pope John Paul II's message to the United Nations on the moral acceptability of deterrence and the need for efforts to reduce "the real danger of explosion" inherent in deterrence. But they also insist that in the pursuit of peace, we must realize that if the violation of human rights is tolerated, rationalized, and even publicly applauded—an obvious reference to events in Poland—this strengthens injustice while threatening peace and freedom. Repression and totalitarian blackmail, they say, constitute another "explosive tinderbox" in addition to nuclear weapons. The dangers from both tinderboxes, which are related, have to be met simultaneously by political means.[70]

The Bishops' Pastoral Letter in Perspective

Bishops, it should be remembered, are shepherds, not strategists. They are bound to be more concerned with what they see as the morally right and good course at a critical juncture of history rather than with what strategists, international theorists, and policy-makers (who are also in their own way no less interested than the bishops in preserving justice and peace) may regard as politically prudent under existing circumstances. Moreover, the bishops are sharply distinguished from the latter group by virtue of a mandate, given long ago, to preach, in unity with the Bishop of Rome, the Successor of St. Peter, a spiritual message entrusted to them by the Holy Spirit. When they gather to deliberate about a pastoral letter, they do a good deal of praying for guidance, ostensibly more than the other group is known to do as a corporate body. This is a factor not to be ignored. The bishops presumably pay more attention to what they experience as the promptings of the Holy Spirit than to what they read or hear from the experts, however important and difficult it may be concretely to discern the difference between promptings and personal predilections for this or that source of expertise, idea, theory, and political position.

Many of the bishops are undoubtedly keenly aware of the profound dilemmas posed by nuclear deterrence as well as by the twin dangers of nuclear war and totalitarian tyranny. They realize that by examining nuclear strategies in light of the Gospel and the traditional moral doctrine of the just war, they might be contributing to the spread of a "sentimental pacifism" among American Catholics, a pacifism which would begin in the nuclear dimension and gradually evolve toward that absolute pacifism which the Catholic New Left (including several bishops) has been expounding as a moral imperative for the NATO nations but not for those countries where liberation theology is appropriate. If this were to happen, it would vitiate the will of the democratic societies to defend themselves militarily and render them more vulnerable to political intimidation by an increasingly powerful communist system to the east. This is a potential consequence to which the bishops do not address themselves.

A prominent West Christian Democrat, Alois Mertes, State Secretary in the Ministry of Foreign Affairs of Chancellor Helmut Kohl, said of the American bishops' second draft: "The effect will be that it is extremely welcome to all those who fight the Western strategy ... They favor in nonnuclear Germany the strategy of the neutralists, the pacifists and the Soviet Union, because they weaken the credibility of the American deterrent."[71]

The bishops are intelligent enough to assume that their teaching *will* have an impact in the United States and Western Europe; they do not expect it to have any significant effect in the communist countries, except to be used as evidence that the Church is becoming more critical of U.S. military policy. The irony is that the West provides an atmosphere of political and spiritual freedom in which the Church can define its own mission, whereas the Soviet system either persecutes the Christian churches or barely tolerates them out of condescending compassion for the ignorant and superstitious masses or concern for foreign opinion, all the while strictly controlling and cynically manipulating religion for internal and external tactical purposes. The Russian Orthodox Church has no choice today but to praise the efforts of the officially atheist Soviet government to prevent nuclear war and strengthen world peace by opposing U.S. and NATO nuclear weapons. Most of the bishops scarcely need to be reminded of the travail and suffering of such Catholic churchmen as Budkiewicz, Slipyi, Beran , Mindszenty and Wyzszynski. Yet they have a hope, grounded in faith, that by taking a prophetic stand on nuclear war which their consciences dictate, they might help infuse the West with renewed spiritual strength without inviting the dire political and military consequences feared by strategic analysts.

Bishops as a whole are neither utopians nor altruists. They are just as complex as ordinary human beings and act out of a variety of assumptions. Some of them probably assume—not unrealistically— that U.S. and NATO strategic policy will not undergo any rapid or drastic change as a result of their pastoral letter. Their intention may be not to bring about the collapse of the Western edifice of nuclear deterrence, but only to reduce the likelihood of a quick or easy resort to nuclear weapons. The motives for which the bishops have taken their stand on specific policies vary widely. Many are concerned about the credibility of their respect for the sacredness of human life in regard to the question of abortion. Many are anxious not to be caught in the position of the German bishops in World War II who appeared to bless the policy of their government regardless of its moral quality. Only a few of the most radicalized bishops, however, are ready to equate the U.S. government with that of Nazi Germany. Many are seeking to do for their own dioceses what Paul VI tried to do for the whole Church—preserve unity in the midst of change and ideological-political polarization of Catholics in regard to nuclear deterrence and other issues. Some wish to keep the extreme Catholic pacifist Left from separating completely from the Church. For this purpose, they are willing to risk irritating the more conservative regular church-attending middle classes who are not very likely to become alienated from the source of their sacramental life regardless of how much they might disagree with the specific political recommendations of the American hierarchy.

Most of the bishops, following the popes and Vatican II, would insist upon multilateral, reciprocal, and safeguarded nuclear disarmament. Only a minority would agree at present with Detroit Bishop Thomas Gumbleton that the United States should dismantle its nuclear arsenal unilaterally even if the Soviet Union proves unwilling to disarm, and that it would be preferable for the Soviet Union to dominate the United States and its allies than for the West to possess and use nuclear weapons in self-defense.[72] Who knows? Perhaps a few are still intrigued by the highly questionable hypothesis (which has been around for many years) that Western Christianity today finds itself in a situation analogous to that of the fifth century, when a decadent Roman Empire was collapsing while its gates were being stormed by barbarians who later received baptism and became the builders of cathedrals and universities. Most of the bishops are not yet willing to advise American Catholics or, more immediately, West European Catholics, to prepare themselves either for martyrdom or subjugation by communist totalitarianism.

Yet there are substantial parts of the pastoral letter, inserted at the behest of the Pax Christi bishops, which are likely to give rise in the minds of many believers to that false dichotomy of old: "Red or dead." The highest and most delicate task of Western governments is to make sure that they never come to the point of having to choose between such extremes. The appropriate motto is, "Better neither than either," and the proper formula is deterrence. It is understandable that some radical Christian pacifists, today as always throughout history, might wish to escape from the tension, uncertainties, and dilemmas which inhere in the human situation and achieve a sense of inner spiritual purification, certitude, and salvation here and now by pitting the Sermon on the Mount against the rational policy of the state viewed as the detested *Realpolitik* or *raison d'etat* and presumed (in contravention of the Augustinian-Thomistic tradition) to be diabolical. This, as Eric Voegelin pointed out a quarter century ago, is the essence of the gnostic mentality, which has something in common with all the political salvation ideologies of the modern era. A Christian should have no difficulty understanding how some religious pacifists might, in the present environment, harbor a yearning for a face-to-face confrontation with that critical choice of nuclear war or submission to totalitarianism, in short, the choice of the person who becomes a martyr for the faith. But that is not an alternative relevant and available to governmental decisionmakers.

It is the function of rational democratic politics, of course, to pursue intelligent policies and commonsense compromises which will avert the cataclysmic choice between Armageddon and the loss of freedom. The pastoral letter, by focusing principally upon the dangers of nuclear war and considerably less on the dangers of Soviet expansionism and the requirements of stable deterrence through a judicious mixture of military modernization and arms control negotiations by the superpowers, seems in several places to pose the stark and far from necessary choice between war and surrender.

Only governmental strategic planners and policymakers, acting on the basis of political experience, intelligence, and pressures from a variety of domestic and foreign sources, can make the practical judgments needed concerning stabilizing and destabilizing weapons modernization programs in relation to nuclear balances and effective arms control negotiating positions; for these are in the last analysis empirical rather than moral judgments.

Some may well argue that the Soviet Union requires, from a psychopolitical standpoint, more military power than does the United States for a self-confident sense of security. This is because a sociologically rigid totalitarian state, especially given the history of war which the Russian people have known in this century, is bound to be much more paranoid than an open, democratic society like that of the United States, which has never really known a foreign aggressor on its own soil. To say that Soviet attitudes ought to be taken into account by the U.S. government is not to suggest that the United States, while remaining patiently tolerant of those who criticize its own defense policies, can allow the Soviet Union to amass such margins of strategic and Eurostrategic military capabilities as to upset the international political and military equilibrium and subject the European allies of the United States to political intimidation by projecting an ominous military shadow against an American defense pledge of declining credibility.

The West cannot be expected to accept the Soviet definition of "equal security," which would justify the accumulation of military power by the USSR equivalent to the combined power of all its presumed adversaries—the United States, Western Europe, Japan, China, and any other countries which might oppose Soviet policies in coming decades. Many Western pacifists, when they have explained to them what "equal security" means in the Soviet strategic lexicon, nod their heads approvingly and concede that Moscow has a point. Responsible Western governments, however, cannot subscribe to such a nonsensical formula. Why not? Because it implies that there are not *two* superpowers, each the head of a politically distinctive coalition, engaged in the extremely difficult task of negotiating security on the basis of military power parity. According to the Soviet view, there is only *one* superpower by "divine right" in the Marxist-Leninist sense. That is the Soviet Union, which must be allowed to become first of all equal and eventually superior to a combination of all the democratic nations and the most populous communist power as well, so that it will be able to dictate to them, as its preferred operational strategy prescribes, without war, much as it has been able to direct the course of events in Finland for many years, or in Poland during recent years, without actually invoking military force. Rather than allow Moscow to perpetrate such a gigantic deception under the guise of fairness, Western governments have no choice but to pursue a mix of political, economic, military, and other policies designed to convince the leaders in the Kremlin that they would be much better off to behave in a way that does not turn everybody else in the world into their potential enemies.

Both superpowers profess to aim at parity. But one power has been moving for several years from superiority to parity or something less; the other, from inferiority to parity or something more. International theorists know that tension rises as the power curves of the two rivals approach intersection. The strategic experts are far from being perfectly agreed on whether the Soviet Union has now actually overtaken and surpassed the United States in total military capabilities. This is hard to say in a world of fluctuating and sometimes compensating asymmetries. But the most expert and objective research institutes in the West, particularly the International Institute for Strategic Studies in London, which annually publishes *The Military Balance* and *Strategic Survey*, have had no doubts during the past decade or more as to the general direction of the trends in military power. No one has suggested that the long-term shift in the military balance has been in favor of the West. Only the uninformed can dismiss as unwarranted the concern of Western defense analysts. More important than the endless statistics relating to numbers, ranges, survivability, reliability, accuracy, yield, and kill-capability of various nuclear delivery systems and warheads, and of their total throw-weight and megatonnage, and other quantitative factors which enter into the calculus of the strategic equation, are the perceptions of governments, elites, and publics concerning the tilting military balance. Ever since the 1960s, the perceived gap between American and Soviet military strength has been widening throughout Western Europe. If the perceived gap becomes too wide—and the United States should avoid overestimating whatever gap may be opening—the danger that calm decision making will give way to miscalculation in a crisis grows. The United States, as a democratic state whose people have ways of making governmental action conformable to their moral values, has a greater responsibility to act rationally and to avoid irrational action of any kind, pacifist or bellicist.

Analysts who have spent many years—indeed, most of their professional lives—studying the requirements of nuclear deterrence can identify sympathetically with the bishops when they call for steps to reduce the dangers of war and warn against strident public rhetoric (as distinct from prudent planning) relating to fighting, limiting, and winning a protracted nuclear war—rhetoric which may or may not frighten our adversaries as much as we know it does our allies.

The rhetoric of nuclear war wageability and winnability was fashionable during the last year of Carter and the first year of Reagan. In fact, there appears to have been a causal nexus between that rhetoric and the decision of the NCCB to draft its pastoral letter. Most of the bishops were probably unaware that Soviet strategic writers had been bandying the idea about, in connection with their own doctrine of the preemptive nuclear strike, for at least fifteen years prior to its emergence in the United States. During the whole decade of SALT, the United States had tried with singular lack of success to "educate" the Soviet Union and "bring it around" to the American philosophy of deterrence and arms control based on the concept of Assured Destruction in a retaliatory strike.[73] Only when that failure became luminously clear did the American community of strategic analysts begin to shift toward the advocacy of a different approach, calculated to alter the pattern of incentives infusing Soviet policy. U.S. policymakers have no choice but to take necessary steps, in the face of a steady Soviet buildup, to maintain a stable political-military equilibrium in the superpower relationship and to convince itself and its allies, after years of growing uncertainty and doubt, that its ability to deter both strategic nuclear war and *any* war in Europe remains unimpaired. Such steps, involving an integrated combination of long-planned modernization programs and negotiation strategies for superpower arms reductions do not deserve to be characterized as efforts to accelerate an unbridled arms race.

In any event, the rhetoric which reached a point of intensity in late 1981 may have had a salutary effect on both parties, making each probe more honestly than heretofore into the dreadful uncertainties of the present situation. The rhetoric has become alternately more muted and more strident on both sides since 1982. The prospects for arms negotiations in which each side takes adequate stock not only of its own security needs but also the legitimate security apprehensions of the other seem better now than at any previous time. It is to be hoped that the bishops' pastoral will have a positive, reinforcing effect upon these trends.

What is the impact of the U.S. bishops' pastoral letter likely to be? This is difficult to predict. The attention span of the mass media had already peaked within a few weeks of the Chicago meeting. its immediate effect on U.S. policy was not dramatic. President Reagan said that "it really is a legitimate effort to do exactly what we're doing, and that is to try to find ways toward world peace."[74] Many of the bishops, of course, would have disagreed. Gerald P. Fogarty, a historian of the American Catholic Church called the pastoral "shocking" precisely because it criticizes and challenges governmental policy.[75]

The New York Times found the bishops' sense of moral concern admirable and many of their strategic judgments beyond dispute— here some strategists would disagree—even though in their support for a weapons freeze they "come perilously close to an undesirable involvement of the church in political action."

... But their letter also contains ambiguities, contradictions and dubious policy counsel that other advocates of arms control will surely want to question... They are not only attacking the main doctrines of the Reagan Administration but also straying far from the prevailing theories of the arms control community.[76]

The newspaper was incorrect in saying that they "characterize any use of nuclear weapons as immoral—thus emboldening Archbishop John Quinn to call upon Catholics in the armed forces to reject any order to fire them." Archbishop Quinn had wanted the letter to brand any use as immoral, but his amendment was finally rejected, and his appeal to Catholics in the military was a personal one.[77] *The New York Times* went on:

> In supporting a nuclear weapons freeze, the bishops seem unmindful of the risk that such negotiations, if successful, could end up freezing the existing nuclear instabilities and actually add to the risk of war. And by repudiating NATO's threat that it may have to use nuclear weapons against a massive Soviet conventional attack, they oppose not only the views of allied governments but of the bishops of West Germany and France.
>
> Fundamentally, the American bishops' approach falters on the assumption that the nuclear dilemma can eventually be resolved by eliminating rather than controlling nuclear weapons. But there is no known way to get rid of The Bomb, no way to guard against all possible production or concealment of warheads. That is why, for a quarter-century, negotiations have focused on limiting and reducing delivery systems.
>
> Even reductions of Soviet and American nuclear weapons, while useful, are less important than achieving a stable nuclear balance. Too much reduction could add to instability; a small number of concealed weapons could make one side dominant.
>
> None of this means mankind has to learn to love The Bomb. But it does have to learn how to live with it and manage the problems it poses. There's no place to hide, even in morality.[78]

Although the bishops appeared to be skeptical of all new nuclear weapons programs, including the MX and new missiles for NATO, within a few weeks after the letter was issued, the Reagan administration won a congressional test vote on the MX and, at the Williamsburg Summit, allied approval for the deployment of cruise and Pershing-2 missiles on schedule. These programs are not likely to be substantially modified as a result of the bishops' moral warnings about nuclear war. They might well be modified, however, by budgetary considerations and/or progress in arms negotiations.

How will Catholics in general react to the letter? We have already seen that the European bishops are quite interested in it, more for its political portents than its theological contents, which apparently do not impress them all that much. Cardinal Bernardin thought that the American initiative might inspire the West Europeans to become bolder and follow suit. The Pax Christi bishops require little encouragement along that line. The other bishops, who tend to think that present circumstances make a sense of political responsibility and prudence a more urgent Christian demand than that form of religious enthusiasm which leads one to stress moral imperatives above political subtleties, are not likely to cave in, unless the situation becomes desperate—and it need not. Much will depend upon signals from the pope.

What about the reaction of American Catholics? There was a time, prior to Vatican II, when American Catholics would have been in the forefront among Catholics of the world—no questions asked—in professing their loyalty to the pope and all the bishops of the universal Church, fully united, consistent, and clear in their moral teaching. In the post-conciliar era, the teaching of the Church on social, political and strategic questions has begun to fragment. National episcopal conferences now "nuance" their moral and political teaching in different ways. We may be moving into a period when the traditional Catholic political philosophy of a homogeneous, universal Church is becoming a mixed congeries of national perspectives in a sort of ecclesiastical United Nations. This development would mark the ultimate triump of Gallicanism.

The overwhelming majority of adult American Catholics, of course, will not be expected to read a letter considerably in excess of 30,000 words. Gerald Fogarty suggested that Catholics will perhaps pay no more heed to this teaching than they did to *Humanae vitae*.[79]

Fogarty's observation may be misleading, since nuclear pacifism is today a much more popular and "trendier" issue than sexual abstinence or continence. Some Catholics in the armed services, nuclear arms industry, and government began immediately to consider the implications of the pastoral for their consciences. But even bishops who support the letter are disagreed on the precise distinction between what is binding and what kinds of personal decisions remain within the realm of choice for the sincere conscience. The consensus is that the letter leaves considerable latitude on practical applications by the laity and the priests who advise them.[80] It is nevertheless likely that future Catholic candidates for President and Vice President, or for appointment to defense, national security, and high military posts will be questioned concerning their attitude toward specific policy recommendations in the letter.

The bishops expect their pastoral to become a major tool of education on the subject of war and peace. Undoubtedly, the long-term impact of the letter will be felt gradually, as the result of its use within the Church's system of parishes and schools. The letter's influence on younger Catholics could be quite significant over the course of years. Naturally, the emphasis will vary from one diocese and even one parish to another. The bishops will quickly discover how hard it is to develop balanced and objective educational programs. Since the document, in a sense, contains two different approaches side by side, it will be easy for left and right, doves and hawks, pacifists and advocates of just war/deterrence, to emphasize the parts most congenial to them.[81] It is probable, however, that in the long run the pacifists, who have had the momentum in recent years, will dominate the instructional process.

Perhaps the bishops themselves will develop their thinking as they learn more about the political, psychological, and military complexities of deterrence and negotiating strategies. In this regard, they would be wise to intensify their dialogue with European national conferences of bishops who are much more sensitive to the present international political realities of deterrence. Otherwise, the net result seems almost certain to be an increase in Catholic nuclear pacifism, increasing skepticism over deterrence and military defense expenditures in general, and a gradual slide toward absolute pacifism. We could also expect the pastoral to become a sort of theological rationalization for neoisolationism in the United States and add to the pressures for U.S. military disengagement from Europe. Thoughtful Europeans rightly regard this as a dreadful prospect.

It would be most regrettable from the standpoint of Christian political philosophy if the just war theory, which was conceived by great Christian intellects to protect a social order of justice and lives of innocents against unjust aggression, either by overt attack or by gradual intimidation and subordination to a totalitarian regime, should now be converted into a theory that does injustice to the democratic nations of the West. Yet that is what could happen if care is not taken. This would be done by people in the peace movement who profess to be acting out of the sublimest Christian motives— there is no reason to disbelieve them—but whose understanding of how the international political system operates scarcely extends beyond what they have been able to imbibe from organizations such as Ground Zero, Physicians for Social Responsibility, and the Union of Concerned Scientists. Were St. Augustine and St. Thomas here, they would probably say: "If nuclear deterrence is rational, then it is moral." That is essentially what Pope John Paul II declared, without attaching a list of caveats, reservations, and hypothetical conditions. We had better not start peeling deterrence away, layer by layer, as if it were an onion. One who does that begins with an onion and ends with nothing but tears.

There has been a good deal of critical comment in this book— not unfair, the author hopes—about some of the specific recommendations in the pastoral letter. Strategists would do well not to confine themselves to negative carping and nit-picking, but to give the bishops their due. The bishops are to be admired for adopting a courageous prophetic stance, for raising some tough questions about their own government's policy, and for introducing a strong moral tone into the national debate about nuclear strategies. They have reminded all of us, and not Catholics only, that "politics" in the highest classical sense as defined by Plato and Aristotle, especially politics in a democratic state, cannot allow the public deliberation of the most important issues to be insulated from the deeply held religious and ethical convictions of the people.

Until rather recently, there was a definite tendency in this country to draw a sharp line of separation between religion and politics, simply because most Church and State issues were seen as politically divisive, pitting one religious group against another. In our pluralist society, it appeared advisable to most politicians and religious leaders to maintain a general distinction (disregarding a few anomalies) between religious beliefs and secular civil policies. But in the ecumenical era of the last two decades, Catholic, Protestant, and Jewish believers have drawn closer together on certain matters to form a more united front against secularism, materialism, and atheism, although it must be admitted that several areas of friction among the religious groups remain. War and peace have become more unitive than divisive issues, and many (but not all) Protestant religious bodies congratulated the bishops for their pastoral letter[82] and for taking a stand which some may have regarded as a bit belated.

It is right and proper for the bishops to preach a message of international reconciliation, not confrontation or the heightening of tensions, a message more conducive to spiritual attitudes that lead to peace rather than war. We expect them to warn against indiscriminate use of nuclear weapons, even in retaliation, and against an excessive reliance upon modes of deterrence which darken the shadow of fear in which the peoples of the world live. We should pay heed to them when they point out that the prevention of war is a moral imperative which demands a fresh appraisal of the problem, but that the avoidance of war, either nuclear or conventional, does not exhaust the content of Catholic teaching and is not by itself a sufficient conception of international relations today.

We need a more positive vision of justice, peace, and order in the world. While eschewing utopianism, the bishops tell us that there must be a better way of building peace than merely piling up stockpiles of armaments—a way that leads toward a more integrated international system based upon an awareness of the growing political and economic interdependence of the human family throughout the whole world. The bishops tolerate deterrence as a policy which buys time in which the world's political leaders can use their political reason to work out a more constructive approach to and design of a far more solid international order than now exists or even looms on the horizons at the present time. The world stands at a crossroads. Deterrence provides it with *Gnadenzeit* (a "time of grace" as Carl Friedrich von Weiszacker termed it) for discerning choice by both superpowers, not just one. How to use this time wisely is only hinted at in the bishops' letter, for they see avoidance of war as a more urgent matter. But perhaps this is a subject for another pastoral letter and another book.

NOTES

Chapter 1

1. Pius XII, Christmas Radio Message, December 24, 1944. In Harry W. Flannery, ed., *Pattern for Peace: Catholic Statements on International Order* (Westminster, Md.: Newman Press, 1962), p. 126.

2. *Findings and Decisions: First Assembly of the World Council of Churches,* Amsterdam, Holland, August 22–September 4, 1948 (New York: World Council of Churches, n.d.), p. 54ff.

3. Address to the Peoples Assembled in St. Peter's Square, Easter, April 18, 1954, in Flannery, *Pattern For Peace*, 235, and Address to Delegates to the Eighth Congress of the World Medical Association, Rome, September 30, 1954, ibid., 236–37.

4. Provisional Study Document, *Christians and the Prevention of War in an Atomic Age—a Theological Discussion* (Geneva: World Council of Churches, 1958), Section 66.

5. Ralph B. Potter, *War and Moral Discourse* (Richmond, Va.: John Knox Press, 1969), pp. 112–13.

6. Works from that period which are still considered classics, some of which will be referred to in later sections of this study, include: Reinhold Niebuhr's pre-World War II essay: "Why the Christian Church is Not Pacifist," Chapter I in *Christianity and Power Politics* (New York: Charles Scribner's Sons, 1940) and "God Wills Both Justice and Peace" (written with Angus Dun), *Christianity and Crisis* 15 (13 June 1955); John C. Bennett, ed., *Nuclear Weapons and the Conflict of Conscience* (New York: Charles Scribner's Sons, 1962); Paul Ramsey, *War and the Christian Conscience: How Shall Modern War be Conducted Justly?* (Durham, N.C.: Duke University Press, 1961); John Courtney Murray, S.J., "Theology and Modern War," in William J. Nagle, ed., *Morality and Modern Warfare: The State of the Question* (Baltimore, Md.: Helicon Press, 1960); William Clancy, ed., *The Moral Dilemma of Nuclear Weapons*; Essays from *Worldview: A Journal of Religion and International Affairs* (New York: The Church Peace Union, 1961); Ulrich S. Allers and William V. O'Brien, eds., *Christian Ethics and Nuclear Warfare* (Washington, D.C.: Institute of World Policy, Georgetown University, 1963).

7. See F. H. Drinkwater, "The Morality of Nuclear War," *Commonweal* 61 (18 March 1955). See also E. I. Watkin, "Unjustifiable War," in Charles S. Thompson, ed., *Morals and Missiles: Catholic Essays on the Problem of War Today* (London: James Clarke, 1959); Walter Stein, ed., *Nuclear Weapons and Christian Conscience* (London: Merlin Press, 1961), published in the United States under the title *Nuclear Weapons: A Catholic Response* (New York: Sheed and Ward, 1962); Justus George Lawler, *Nuclear War: The Ethic, the Rhetoric, the Reality* (New York: Sheed and Ward, 1962).

8. Thomas Merton, "Nuclear War and Christian Responsibility," *Commonweal* 75 (9 February 1962) and the book he edited, *Breakthrough to Peace* (New York: New Direction Books, 1962); James W. Douglass, *The Non-Violent Cross* (New York: Macmillan, 1966); and Gordon C. Zahn, *War, Conscience and Dissent* (New York: Hawthorn Books, 1967).

9. James V. Schall, S.J., "The Political Consequences," in the symposium, "From the University: American Catholics and the Peace Debate," *Washington Quarterly* 5 (Autumn 1982): 127.

10. The 1980 General Meeting of the NCCB created an ad hoc Committee on War and Peace to study the issues and prepare a pastoral letter. The Committee consisted of Archbishop Joseph L. Bernardin of Cincinnati (now a Cardinal in Chicago), Chairman; and Bishops George Fulcher of Columbus, Thomas Gumbleton of Detroit, John O'Connor of New York (now Archbishop), and Daniel Reilly of Norwich. The Committee was assisted by Edward Doherty, Rev. J. Bryan Hehir of the United States Catholic Conference and Bruce Russett, professor of political science at Yale University. The Committee also consulted a number of theologians, academic strategic analysts, and government policymakers, especially from the Department of Defense, the National Security Council, and the Arms Control and Disarmament Agency. The first draft was presented to the Bishops assembled at Collegeville, Minnesota, in June 1982. The Committee received and reviewed more than 700 sets of critical comments on the first draft. A second draft was circulated in October 1982, but the ad hoc Committee requested that—contrary to the original plan—the bishops not vote on the document at their annual Washington conference in November.

11. Speech of Archbishop Raymond G. Hunthausen to Pacific North West Synod, Lutheran Church in America at Pacific Lutheran University, Tacoma, June 12, 1981, in *Catholic Northwest Progress*, July 2, 1981, Cf. also Kenneth A. Briggs, "Religious Leaders Objecting to Nuclear Arms," *The New York Times*, 5 September 1981.

12. "Texas Catholic Bishops Reject Neutron Bomb," *The New York Times*, 13 September 1981.

13. The following samples illustrate the attention given by the press: Richard Halloran, "Bishops Joining Nuclear Arms Debate," *The New York Times*, 4 October 1982 and "Proposed Catholic Bishops' Letter Opposes First Use of Nuclear Arms," *The New York Times*, 26 October 1982; Michael Getler, "Bishops Challenge A-Strategy," *The Washington Post*, 23 October 1982; "A Blast from the Bishops," *Time*, 8 November 1982; James L. Franklin, "U.S. Catholic Bishops Raise Nuclear Alarm," *The Boston Globe*, 14 November

1982; Kenneth A. Briggs, "Catholic Bishops Are to Open Nuclear Arms Debate Today," *The New York Times*, 15 November 1982; Marjorie Hyer, "Bishops Appear Divided on Proposed A-War Letter," *The Washington Post*, 16 November 1982; John J. Fialka, "Catholic Bishops' Statement is Expected to Question U.S. Nuclear Defense Policy," *The Wall Street Journal*, 16 November 1982: Herman Kahn, "Bishops and the Bomb," *The New York Times*, 9 December 1982; Robert Nowell, "Catholic bishops on the disarmament brink," *The Times* (London), 13 December 1982: W. J. Weatherby, "How America's bishops learned to loathe the bomb," *The Manchester Guardian Weekly*, 2 January 1983.

14. "The bishops offer reason where others talk of war," *Philadelphia Inquirer*, 1 November 1982; "A document of faith and hope," Editorial, *The Boston Globe*, 17 November 1982; James Reston, "Church, State and the Bomb," *The New York Times*, 27 October 1982; and "The Bishops and the Bomb," *Time*, 29 November 1982.

15. Michael Novak, "Arms and the Church," *Commentary* (March 1982): 39–40. Edwin M. Yoder, Jr. wrote sarcastically: "With all respect, my own churlish suspicion is that the opinion of bishops on the fine points of deterrence is approximately as valuable as the opinion of generals on the fine points of transubstantiation." "What do Bishops Know of Bombs?" *The Washington Post*, 3 November 1982. Herman Kahn said that the second draft did not reflect the kind of thoughtful and accurate strategic assessment which was necessary if the bishops were to make sound moral judgments. "Bishops and the Bomb," *The New York Times*, 9 December 1982.

16. Kenneth A. Briggs, "Prelates Backed in Dispute on Arms," *The New York Times*, 18 November 1982. Signers of the statement included William E. Colby, Robert Dahl, Hans Bethe, Mark O. Hatfield, Bruce Russett, Glenn T. Seaborg, Herbert Scoville, Gerard C. Smith, Paul Warnke, and Jerome Wiesner.

17. John F. Lehman, Jr., "The U.S. Catholic Bishops and Nuclear Arms," *The Wall Street Jornal*, 15 November 1982.

18. Richard Halloran, "U.S. Tells Bishops Morality is Guide on Nuclear Policy," and text of Clark Letter, *The New York Times*, 17 November 1982.

19. "24 Catholics in House Oppose Bishops on A-Arms," *The New York Times*, 23 December 1982. The full text of the letter from the Honorable Henry J. Hyde and twenty-three Catholic members of the U.S. Congress was published in a pamphlet *Peace Without Justice Is Moral Violence* by the National Committee of Catholic Laymen, Inc., New York.

20. Stephen S. Rosenfeld, "The Bishops and the Bomb," *The Washington Post*, 29 October 1982.

21. Talk at a Colloquium on Nuclear Weapons in Washington, D.C., sponsored by the Bishops' Committee on Sacred Doctrine and the Council of Catholic Scholars and Learned Societies, September 23–25, 1982. Cf. also "Battle of the Bishops: Should Church Oppose Nuclear Arms?" Interviews with Bishop Thomas Gumbleton (YES) and Archbishop Philip M. Hannan (NO), *U.S. News and World Report*, 20 December 1982.

22. George Weigel, Open Letter to Archbishop Joseph L. Bernardin,

Catholicism in Crisis—A Journal of Catholic Lay Opinion 1 (January 1983): 15. Archbishop Oscar Lipscomb of Mobile, Alabama, spoke in a similar vein: "We seem to assign the human species itself a right to eternity. This is certainly not the 'biblical vision of the world at the heart of our religious heritage.' The worst evil that can befall us is not the loss of life, or even of all human life. It is sin and the consequent loss of life in the Father through Christ by means of the Spirit that we rightly call 'life everlasting.' Should this world and our species remain in such a way that such life in the Father is not possible to the generations that would follow, then we have threatened not just the Sovereignty of God over the world, but the victory of Christ over sin and death." Quoted in *The New York Times*, 19 November 1982.

23. Thomas C. Fox, "Bishops retreat on nuclear deterrence—U.S. nuclear policy's basic tenets upheld," *National Catholic Reporter*, 15 April 1983, and Steve Askin, "Administration: 'Draft substantially improved'; claims bishops 'allies,'" *National Catholic Reporter*, 15 April 1983.

24. *Time*, 29 November 1982; Marjorie Hyer, "Bishops Appear Divided on Proposed A-War Letter," *The Washington Post*, 16 November 1982. For earlier speculation on this question, see John J. Fialka, "Atom-Weapons Issue Stirs Divisive Debate in the Catholic Church," *The Wall Street Journal*, 9 June 1982.

25. Roland H. Bainton, *Christian Attitudes Toward War and Peace: A Historical Survey and Critical Re-Evaluation* (Nashville: Abingdon Press, 1960), p. 14.

26. L. Bruce van Voorst argues that "Catholic teaching has been characterized by two essentially contradictory forces: pacifism and 'just war' theory" and that the pastoral letter in its second draft reflected "a tug of war between these two schools of thought." "The Churches and Nuclear Deterrence," *Foreign Affairs* 61 (Spring 1983): 832.

27. Philip F. Lawler, ed., *Justice and War in the Nuclear Age*, for the American Catholic Committee (Lanham, Md.: University Press of America, 1983), p. 2.

Chapter 2

1. Peter Brock, *Pacifism in Europe to 1914* (Princeton, N.J.: Princeton University Press, 1972), p. 3. In ancient China, the followers of Mo-Ti (or Mo-tzu), regarded by historians as convinced pacifists, sought to avoid wars but also defended cities subect to unjust attack by force of arms. Jacques Gernet, *A History of Chinese Civilization*, trans. J. R. Foster (Cambridge: Cambridge University Press, 1983) p. 88. According to Lin Mousheng, the Mocian anti-war position was essentially utilitarian, not religious. Lin Mousheng, *Men and Ideas: An Informal History of Chinese Political Thought* (Port Washington, N.H.: Kennikat Press, 1942, 1969), p. 93. In ancient India, the Buddhist doctrine of

ahimsa, or "harmlessness toward all living things," famous in modern times as one of the principal sources from which Gandhi derived the creed of non-violent resistance, was not originally taken to forbid the waging of war. It promoted vegetarianism (based on reverence toward animal life) long before it promoted pacifism. A. L. Basham, "Some Fundamentals of Hindu State-craft," in Joel Laurus, ed., *Comparative World Politics: Readings in Western and Pre-Modern Non-Western International Relations* (Belmont, Calif.: Wadsworth Publishing Co., 1964), p. 48.

2. "Those who live by the sword shall perish by it." Mt. 26:52. Whether this was a mere statement of probability or a moral admonition is uncertain. Shortly before Christ said this, as he left the cenacle for Gethsemane, He asked whether the disciples were carrying arms and was told that there were two swords. He replied: "It is enough." Lk. 22:38. There is also the episode in which Jesus fashioned a whip of cords to drive the moneylenders from the temple. Jn. 2:15. These scriptural passages have provoked much inconclusive debate.

3. Cecil John Cadoux, *The Early Church and the World* (Edinburgh: T. & T. Clark, 1925), p. 36. Christ did, however, employ military similes on occasion. See Mt. 26:7 and Lk. 14:31–33. Cf. Also Cadoux, pp. 51–57.

4. Bainton, *Christian Attitudes Toward War and Peace,* 53.

5. James E. Dougherty, "The Catholic Church, War and Nuclear Weapons," *Orbis* 9 (Winter 1966): 846.

6. Jules Lebreton and Jacques Zeiller, *The History of the Primitive Church* (New York: Macmillan, 1949), 2: 1159.

7. Bainton, *Christian Attitudes,* 67–68 and Brock, *Pacifism in Europe to 1914,* 4.

8. G. I. A. D. Draper, "The Origins of the Just War Tradition," *New Blackfriars* (November 1964): 84. This resembles somewhat the interpreta-tion set forth by Reinhold Niebuhr, that group behavior, unlike the action of individuals, is dictated more by considerations of power rather than morality. Reinhold Niebuhr, *Moral Man and Immoral Society* (New York: Scribner's, 1947).

9. See Brock, *Pacifism in Europe to 1914,* and Knut Willem Ruyter, "Pacifism and Military Service in the Early Church," *Cross Currents* 32 (Spring 1982): 58.

10. Only a few of many scriptural texts need to be cited: Jgs. 7:2–22; Ex. 15:3, 17:6; Dt. 23:15; Jos. 2:24; II Sm. 5:24. See also Everett F. Gendler, "War and the Jewish Tradition," in James Finn, ed., *A Conflict of Loyalties: The Case for Selective Conscientious Objection* (New York: Pegasus, 1968), p. 78. George Foot Moore, *Judaism* (Cambridge: Harvard University Press, 1966), Vol. 2, p. 106. See also Roland de Vaux, *Ancient Israel: Its Life and Institutions* (New York: McGraw-Hill, 1961), pp. 213–267.

11. Dt. 20:1–9, For an account of Gideon's call to arms against the Midianites, cf. Jgs. 7:2–3.

12. II Sm. 24:1–10.

13. Dt. 20:10–18. For descriptions of how the rules of *herem* were applied in the holy wars, see Jos. 6 and Giuseppe Ricciotti, *The History of Israel*, trans. Clement Della Penta and Richard T. A. Murphy (Milwaukee: Bruce, 1955), Vol. I: *From the Beginning to the Exile*, pp. 225–40. Cf. also "War," Article in the *Jewish Encyclopaedia* (London: Funk and Wagnall, 1907), Vol. 12, pp. 463–66; "Peace *(shalom)*," Article in *The Encyclopaedia Judaica* (Jerusalem: Keter Publishing Co. and New York: Macmillan, 1971), Vol. 13 pp. 274–82; and George Foot Moore, *Judaism*, 2; 106–7.

14. Is. 2:1–5; 5:25–30; 22:8–11; 30:15–17; Jer. 21:3–10; 25; 34:1–5; Hos. 8:14; 10:13–14; Am. 2:14–16.

15. Otto Bardenhewer, *Patrology: The Lives and Works of the Fathers of the Church*, trans. by Thomas J. Shahan (St. Louis, Mo.: B. Herder, 1908), pp. 79–80; and Johannes Quasten, *Patrology* (Westminster, Md.: Newman Press, 1950), Vol. I. p. 270.

16. Isaiah 28:6.

17. See. A. J. and R. W. Carlyle, *A History of Medieval Political Theory in the West* (London: William Blackwood and Sons, 3rd impression, 1950), Vol. I, p. 82: George H. Sabine, *A History of Political Theory* (New York: Holt, 1950), p. 180; and Charles H. McIlwain, *The Growth of Political Thought in the West* (New York: Macmillan, 1932), pp. 149–50.

18. I Pt. 2:13–14 and Rom. 13:1–5.

19. I Cor. 7:20. St. Clement of Alexandria later cited this passage in urging those who were soldiers at the time of embracing the faith merely "to listen to the leader whose watchword is justice." *Proterepticus*, X, 100. Quoted in Lebreton and Zeiller, *The History of the Primitive Church*, Vol. 2: 1159. See also Acts 10:47.

20. Tertullian, *De idolotria*, Chapter xix. Excerpted in Ernest Barker, trans. and ed., *From Alexander to Constantine: Passages and Documents Illustrating the History of Social and Political Ideas* (Oxford: Clarendon Press, 1956), p. 105. This work, incidentally, provides evidence that there were Christians in the army who were baptized before they enlisted. Tertullian asks how a Christian can make war or serve as a soldier in peacetime without the sword the Lord has taken away. "Christ in disarming Peter ungirt every soldier." Brock, *Pacifism in Europe to 1914*, 10–11.

21. See, e.g., *The Letter of St. Clement to the Corinthians* in *The Fathers of the Church: A New Translation*, Vol. I, *The Apostolic Fathers*, trans. by Francis X. Glimm *et al.* (Washington, D.C.: The Catholic University of America Press, 1962), p. 56. See also the statement by the 2nd century bishop of Lyons, St. Irenaeus, *Adversus haereses*, Chap. 24, in a *Select Library of the Ante-Nicene Fathers of the Christian Church*, ed., Philip Schaff (Buffalo, 1887).

22. From Origen's *Contra Celsum*, 8, 68–69, as quoted in Bainton, *Christian Attitudes Toward War*, 68.

23. Jean Danielou, *Origen*, trans. Walter Mitchell (New York: Sheed & Ward, 1955) p. 115.

24. *Contra Celsum*, 8, 73, as quoted in Franziskus Stratmann, *War and*

Christianity Today, trans. John Doebele (Westminster, Md.: Newman Press, 1956), p. 105.

25. For a pacifist statement by Cyprian remarkably similar to Mo-Ti, see Cyprian, *Ad Demetrianum,* 3, 17. Quoted in Edward A. Ryan, S.J., "The Rejection of Military Service by the Early Christians," *Theological Studies* 13 (March 1952):14. *Epist.* I, 6, *Patrologia Latina,* 4, p. 205. Quoted in Igino Giordani, *The Social Message of the Early Church Fathers,* trans. Alba I. Zizzamia (Paterson, N.J.: St. Anthony Guild Press, 1944), p. 178. For the similarity between Cyprian and Voltaire, see Frank M. Russell, *Theories of International Relations* (New York: Appleton-Century-Crofts, 1936), pp. 26–27.

26. Bainton, *Christian Attitudes Toward War,* 70.

27. Brock, *Pacifism in Europe to 1914,* 57.

28. Ruyter, "Pacifism and Military Service in the Early Church," 60.

29. Actually, St. Martin did not renounce military service for two years after his baptism, because of the prayers of his tribune, who promised to renounce the world upon the termination of his tribunate. Sulpicius Severus, *Life of St. Martin, The Fathers of the Church,* Vol. 7 (New York: Fathers of the Church, Inc., 1949), p. 108. See also Alexander F. Webster, "Varieties of Military Saints: From Martyrs Under Caesar to Warrior Princes," *St. Vladimir's Theological Quarterly* 24, 1 (1980): 3–35.

30. The non-doctrinal reasons for abstention from military service are summarized here from several sources where ample documentation can be found. Most notable are Edward A. Ryan, S.J., "The Rejection of Military Service"; Chapter 5 in Roland H. Bainton, *Christian Attitudes*; Peter Brock, *Pacifism,* Chapter 1; Knut Willem Ruyter, "Pacifism and Military Service"; and "The Development of the Christian Attitude toward War Before Aquinas," Chapter 1 in Joan D. Tooke, *The Just War in Aquinas and Grotius* (London: SPCK, 1965), pp. 1–20.

31. 13th Canon of St. Basil, Letter 188 to Amphilocius, in *St. Basil Letters,* trans. Sr. Agnes Clare Way, with notes by Roy J. Deferrari (New York: Fathers of the Church, Inc., 1955), Vol. 2, 23.

32. Letter 138 to Marcellinus, *Saint Augustine Letters,* Vol. 3 (nos. 131–64), translated by Sr. Wilfred Parsons, ed. Roy J. Deferrari (New York: Fathers of the Church, Inc., 1953), p. 47.

33. L. L. McReavy, "Pacifism," *New Catholic Encyclopedia* (New York: McGraw-Hill, 1967) 10: 855.

34. See the discussion of the just war doctrine in Heinrich A. Rommen, *The State in Catholic Thought* (St. Louis: B. Herder, 1947), pp. 652–57, esp. p. 653.

35. Igino Giordani, *The Social Message of the Early Church Fathers,* 18.

36. *Writings of St. Justin Martyr,* ed. and trans. by Thomas B. Falls (New York: Christian Heritage, Inc., 1948), The First Apology, Chapter 46, pp. 83–84. Saint Justin pointed out several parallels between Plato and Old Testament revelation, ibid., pp. 55–58 and 97–101.

37. Lebreton and Zeiller, *The History of the Primitive Church*, 2: 909. For the problem of "Christian Philosophy," see Frederick Copleston, S.J., *A History of Philosophy* (Westminster, Md.: Newman Press, 1952), 2, Chapter 2 and Etienne Gilson, *The Spirit of Mediaeval Philosophy* (New York: Scribner's, 1940), Chapters 1 and 2.

38. Ernest Barker, *The Political Thought of Plato and Aristotle* (New York: Dover, 1959), p. 429. See Plato, *The Republic*, Book 2 and *The Laws*, Book 5; Aristotle, *The Politics*, Book 1, Chapter 6; Book 2, Chapter 9; and Book 7, Chapters 4 to 6.

39. Coleman Phillipson, *The International Law and Custom of Ancient Greece and Rome* (London: Macmillan, 1911, Vol. II, pp. 192–93.

40. G. I. A. D. Draper, "The Origins of the Just War Tradition," *New Blackfriars*, (November 1964): 82.

41. Phillipson, *The International Law and Custom*, 2: 223. The Roman tradition of restraint did not always prevail. Rome treated Spain with harsh brutality, reduced civilized people to slavery, and succumbed to Cato's oft-repeated admonition, *Carthago delenda est*, by annihilating her former rival.

42. Heinrich Rommen, *Natural Law*, trans. Thomas R. Hanley, O.S.B. (St. Louis, Mo.: B. Herder, 1948), pp. 3–69.

43. William V. O'Brien, *The Conduct of Just and Limited War* (New York: Praeger, 1981), pp. 22–23.

44. Tooke, *The Just War in Aquinas and Grotius*, 7–8. Bainton, p. 81, presents a different interpretation.

45. Letter to Emperor Theodosius in *St. Ambrose: Letters*, trans. Sr. Mary Melchior Beyenka, O.P. (New York: Fathers of the Church, Inc., 1954), viii and pp. 20–26.

46. Ambrose writes to Studius in reply that some Christian judges stay away from Communion of their own accord, but he himself observes the authority of the apostle Paul who said "For not without reason does he carry the sword who gives judgment" (Rom. 13:4) and does not refuse such judges Communion. Ambrose was by no means an exponent of capital punishment. He tenderly cited the example of the woman taken in adultery and how Christ dealt with her accusers. "I have heard some heathens say that they returned from governing their province with ax unstained by blood. If heathens say this, what should Christians do?" But he concludes noting that "our predecessors preferred to be rather indulgent toward judges, so that, while their sword was feared, the madness of crime was checked and not aroused." Letter to Studius, ibid., pp. 492–94.

47. *De officiis*, i, 139 and iii, 54–56, 67–69 and 86–87. Cited in F. Homes Dudden, *The Life and Times of Saint Ambrose* (Oxford: Clarendon Press, 1945), 2: 538–39. Bainton exhibits a slight bias against the Ambrosian teaching by noting that "he never entertained any scruples against military service because he had been the praetorian prefect of northern Italy before being impressed into the bishopric of Milan" and "because the defense of the Empire coincided in his mind with the defense of the faith." *Christian Attitudes Toward War and Peace*, pp. 89–90.

48. Bainton, *Christian Attitudes*, 91.

49. Augustine, *The City of God*, Book 4, Chapter 15. Trans. Demetrius B. Zema, S.J. and Gerald G. Walsh, S.J. (New York: Fathers of the Church, Inc., 1950), p. 193.

50. Augustine, *The City of God*, Book 19, Chapter 12.

51. Letter 189 to Boniface, *Saint Augustine: Letters*, trans. by Sr. Wilfred Parsons, S.N.D. (New York: Fathers of the Church, Inc., 1955), Vol. 4: 268–69.

52. Gustave Combès, *La doctrine politique de Saint Augustin* (Paris, 1927), cited in Bainton, *Christian Attitudes*, 7.

53. Passages drawn from St. Augustine's Letter 138 and one of his Sermons, quoted in Bainton, *Christian Attitudes*, 97. Paul Ramsey has argued that, although Augustine saw a difference of justice between killing an innocent person and killing an unjust aggressor, he did not justify Christian participation in warfare on the grounds of justice alone, but *caritas* as well. It is from love that the Christian renounces private self-defense but wages a just war to defend the common good. Paul Ramsey, *War and the Christian Conscience: How Shall Modern War Be Conducted Justly?* (Durham, N.C.: Duke University Press, 1961), pp. 36–38. Ramsey faults such Late Scholastics as Victoria and Suarez for formulating the just war theory exclusively in terms of justice and forgetting "the genesis of [that] theory in the interior of an ethic of Christian love." Ramsey, *The Just War: Force and Political Responsibility* (New York: Charles Scribner's Sons, 1968), pp. 206–7.

54. St. Augustine, Letter 47. Quoted in Bainton, *Christian Attitudes*, 98.

55. In addition to the works by Tooke, O'Brien, and Ramsey previously cited, see James Turner Johnson, *Just War Tradition and The Restraint of War: A Moral and Historical Inquiry* (Princeton, N.J.: Princeton University Press, 1981), and Frederick Russell, *The Just War in the Middle Ages* (Cambridge: Cambridge University Press, 1975).

56. Johnson, *Just War Tradition*, 122–23.

57. St. Thomas Aquinas, *Summa Theologica*, 2–2ae, Quest. 40, Art. 1, in Aquinas, *Selected Political Writings*, trans. J. G. Dawson (Oxford: Blackwell, 1948), p. 159.

58. Ibid.

59. O'Brien, *The Conduct of Just and Limited War*, 22.

60. See Francisco de Victoria, *De Indis et De Iure Belli Relectiones*, trans. John P. Bate (Washington: Carnegie Endowment for International Peace, 1917); and Francisco Suarez, *De Triplici Virtutate Theologica*, Disputation 8, "De Bello," in *Selections from Three Works* (Oxford: Clarendon Press, 1944). Both works are in the Classics of International Law Series, James Brown Scott, ed. For a good summary of the thought of Victoria and Suarez, see E. B. F. Midgley, *The Natural Law Tradition and the Theory of International Relations* (New York: Barnes and Noble, 1975), pp. 62–93. See also O'Brien, *The Conduct of Just and Limited War*, 37ff and James R. Childress, "Just War Theories," *Theological Studies* 39 (September 1978): 427–45.

61. O'Brien, *The Conduct of Just and Limited War*, 27.

62. Johnson, *Just War Tradition*, 124–31. By the mid-thirteenth century, Hostiensis reflected the general canonical opinion that all weapons were permissible in a just war.

63. Ibid., 127, 131–150.

64. In the modern international law of war, Georg Schwarzenberger stresses the value of civilization, while Myers McDougall and Florentino Feliciano emphasize humanitariansim. Cf. Johnson, *Just War Tradition*, 79–94; O'Brien, *The Conduct of Just and Limited War*, 222–28. Johnson concludes on p. 199 that it is not at all clear from his study of the Middle Ages that the "protection to be given noncombatants must be absolute." O'Brien, on p. 45, writes in a similar vein: "It is my contention that the moral, just-war principle of discrimination is not an absolute limitation on belligerent conduct. There is no evidence that such a principle was ever seriously advanced by the Church, and it is implicity rejected when the Church acknowledges the continued right of legitimate self-defense, a right that has always been compatible with observance of an absolute principle of discrimination."

65. John Courtney Murray, "Theology and Modern War," quoted in O'Brien, *The Conduct of Just and Limited War*, 28.

66. David Wood, *Conflict in the Twentieth Century*, Adelphi Papers, no. 48 (London: Institute for Strategic Studies, 1968), p. 26.

67. Robert W. Tucker, *The Just War: A Study in Contemporary American Doctrine* (Baltimore: The Johns Hopkins University Press, 1960), pp. 97–162; Richard A. Falk, *Legal Order in a Violent World* (Princeton: Princeton University Press, 1968), p. 136.

68. See John U. Nef, *War and Human Progress* (Cambridge: Harvard University Press, 1950), pp. 250–59. See also Richard A. Preston and Sydney F. Wise, *Men in Arms: A History of Warfare and Its Interrelationships with Western Society*, 4th ed. (New York: Holt, Rinehart and Winston, 1979), Chap. 9.

69. See Paul Hazard, *European Thought in the Eighteenth Century*, trans. J. Lewis May (New York: World Publishing Co., 1963), p. 18, and Kingsley Martin, *French Liberal Thought in the Eighteenth Century* (New York: University Press, 1954), Chapter 11.

70. Allocution to the Sacred College, February 11, 1889. Quoted in Emile Guèrry, *The Popes and World Government*, trans. Gregory Roettiger, O.S.B. (Baltimore: Helicon Press, 1964), p. 144.

71. Walter H. Peters, *The Life of Benedict XV* (Milwaukee: Bruce, 1959), Chapters 14 and 15.

72. See, e.g., J. Elliott Ross, *Christian Ethics* (New York: Devon-Adair, 1924), pp. 446–71; Cyprian Emanuel, O.F.M., *The Ethics of War* (Washington: C.A.I.P., 1932); John Eppstein, *Must War Come?* (London: Burns, Oates & Washbourne, 1935).

73. The Code of International Ethics in John A. Ryan and Francis J. Boland, *Catholic Principles of Politics* (New York: Macmillan, 1940), p. 255;

International Relations from a Catholic Standpoint, trans. from *La Societé Internationale*, ed. Stephen J. Brown, S.J. (Dublin: Brown and Nolan, 1932), p. 61.

74. John C. Ford, S.J., "The Morality of Obliteration Bombing," *Theological Studies* 6 (September 1944): 261–309.

75. See Chapter 1, Note 1 for source.

76. John Courtney Murray, "Theology & Modern War," in William J. Nagle, ed., *Morality and Modern Warfare* (Baltimore: Helicon, 1960), p. 77.

77. James W. Douglass, *The Non-Violent Cross: A Theology of Revolution and Peace* (New York: Macmillan, 1968), pp. 177–178.

78. Richard T. McSorley, S.J., "The Gospel and the Just War," in William H. Osterle and John Donaghy, eds., *Peace Theology and the Arms Race*, College Theology Society Sourcebook Series, I (mimeographed), 1980, p. 141.

79. Peter J. Riga, "Selective Conscientious Objection," *The Catholic World* 211 (July 1970): 21.

80. David Hollenbach, S.J., "Nuclear Weapons and Nuclear War: The Shape of the Catholic Debate," *Theological Studies* 43 (December 1982): 584.

81. There was, of course, a moderate theory of the right of revolution in St. Thomas Aquinas' *De Regimine Principum*. The modern New Left theologians' theory, in which Christian and Marxist-Leninist ideas are fused, has little in common with the political philosophy of Thomism, which they specifically reject as inadequate in the present situation. See Eric Willenz, "Revolutionary War: Challenge to Just War;" Paul J. Weber, S.J., "A Theology of Revolution;" and Peter J. Riga, "Violence: A Christian Perspective;" all in *Worldview* (October 1968); 6–16. Cf. also Gustavo Gutierrez, "Liberation and Development," *Cross Currents* 21 (1971): 243 56; Philip E. Berryman, "Latin American Liberation Theology," *Theological Studies* 34 (December 1973), 357–95; and Guenther Lewy, *Religion and Revolution* (New York: Oxford University Press, 1974): 504–36; and the citations in Notes 19 and 23 for Chapter 4.

82. Paul J. Weber, S.J., "A Theology of Revolution," 11.

Chapter 3

1. Pope Pius XII, Christmas Message, December 23, 1956. Text in Flannery, ed., *Pattern for Peace* 283. It is worth noting that the pope calls attention here to the defensive decisions of a democratically elected government. Although aristocratic in background and bearing, Pius XII was more attracted than any of his predecessors to constitutionally limited parliamentary government which recognizes and safeguards individual human and civil rights. Whereas Pius X had said in 1910 that "the advent of universal democracy does not concern the action of the Church in the world,"

Pius XII in 1944 wrote that "the democratic form of government appears to many a postulate of nature imposed by reason itself." The quotation of Pius X is from his *Letter on Sillon* to Marc Sangnier, August 25, 1910, in Jacques Maritain, *The Things That Are Not Caesar's*, trans. J. F. Scanlan (New York: Charles Scribner's, 1931), p. 64. That of Pius XII is from his Christmas Message, December 24, 1944, in *Pius XII and Democracy*, trans. John B. Harney, C.S.P. (New York: Paulist Press, 1945), p. 8. Throughout the late 1940s and the 1950s, Pius XII was widely regarded throughout Europe as the spiritual symbol of Christian democracy.

2. *Pacem in Terris,* Encyclical Letter of Pope John XXIII, April 11, 1963, Washington: National Catholic Welfare Conference, n.d., p. 30. It is interesting to note that out of a total of seventy-three documentary references in the encyclical, Pius XII is cited thirty-two times, far more frequently than all other papal predecessors combined. For a further comparison of Pius XII and John XXIII, see James E. Dougherty, "The Catholic Church, War and Nuclear Weapons," *Orbis* 9 (Winter 1966): 860–78.

3. *Pacem in Terris,* p. 27.

4. The General Assembly of the United Nations approved a definition of aggression by consensus resolution, without a vote, on December 14, 1974, which fails to deal with the problem of a threatened or impending use of force that might warrant a preemptive response. Moreover, according to communist international law, wars of national liberation against capitalist imperialism are by definition just and nonaggressive, whereas any intervention against communist insurgents is unjust and illegal. The UN members had no difficulty approving the General Assembly resolution, since such resolutions do not create binding rules of international law. Thus the United Nations took no action when the Soviet Union invaded Afghanistan in late 1979. See Gerhard von Glahn, *Law Among Nations*: *An Introduction to Public International Law*, 4th ed. (New York: Macmillan, 1981), Chapter 24, "Legal Nature of War Today," esp. pp. 581-87. In discussing the British response of April 1982 to the seizure of the Falkland-Malvinas Islands by Argentina, John Eppstein, England's best-known Catholic authority on the just war, who played a key role in drafting the Malines Code of International Ethics in 1937 and its revision in 1947-49, carefully distinguished "between immediate self-defence against attack or invasion and a war deliberately declared thereafter to rectify and vindicate the injury." The effort to reverse the direct effects of aggression at some later time is a more complex matter, and requires that additional conditions be fulfilled if it is to be morally justifiable. Eppstein, "The Ethics of War I: The Principles," *Christian Order* 24 (January 1983): 5.

5. Francisco Suarez, *De bello*, s. iv., 10. Cited in Midgley, *The Natural Law Tradition and the Theory of International Relations*, 65 and 454.

6. Quoted in Francis M. Stratmann, O.P., *War & Christianity Today*, 24–25.

7. Ibid., Chapter 2, "The Immorality of Modern Total War."

8. Christopher Hollis, "The Two Pacifisms: The Old Case and the New," *The Tablet* (London) 1 February 1958.

9. Leslie Dewart, "War and the Christian Tradition," *The Commonweal* 76 (2 November 1962): 145.

10. Thomas Merton, "Nuclear War and Christian Responsibility," *The Commonweal* 75 (9 February 1962) 510–13. Similar views may be found in Walter Stein, ed., *Nuclear Weapons: A Catholic Response* (New York: Sheed and Ward, 1962); E. I. Watkin, "Unjustifiable War," in Charles S. Thompson, ed., *Morals and Missiles* (London: James Clarke & Co., Ltd., 1959); Anthony Kenny, "Counterforce and Counter-Value," *Clergy Review* (December 1962); Karl Stern, "The Case for Christian Pacifism," *The Catholic Worker* (April 1962); Sylvester P. Theisen, "Man and Nuclear Weapons," *The American Benedictine Review (September 1963); James Douglass, "Peace and the Overkill Strategists," Cross Currents* (Summer 1964); Brian Midgley, "Nuclear Deterrents: Intention and Scandal," *Blackfriars* (August 1964).

11. William W. Kaufman, ed., *Military Policy and National Security* (Princeton, N.J.: Princeton University Press, 1956); Henry A. Kissinger, *Nuclear Weapons and Foreign Policy* (New York: Harper, 1957); Robert E. Osgood, *Limited War: The Challenge to American Strategy* (Chicago: University of Chicago Press, 1957); Maxwell Taylor, *The Uncertain Trumpet* (New York: Harper, 1960; James M. Gavin, *War and Peace in the Space Age* (New York: Harper, 1958). An efficient summary of the debate over massive retaliation versus limited war can be found in Russell F. Weigley, *The American Way of War: A History of United States Strategy and Policy* (Bloomington, Ind.: Indiana University Press, 1973), pp. 410-24.

12. F.H. Drinkwater, "The Morality of Nuclear War," *Commonweal* 61 (18 March 1955): 623–26. The three quotations by Drinkwater in this and the succeeding paragraph came respectively from pp. 623, 625, and 626.

13. L. I. McReavey, "Conscience and the H-Bomb," *The Catholic World* (July 1959): 250–51.

14. Thomas Corbishley, S.J., "Can War be Just in a Nuclear Age?" *New Blackfriars* (September 1965): 684–85. Cf. also Pelayo Zemayon, O.F.M., "Morality of War Today and in the Future," *Theology Digest* (Winter 1957).

15. The author previously summarized the debate at the Second Vatican Council, relying on *Council Daybook*, Vatican II, Session 3, edited by Floyd Anderson (Washington: National Catholic Welfare Conference, 1965); the *Council Digest* prepared daily for the Council Fathers of the U.S.A., and mimeographed texts of individual speeches. See Dougherty, "The Catholic Church, War and Nuclear Weapons," *Orbis* 9 (Winter 1966): 878–92. The preceding quotations from Vatican II statements are all taken from that article.

16. *Gaudium et spes*, Pastoral Constitution on the Church in the Modern World, Chapter 5, Section 79. Text in Walter M. Abbott, ed., *Documents of Vatican II* (New York: American Press, 1966), p. 293.

17. Ibid., Section 81, pp. 294–95.

18. Text of Statement of the Holy See on Disarmament in *The Pope Speaks*, Vol. 22, 1976, p. 245. For a fuller discussion of post-conciliar Papal

statements on the problem of nuclear weapons, see the author's article, "Disarmament" in *The New Catholic Encyclopedia* (Washington, D.C.: Catholc University of America, 1981) Vol. 17, pp. 187–89.

19. See, e.g., O'Brien, *The Conduct of Just and Limited War*, 127–41.

20. Paul Ramsey, *The Limits of Nuclear War* (New York: Council on Religion and International Affairs, 1963), p. 10. See also his *The Just War: Force and Political Responsibility* (New York: Charles Scribner's Sons, 1968) pp. 302–7.

21. Murray wrote that "since nuclear war may be a necessity, it must be made a possibility. Its possibility must be created." To say that war cannot be limited "is to succumb to some sort of determinism in human affairs." "Theology and Modern War," in Nagle, *Morality and Modern Warfare: The State of the Question*, 77.

22. Alexander L. George and Richard Smoke, *Deterrence in American Foreign Policy: Theory and Practice (New York: Columbia University Press, 1974), p. 11. See also Bernard Brodie, "The Anatomy of Deterrence," World Politics* 11 (January 1959): 174; Patrick M. Morgan, *Deterrence: A Conceptual Analysis* (Beverly Hills, Calif.: Sage, 1977): Chapter 1; Donald M. Snow, *Nuclear Strategy in a Dynamic World* (University, Ala.: University of Alabama Press, 1981), Chapters 1 and 2.

23. George Quester, *Deterrence Before Hiroshima* (New York: Wiley, 1966); George and Smoke, *Deterrence in American Foreign Policy*, 11–34.

24. Bernard Brodie presented the classic argument for strategic nuclear deterrence in 1959. The rejection of a preventive war or "first strike" strategy, he said, commits the United States to a deterrent or "second strike" strategy, which in turn requires a secure retaliatory force sufficient to dissuade any rational adversary from attempting a surprise knockout blow. "Known ability to defend our retaliatory force constitutes the only unilaterally attainable situation that provides potentially a perfect defense of our home land. Conversely, a conspicuous inability or unreadiness to defend our retaliatory force must tend to provoke the opponent to destroy it; in other words, it tempts him to an aggression he might not otherwise contemplate." Brodie, *Strategy in the Missile Age* (Princeton, N.J.: Princeton University Press, 1959), pp. 176, 185. Brodie was building in part on ideas put forward at the same time by Albert Wohlstetter in "The Delicate Balance of Terror," *Foreign Affairs* 37 (January 1959): 211–34. Wohlstetter argued that deterrence, once achieved, did not remain automatically stable for an indefinite period, because technological advances by one side could bring disproportionate strategic advantages and offer an incentive to reap the gains inherent in a first-strike strategy. Oskar Morgenstern wrote in a similar vein that the United States would need an invulnerable second-strike capability in order to avoid becoming subject in the future to Soviet "threats, ultimatums, blackmail: open or veiled." Morgenstern, *The Question of National Defense* (New York: Random House, 1959), p. 286.

25. "Dreams and Delusions of a Coming War," Chapter 3 in Geoffrey Blainey, *The Causes of War* (New York: The Free Press, 1973); John G.

Stoessinger, *Why Nations Go to War* (New York: St. Martin's Press, 1974), pp. 223–24.

26. Besides the sources cited in Notes 22 and 24 above, see Glenn H. Snyder, *Deterrence and Defense: Toward a Theory of National Security* (Princeton, N.J.: Princeton University Press, 1961); Raymond Aron, *The Great Debate: Theories of Nuclear Strategy*, trans. Ernst Pawel (Garden City, N.Y.: Doubleday, 1965), esp. Chapter 2 and 6; and Thomas C. Schelling, *Arms and Influence* (New Haven, Conn.: Yale University Press, 1966), Chapter 1.

27. Henry A. Kissinger, "Domestic Structure and Foreign Policy," in *American Foreign Policy: Three Essays* (New York: W. W. Norton, 1969), p. 15.

28. On the complex relationship between rationality and deterrence, see Patrick M. Morgan, *Deterrence*, Chapter 4; Thomas C. Schelling, *Arms and Influence*, pp. 36–43; Ole R. Holsti, *Crisis, Escalation, War* (Montreal: McGill-Queens University Press, 1972); Thomas Millburn, "The Concept of Deterrence: Some Logical and Psychological Considerations," *Journal of Social Issues* 17, no. 3 (1961): 3–11. John D. Steinbruner rejects the rational-analytical model in "Beyond Rational Deterrence: The Struggle for New Conceptions," *World Politics* 28 (January 1976). See also Jack L. Snyder, "Rationality at the Brink: The Role of Cognitive Processes in Failures of Deterrence," *World Politics* 30 (April 1978). These and related sources are summarized in James E. Dougherty and Robert L. Pfaltzgraff, Jr., *Contending Theories of International Relations: A Comprehensive Survey*, 2d ed. (New York: Harper & Row, 1981), pp. 375–87 and 386–89.

29. Glenn H. Snyder, *Deterrence and Defense*, 3–7. The quotation is from p. 6.

30. The author of this study has published several works on the problems of disarmament and arms control: "The Disarmament Debate: A Review of Current Literature" (Parts One and Two), *Orbis* 5 (Fall 1961 and Winter 1962); "Nuclear Weapons Control," *Current History* 47 (July 1964); "The Status of Arms Negotiations," *Orbis* 9 (Spring 1965); "Soviet Arms Control Policy" and "Soviet Arms Control Negotiations" in Eleanor L. Dulles and Robert D. Crane, eds., *Detente: Cold War Strategies in Transition* (New York: Praeger, 1965); *Arms Control and Disarmament: The Critical Issues* (Washington: Georgetown Center for Strategic Studies, 1966); "The Non-Proliferation Treaty," *The Russian Review* 25 (January 1966); co-editor, *Arms Control for the Late Sixties* (Princeton: Van Nostrand, 1967); "What Shape a Strategic Arms Agreement Might Take," *War/Peace Report* (December 1969); "Arms Control in the 1970s," *Orbis* 15 (Spring 1971); "SALT and the Future of International Politics," in W. R. Kintner and R. L. Pfaltzgraff, Jr., eds., *SALT: Implications for the 1970s* (Pittsburgh: University of Pittsburgh Press, 1972); *How to Think About Arms Control and Disarmament* (New York: Crane, Russak, 1973); "From SALT I to SALT II" in R. L. Pfaltzgraff, Jr., ed., *Contrasting Approaches to Strategic Arms Control* (Lexington, Mass.: D. C. Heath, 1974); "Soviet-Western Arms Negotiations: SALT and MBFR," *Brassey's Defence Yearbook 1974*, Royal United Services Institution (London: William Clowes & Sons, Ltd., 1974); *Security Through World Law and World*

Government: *Myth or Reality?* Monograph Series, no. 15 (Philadelphia, Pa.: Foreign Policy Research Institute, 1974); with Paul Nitze and Francis X. Kane, *The Fateful Ends and Shades of SALT* (New York: Crane, Russak, 1979); "A National Arms Control Policy for the 1980s," *The Annals, American Academy of Political and Social Science* 457 (September 1981).

31. Raymond Aron has pointed out that "there is no deterrent in a general or abstract sense; it is a case of knowing *who* can deter *whom, from what, in what circumstances, by what means*," from "The Evolution of Modern Strategic Thought," in *Problems of Modern Strategy*: *Part One*, Adelphi Papers, no. 54 (London: Institute for Strategic Studies, 1969), p. 9.

32. *Arms Control and Disarmament Agreements*: *Texts and Histories of Negotiations* (Washington, D.C.: U.S. Arms Control and Disarmament Agency, 1982), p. 9.

33. James E. Dougherty, "Just War, Nuclear Weapons and Noncombatant Immunity," Review Essay in *Orbis* 26 (Fall 1982): 780. While we should refrain from passing moral judgment upon those who took the decision, we should not try "to throw a mantle of moral approval over the A-bombing of Japan." Ibid., 782.

34. Alain C. Enthoven and K. Wayne Smith, *How Much is Enough? Shaping the Defense Program, 1961–1969* (New York: Harper & Row, 1971), p. 207; Snow, *Nuclear Strategy*, 64–68; Morton Halperin, *Defense Strategies for the Seventies* (Boston: Little, Brown, 1971), pp. 73–76.

35. See Fritz W. Ermarth, "Contrasts in American and Soviet Strategic Thought," *International Security* 3 (Fall 1978); Snow, *Nuclear Strategy*, Chapter 5, "Soviet Strategic Doctrine and Forces."

36. See Richard L. Garwin, "Launch Under Attack to Redress Minuteman Vulnerability?," *International Security* 4 (Winter 1979–1980).

37. For Schlesinger's views, see *Report of the Secretary of Defense to the Congress on the FY 1975 Defense Budget* (Washington: GPO, 4 March 1974), pp. 35–41. The text of PD 59 remained secret but a summary can be found in "Address by Defense Secretary Harold Brown, Naval War College, Newport, Rhode Island," *New York Times*, 21 August 1980.

38. Walter Slocombe, "The Countervailing Strategy," *International Security* 5 (Spring 1981).

39. Ibid., p. 19. It should be noted that less than two years before the countervailing strategy was announced, defense secretary Harold Brown had said it was necessary for the United States to maintain the capability of destroying in retaliation a minimum of two hundred Soviet cities. *Annual Report Department of Defense, Fiscal Year 1979* (Washington, D.C.: USGPO, October 1978) pp. 49, 55.

40. "The Whirlpool of Weapons," Editorial in *Commonweal* 113 (30 January 1981).

41. Cf. Thomas Powers, "After the bombs: where the imagination falters," *Commonweal* 113 (30 January 1981); "Signs of war," ibid., 27 February, 1981 "Spasm war," ibid., 27 March 1981; "Principles of abolition: eight reasons for getting rid of the bomb," ibid., 31 July 1981; "The moral fallacy:

Nuclear war makes our differences pale," ibid., 11 September 1981; John Garvey, "King of Prussia eight: Extremism in the defense of sanity," ibid., 30 January 1981. The title of the last article refers to a defense of Daniel and Philip Berrigan and six others arrested for breaking into the General Electric plant in King of Prussia, Pennsylvania and using hammers to smash missile parts manufactured for the U.S. Government. Similar examples could readily be found in the *National Catholic Reporter*. Comments such as these were quite common in the U.S. Catholic press throughout the period when the bishops' pastoral letter was being drafted.

42. *Arms Control and Disarmament Agreements: Texts and Histories of Negotiations* (Washington, D.C.: U.S. Arms Control and Disarmament Agency, 1982), p. 93.

43. Ibid., p. 241. President Brezhnev gave a similar assurance concerning Soviet intentions.

44. Hedrick Smith, "U.S. Seeking Soviet Parley on Arms Violations," *The New York Times*, 12 August 1983; Henry Trewhitt, "President says Soviets violate pact," *The Sun*, January 24, 1984.

45. Thomas J. Gumbleton, "Chaplains blessing the bombers," *Commonweal* (2 March 1979): 105–7. This article was the negative side in a debate: "Is SALT Worth Supporting?" The affirmative side was taken by J. Bryan Hehir, "Limited but substantial achievements," ibid., 108–10.

46. To Live in Christ Jesus (Washington, D.C.: United States Catholic Conference, 1976), p. 34.

47. The Text of Cardinal Krol's testimony may be found in *Origins*, National Catholic News Service, 1979, pp. 195–99, and in *America* (8 March 1980). See also Francis X. Winters, "The Bow or the Cloud? American Bishops Challenge the Arms Race," *America* (25 July 1981).

48. Excerpts from Terence Cardinal Cooke's letter to military chaplains, *The New York Times*, 15 December 1981. A few days later, a group of priests, brothers, nuns, church officials, and members of the laity of the Archdiocese of New York openly criticized the cardinal's statement and said that his views were "clearly contradicted by the developing position of his fellow bishops." Kenneth A. Briggs, "Letter by Cooke on Arms Policy Prompts Protest," *The New York Times*, 18 December 1981.

49. Message of His Holiness Pope John Paul II, Delivered by His Eminence Agostino Cardinal Casaroli, Secretary of State, on the Occasion of the Second Special Session of the General Assembly Devoted to Disarmament, United Nations, New York, June 11, 1982.

50. Henry Kamm, "Pope Bolsters Bid for Disarmament," *The New York Times*, 2 January 1983. The same points were reiterated two weeks later in the Address of Pope John Paul II to Members of the Diplomatic Corps Attached to the Holy See at the Customary Exchange of New Year's Greetings, January 15, 1983, *The Pope Speaks: The Church Documents Quarterly* 28, no. 2 (1983): 170–79.

51. William Robbins, "Krol Assesses Position in Disarmament Movement," *The New York Times*, 9 June 1982.

Chapter 4

1. Two works on this subject which have attained the status of classics are John Henry Cardinal Newman's mid-nineteenth century *Essay on the Development of Christian Doctrine* (Garden City, N.Y.: Doubleday, 1960) and Henri de Lubac, S.J., *The Splendour of the Church* (New York: Sheed and Ward, 1956).

2. The Catholic faith, declared the pope, must be carefully guarded and is "not to be departed from under the specious pretext of a more profound understanding." Thomas I. McAvoy, C.S.C., *The Americanist Heresy in Roman Catholicism 1895–1900* (Notre Dame, Ind.: University of Notre Dame Press, 1963), pp. 231–32. See also Neil T. Storch, "John Ireland's Americanism after 1899: The Argument from History," *Church History* 51 (December 1982): 434–40.

3. Edward R. Kantowicz, "Cardinal Mundelein of Chicago and the Shaping of Twentieth Century American Catholicism," *The Journal of American History* 68 (June 1981), as summarized in Neil T. Storch, "John Ireland's Americanism after 1899," 443–44.

4. John Tracy Ellis, *American Catholics and Peace: An Historical Sketch*, Pamphlet (Washington, D.C.: Division of World Justice and Peace, United States Catholic Conference, 1970), pp. 4–12.

5. Introduction in James Finn, ed., *A Conflict of Loyalties: The Case for Selective Conscientious Objection*, viii-x. The Lutherans made a somewhat more qualified statement. Their Fourth Biennial Convention in Atlanta in 1968 rejected conscientious objection as ethically normative and required that ethical decisions in political matters be made in the context of the competing claims of peace, justice and freedom, but within this context they called for legal protection of the status of the CO and the SCO not as a right but as a privilege which could be revoked in situations of clear danger to the public order. "Conscientious Objection," Social Statements of the Lutheran Church in America, n.d.

6. Pius XII, Christmas Message, December 23, 1956. In Flannery, ed., *Pattern for Peace*, 283.

7. *Gaudium et spes*, Pastoral Constitution on the Church in the Modern World, December 8, 1965, Section 79, in Abbott, *Documents of Vatican II*, 292.

8. Bishops' Statement on Vietnam, quoted in James O'Gara, "Peace and the Bishops," *Commonweal* (23 December 1966): p. 338.

9. John Courtney Murray, "War and Conscience," Commencement Address, Western Maryland College, June 1967. Reprinted in Finn, ed., *A Conflict of Loyalties*, 22–24.

10. Ibid., 24.

11. Ibid., 27.

12. Gillete v. United States and Negre v. Larsen. Excerpts from opinion by Justice Thurgood Marshall, *The New York Times*, 9 March 1971.

13. See November 1968 Pastoral Letter, "Human Life in Our Day;" Statement on "The Catholic Conscientious Objector," October 15, 1969; Statement on Military Conscription by Monsignor Marvin Bordelon, Director of Department of International Affairs, United States Catholic Conference, Submitted to the House Armed Services Committee, March 5, 1971; "Declaration on Conscientious Objection and Selective Conscientious Objection," October 21, 1971—all published by the United States Catholic Conference, Washington, D.C.; Peter J. Henriot, "American Bishops and Conscientious Objection," *America* (4 January 1969): 18. See also Leonard Marion, *Country, Conscience and Conscription* (Englewood Cliffs, N.J.: Prentice-Hall, 1970); "The Draft and Conscience," Editorial in *Commonweal* (21 April 1967); "Selective Conscientious Objection," Symposium with Staughton Lind, Paul Ramsey, William V. O'Brien, and others, *Worldview*, 10 (February 1967); Peter J. Riga, "Selective Conscientious Objection," *Catholic World* (July 1970); Edward R. Cain, "Conscientious Objection in France, Britain and the United States," *Comparative Politics*, 2 (January 1970).

14. The author of this book pointed out these practical difficulties of SCO in a memorandum to the International Affairs Committee of USCC on March 31, 1971. The President's Commission majority concluded: "A determination of the justness or unjustness of any war could only be made within the context of that war itself. Forcing upon the individual the necessity of making that distinction . . . could put a burden heretofore unknown on the men in uniform and even on the brink of combat, with results that could be disastrous to him, to his unit, and to the entire military tradition." From the Report of the President's National Advisory Commission on Selective Service, *In Pursuit of Equity—Who Serves When Not all Serve?*, p. 4.

15. *The Official Catholic Directory Anno Domini 1982* (New York: P. J. Kennedy & Sons, 1982), pp. 1188–94.

16. See Marjorie Hyer, "How Our War-Blessing Catholic Bishops Got Religion on Nukes," *The Washington Post*, 1 May 1983. George Weigel has written that there "used to be a quality of argument in the Catholic community that distinguished it from other types of religious involvement with public policy issues . . . . summed up in the old Roman virtues of *pietas* and *gravitas*: mature patriotism and a sense of the moral weight of public affairs . . . . *Pietas* has been replaced, in some quarters, by an attempt to get as much distance as possible between the Church and American society, as if counter-cultural values were more expressive of a genuinely Catholic social ethic." "The Catholic 'Peace' Bishops," *Freedom at Issue* no. 67 (July–August 1982): 14.

17. Speaking of the controversy over Pope Paul VI's 1968 Encyclical *Humanae Vitae*, which dealt with contraception, Charles E. Curran, professor of moral theology at Catholic University, shocked orthodox theologians by holding that "a Catholic can dissent from an authoritative, noninfallible hierarchical teaching when one discerns there are sufficient reasons for overturning the presumption in favor of the official teaching." "Challenge of Pluralism," *Commonweal* (30 Janury 1981): 45. He demanded

academic freedom for theologians and objected to "recent Roman regulations and proposed new Code of Cannon Law . . . designed to put theology under the jurisdiction of the hierarchy." Ibid. George MacRae, S.J., professor of Roman Catholic theological studies at Harvard Divinity School, said that building Catholic theology for our own time has become "an urgent task now that a particular scholastic theology has been relegated to history." MacRae referred to "the relativity of the older formulations" and to "a loss of the familiar absolutes in theological reflection." "Limits of Formulations," ibid., p. 43.

Such views were not new. A few theologians in Europe and the United States had been propounding them for more than a decade. Even earlier, such distinguished theologians as Henri de Lubac, Karl Rahner, Yves Congar, and John Courtney Murray had been forbidden to publish their research and interpretative conclusions which differed from the teachings of Rome on questions then undergoing refinement in light of historical developments. The theologians just mentioned, however, neither expounded a theological pluralism nor denied Rome's authority to silence them until the issues had been clarified. All of them were eventually vindicated and "rehabilitated." What was new in the post-conciliar period was a confusion between the unquestionable right of theologians to conduct research into any matters whatsoever and the questionable right of those theologians, in the name of academic freedom, to teach their own "optional interpretations" even though they are in conflict with the authority of the ecclesiastical magisterium. Cf. Bishop David M. Maloney, "The Magisterium, the Bishops and the Theologians," in Monsignor John J. O'Rourke and S. Thomas Greenburg, eds., *Symposium on the Magisterium: A Positive Statement*, for the Institute of Catholic Higher Education and the Archdiocese of Philadelphia (Boston: St. Paul Edition, 1978), pp. 63–69.

18. Andrew M. Greeley, "Selective Catholicism: How They Get Away with It," *America* (30 April 1983).

19. Francis P. Fiorenza, "Political Theology and Liberation Theology: An Enquiry into Their Fundamental Meaning," in Thomas M. McFadden, ed., *Liberation, Revolution and Freedom: Theological Perspectives* (New York: Seabury Press, 1975), p. 5.

20. Ibid., pp. 6–15; Richard P. McBrien, *Catholicism*, Study Edition (Minneapolis, Minn.: Winston Press, 1981), pp. 60, 318, 697, 973; Johannes Metz, *Theology of the World* (New York: Herder and Herder, 1969), pp. 93–95; Charles E. Curran, "Theological Reflections on the Social Mission of the Church," in Edward R. Ryle, ed., *The Social Mission of the Church* (Washington, D.C.: Catholic University of America Press, 1972), pp. 31–54; and Michael Fahey, "The Mission of the Church: To Divinize or to Humanize?" *Proceedings of the Catholic Theological Society of America* (1976), pp. 56–69.

21. Rosemary Radford Ruether, e.g., one of the most outspoken advocates of a feminist theology, has attributed "social sin" to both the United States government and the Roman Catholic Church because of "the massive

and chronic contradictions" between their professed ideas and operating procedures. "Social Sin," *Commonweal* (30 January 1981).

22. Fiorenza, "Political Theology and Liberation Theology," 15–17.

23. Leonardo Boff, *Jesus Christ Liberator: A Critical Christology for Our Time* (Maryknoll, N.Y.: Orbis Books, 1978), pp. 279–80. Cited in McBrien, *Catholicism*, 491. Other principal Latin American sources of liberation theology include Gustavo Gutierrez, *A Theology of Liberation*, trans. Caridad Inda and John Eagleson (Maryknoll, N.Y.: Orbis Books, 1976) and Juan Luis Segundo, *Theology for Artisans of a New Humanity*, trans. John Drury, 5 vols. (Maryknoll, N.Y.: Orbis Books, 1973–1974).

24. Boff, cited in McBrien, 491.

25. McBrien, 128. Richard Neuhaus, a Lutheran, thinks that the liberation theologians ultimately equate the mission of the Church with revolutionary struggle. "Liberation Theology and the Captivities of Jesus," *Worldview* 16 (1973): 41–48. Cited in Fiorenza, "Political Theology and Liberation Theology," 24.

26. McBrien, *Catholicism*, 317–18.

27. James V. Schall, S.J., "The Changing Catholic Scene," in Carol Friedley Griffith, ed., *Christianity and Politics: Catholic and Protestant Perspectives* (Washington, D.C.: Ethics and Public Policy Center, 1981), pp. 19–38. Dennis P. McCann has called liberation theology flawed because it cannot distinguish between religious transcendance and political enthusiasm. Cf. his *Christian Realism and Liberation Theology* (Maryknoll, N.Y.: Orbis Books, 1981).

28. *Justice in the World*, Statement of the Synod of Bishops (Washington, D.C.: United States Catholic Conference, 1972), p. 34.

29. All of the documents of Vatican II can be found in Walter M. Abbott, S.J., ed., *Documents of Vatican II*. For an analysis of the documents by more than fifty authoritative specialists (including some non-Catholic), cf. John H. Miller, C.S.C., ed., *Vatican II: An Interfaith Appraisal* (Notre Dame, Ind.: University of Notre Dame Press, 1966).

30. Edward B. Fiske, "The Reign of Pope Paul: A Bridge Between Eras," *The New York Times*, 7 August 1978; *Catholic Trends* (National Catholic News Service, Washington) 9 (August 19, 1978): 1–2.

31. John Tracy Ellis, "From the Enlightenment to the Present: Papal Policy Seen Through the Encyclicals: A Review Essay," *Catholic Historical Review* 69 (January 1983): 57.

32. *On The Development of Peoples*, March 26, 1967, United States Catholic Conference, n.d.

33. Ibid., p. 20.

34. Quentin L. Quade, Editor's Introduction to *The Pope and Revolution: John Paul II Confronts Liberation Theology* (Washington, D.C.: Ethics and Public Policy Center, 1982), p. 6.

35. Ibid., 6–7.

36. Medellin, *Conclusiones*, Document on Justice. Quoted in John Drury,

trans. and John Eagleson, ed., *Christians for Socialism* (Maryknoll, N.Y., Orbis Books, 1975), Introduction (By "Anonymous Priest"), viii.

37. "Declaration of the 80," ibid., 4.

38. "Declaration of the Bishops of Chile," April 22, 1971, 12–13.

39. Ibid., 13.

40. Ibid., 14.

41. Medellin, *Conclusiones*, quoted in Philip E. Berryman, "Latin American Liberation Theology," in Sergio Torres and John Eagleson, eds., *Theology in the Americas*, (Maryknoll, N.Y.: Orbis Books, 1976), p. 23.

42. Robert McAfee Brown, "A Preface and a Conclusion," in Torres and Eagleson, eds., *Theology of the Americas*, ix–xxviii.

43. Gregory Baum, "The Christian Left at Detroit," in ibid., 399–429. "Praxis," says Baum,". . . is practice associated with a total dynamics of historical vision and social transformation. Through praxis, people enter their historical destiny. . . . The dialectics of truth begins with praxis." Ibid., p. 407.

44. The author of this study was a delegate to the Detroit conference.

45. The survey, completed in early 1982, was conducted by the Roper Center at the University of Connecticut under a grant from the Institute for Educational Affairs. Out of 2,000 randomly sampled professors to whom questionnaires were sent, 1,112 replied, including 221 Catholics. See "What Theologians Believe: The IEA/Roper Center Theology Faculty Survey," *This World* no. 2 (Summer 1982): 28–108.

46. J. Bryan Hehir, "Nuclear weapons: the two debates," *Commonweal*, 13 March 1981: 135.

47. In *Populorum Progressio* he said that a revolutionary uprising "produces new injustices, throws more elements out of balance and brings on new disasters. A real evil should not be fought against at the cost of greater misery." *On the Development of Peoples*, USCC, 22–23.

48. See Jacques Rupnik, "The Vatican's new *Ostpolitik* and Church-State relations in Eastern Europe," *The World Today* (July 1979): 286–294; and Dennis J. Dunn, "The Vatican's *Ostpolitik*," *Journal of International Affairs* 36 (Fall/Winter 1982/83).

49. Letter from His Holiness Pope Paul VI to Maurice Cardinal Roy, Archbishop of Quebec and President of the Pontifical Commission for Justice and Peace, on the 80th anniversary of Leo XIII's Enclyclical *Rerum Novarum*, 1971. Quoted in Peter Hebblethwaite, "The Popes and Politics: Shifting Patterns in 'Catholic Social Doctrine'," *Daedalus* 3 (Winter 1982): 91.

50. See James V. Schall, "The Changing Catholic Scene," and the following articles in Quade, ed., *The Pope and Revolution*: Dale Vree, "'Christian Marxists': A Critique"; and Michael Novak, "Liberation Theology and the Pope." Cf. also the Addresses of Pope John Paul II in the same work. Early in 1983, the pope reiterated that priests should avoid partisan politics and under no circumstances should hold official posts within government. Referring to priests who died after joining guerrilla movements, he said that it is

not worth the effort for a priest to lose his life "for an ideology, for a mutilated or manipulated Gospel, for a partisan option." National Catholic News Service, "Pope's Visit Confronts Central American Issues," *The Catholic Standard and Times* (Philadelphia), 10 March 1983. Quentin Quade, on the first page of his Introduction asks: "What shall be the relation of religion to politics? Specifically, how may the Catholic Church rightly influence particular political and economic issues? .... And the answer...: through believers acting as citizens. The Church may not be a direct political actor. Priests and other Church leaders in their ecclesiastical capacity may not act as politicians or political prophets."

51. Following the anti-Somoza revolution in Nicaragua, members of Congress and of the Carter administration credited the U.S. bishops with staving off efforts to terminate economic aid to the new government. From 1977 onward, the American bishops became deeply disturbed by governmental persecution of the Church, especially the Jesuits, in El Salvador. In 1980, the Carter administration developed a new Salvador policy, designed to identify and support "a progressive middle" that would carry out political, social and economic reforms. Archbishop Oscar Romero of El Salvador, a champion of the poor and of human rights, opposed the new Carter initiative because the government's security forces had not been sufficiently purged and because Marxist guerrilla forces were excluded from the proposed solution. After the assassination of Romero in March 1980, the United States Catholic Conference under the presidency of Archbishop John R. Quinn of San Francisco strongly urged the U.S. government to withhold all economic and military aid from the Salvadoran government for five reasons—every one of which depended upon an empirical political judgment on matters where the USCC was in disagreement with U.S. policy. See Thomas F. Quigley, "The Catholic Church and El Salvador," *Cross Currents* 32 (Summer 1982), esp. 183–90.

Chapter 5

1. The Final Text, or third draft with amendments, was approved by an overwhelming vote of 238–9. Kenneth A. Briggs, "Bishops Endorse Stand Opposed to Nuclear War," *The New York Times*, 4 May 1983. The press reported that as many as 288 bishops were present for the start of the meeting. Some of these were retired and thus had no deliberative vote. Since the debate lasted longer than expected, a small number of bishops departed before the vote. Whether there were any abstentions was not reported.

2. John Garvey wrote: "The most stupid criticism the bishops received was the argument that they are not expert in these issues. Archbishop Bernardin properly pointed out that editorialists sound off every day on any number of issues, ranging from the finer points of economics to every area of

foreign policy. Are they experts on all or any of them?" "The Bishops and the Critics," *Commonweal* (14 January 1983): 7

The answer to that question, of course, is no. But the point is that editorialists do not speak, however much they might wish or pretend to speak, with the moral authority with which a national conference of bishops addresses the faithful. Quentin L. Quade of Marquette University has noted that the formal political teaching of the Catholic Church since 1891 has not on balance either claimed or established a warrant for the Church to give directives for specific action in the political order. During the decade or so from 1967 on, there was a tendency "to think that faith in Christ was sufficient for knowing right political action," but Pope John Paul II has indicated that he means to reverse such a pretension. "A Question of Competence," *Thought* 57 (September 1982): 345.

3. See, for example, Arthur Jones, "Bishops tell how views on nuclear arms formed," *National Catholic Reporter*, 11 December 1981, an account of a symposium at Catholic University, Washington, with Bishops Sullivan, Gumbleton and Matthiesen and Archbishop Hunthausen; and Colman McCarthy, "How the 'Peace Bishops' Got That Way," an interview with Archbishop Hunthausen and Bishop Matthiesen, *The Washington Post*, 27 December 1981.

4. One of the most influential of the pastoral letters was that issued by Bishop Mahony of Stockton, California, "Becoming a Church of Peace Advocacy," December 30, 1981; reprinted in *Commonweal*, (12 March 1982).

5. Former officials were Harold Brown, secretary of defense for President Carter; James Schlesinger, secretary of defense for Presidents Nixon and Ford; Gerard Smith, chief of the U.S. SALT Delegation for President Nixon; Helmut Sonnenfeld, counselor to the Department of State in the Nixon administration; Herbert Scoville, deputy director of the CIA; David Linebaugh of the Arms Control and Disarmament Agency; and Roger Molander, of President Carter's National Security Staff. The Reagan administration officials were Caspar Weinberger, secretary of defense; Lawrence Eagleburger, undersecretary of state for political affairs; Eugene Rostow, former director of the Arms Control and Disarmament Agency; and Ambassador Edward Rowny, chief of the U.S. Delegation to the Strategic Arms Reduction Talks (START).

6. For a profile article on Father Hehir, see Charlotte Hays, "The Voice in the Bishops' Ear," *The Washington Post Magazine*, 3 April 1983. "Many observers of the Catholic scene" regard Hehir, age 42, as "the single most important figure in what *The New Republic* recently called 'the new Catholic politics.'" Ibid., 6.

7. First Draft, Pastoral Letter on Peace and War, *God's Hope in a Time of Fear*, June 11, 1983, Mimeograph, hereafter referred to as First Draft, 28.

8. Ibid., 30. "Our conclusions are less clear than many would have hoped for, but we believe they correspond to the complexity of the problem we face." Ibid., 37. The fact that moral questions have a political dimension is

no excuse for denying the Church's obligation to provide guidance for members' consciences. Ibid., 47.

9. Excerpts from "Comments by Catholic Bishops on Issues of War and Peace," *The New York Times*, 19 November 1982.

10. *Dogmatic Constitution on the Church (Lumen Gentium)*, Chapter 3 "The Hierarchical Structure of the Church, With Special Reference to the Episcopate," in Walter M. Abbott, S.J., ed., *The Documents of Vatican II*, 37–50. The Vatican Council said that "when either the Roman Pontiff or the body of bishops with him defines a judgment, they pronounce it in accord with revelation itself . . . . But they do not allow that there could be any new public revelation pertaining to the divine deposit of faith." Ibid., 49–50.

11. *Decree on the Bishops' Pastoral Office in the Church (Christus Dominus)*, Chapter 3, "Concerning the Cooperation of Bishops for the Common Good of Many Churches, I. Synods, Councils and Especially Episcopal Conferences," ibid., 424–26. Article 38, Section 4 reads: "Decisions of the episcopal conference, provided they have been made lawfully and by the choice of at least two-thirds of the prelates who have a deliberative voice in the conference, and have been reviewed by the Apostolic See, are to have juridically binding force in those cases and in those only which are prescribed by common law or determined by special mandate of the Apostolic See, given spontaneously or in response to a petition from the conference itself." Ibid., 425–26.

12. Francis X. Winters, S.J., "Nuclear Deterrence Morality: Atlantic Community Bishops in Tension," *Theological Studies* 43 (September 1982): 428.

13. Bishop John J. O'Connor, "Bishops Strive for a Credible Peace Letter," *National Catholic Register*, 26 December 1982.

14. "Rome Consultation on Peace and Disarmament: A Vatican Synthesis," Text in *Origins* 12 (7 April 1983): 691–95. Quotation from p. 692. (Hereafter referred to as "Rome Consultation.")

15. Ibid., 692.

16. Ibid., 692.

17. Ibid., 693.

18. The Pastoral Letter on War and Peace, *The Challenge of Peace*: *God's Promise and Our Response*, Text in *Origins*, NC Documentary Service 13 (May 19, 1983): 2–3. (Herafter referred to as Final Text.)

19. John Langan, S.J., "The Debate Identified," in William V. O'Brien, *et al.*, "American Catholics and the Peace Debate," *The Washington Quarterly*, published by the Center for Strategic and International Studies, Georgetown University 5 (Fall 1982): 124–25. See also Langan's "The American Hierarchy and Nuclear Weapons," *Theological Studies* 43 (September 1982).

20. Michael Novak, "Example of open church in practice," *National Catholic Reporter*, 22 April 1983.

21. First Draft, 8.

22. Ibid., 9.

23. Final Text, 1–2. The second and third drafts were substantially the same.

24. Final Text, 3. Whereas the second and third drafts said "To take a human life is to approximate the role reserved to God," the Final Text reads: "God is the Lord of life, and so each human life is sacred."

25. Final Text, 4.

26. Ibid.

27. The metaphor of God as warrior had much meaning for a people smaller and weaker than their neighbors. "No one can deny the presence of such images in the Old Testament nor their powerful influence upon the articulation of this people's understanding of the involvement of God in their history. The warrior God was highly significant during long periods of Israel's understanding of its faith. But this image was not the only image, and it was gradually transformed, particularly after the experience of the exile, when God was no longer identified with military victory and might. Other images and other understandings of God's activity became predominant in expressing the faith of God's people." Ibid., 5.

28. Ibid., 5.

29. Ibid., 6–7.

30. Ibid., 7.

31. "Rome Consultation," 694.

32. Final Text, 9.

33. Ibid., 9.

34. Arthur Jones, "Bishops tell how views on nuclear arms formed."

35. Precis on the Third Draft, ii–iii.

36. Final Text, 10.

37. Ibid.

38. William V. O'Brien, "The Peace Debate and American Catholics," *The Washington Quarterly* (Spring 1982). Reprinted with responses appearing in the Fall 1982 issues in *American Catholics and the Peace Debate*, no page number.

39. "Rome Consultation," 694–95.

40. Final Text, 23.

41. Ibid. The last sentence gives rise to difficulties in the order of foreign policy. The granting of aid can be an instrument for persuading a government to ameliorate its policy on human rights. Some bishops may have El Salvador in mind, but they would probably not wish to suggest that the United States ought to refrain from shipping grain to the Soviet Union for a similar purpose.

42. Ibid.

43. Ibid., 10.

44. Ibid., 10–11. The principle of proportionality, as noted in Chapter 3, requires a constant evaluation throughout the course of the war. The

bishops, who supported the war in 1966, concluded five years later that the mounting level of damage both to the adversary and the United States made its continuation no longer justifiable. Ibid., 11, citing the bishops' *Resolution on Southeast Asia* (Washington, D.C.: United States Catholic Conference, 1971).

45. *De Regimine Principum* (On Kingship), Chapter 6. See Dino Bigongiari, ed. and intro., *The Political Ideas of St. Thomas Aquinas* (New York: Hafner, 1957), pp. 189–92.

46. Final Text, 10.

47. Third Draft, 43 (Omitted from the comparable section of the Final Text, 10). On this point, see the discussion at the end of Chapter 2, pp. 00–00.

48. Final Text, 11.

49. Ibid.

50. This wording from *Gaudium et spes*, Sec. 80, is in the Final Text, 11.

51. The quotation from Clark and a parallel statement from Weinberger were included in the text of the Third Draft, 83–84, but in the Final Text they were reduced to a one sentence summary on p. 17, and the quotations were moved to the Footnotes to the Pastoral Letter (note 81). For earlier references to similar assurances, see Richard Halloran, "Bishops Joining Nuclear Arms Debate," *The New York Times*, 4 October 1982.

52. Final Text, 11.

53. Ibid., 26.

54. Ibid., 12.

55. Albert Wohlstetter says that informed realists in foreign policy establishments should agree with the bishops in opposing indiscriminate threats to kill innocent bystanders—threats which paralyze the West, not the East. See Albert Wohlstetter, "Bishops, Statesmen, and Other Strategists on the Bombing of Innocents," *Commentary* (June 1983): 15.

56. "Rome Consultation," 693.

57. Ibid., 15.

58. Joseph A. Fahey, for example, is not correct when he says that it is "clear from recent papal, conciliar and episcopal statements that the use of nuclear weapons is immoral." "Morality of War," *New Catholic Encyclopaedia* (New York: Publishers Guild-McGraw-Hill, 1979), 17: 701. For an exposition of the view that Vatican II did not affirm a nuclear pacifism, see Robert W. Tucker, *Just War and Vatican II: A Critique* (New York: Council on Religion and International Affairs, 1967) and Robert F. Rizzo, "Nuclear War: the Moral Dilemma," *Cross Currents* 32 (Spring 1982): 71–84. For several years, American Catholic radical pacifists—clerical, religious and lay—have been speaking and writing as if all activities related to nuclear weapons research, testing, production, handling, management, planning and training, are intrinsically evil *(mala in se)*, regardless of any good faith intention of contributing to peace through deterrence. John J. O'Connor, *In Defense of Life* (Boston: St. Paul Editions, 1981), pp. 17–21.

Bishop O'Connor traces much of the current confusion concerning the teaching of the Catholic Church on war and peace to "neo-Gnosticism." "There are those who in their zeal to avert war . . . tend to convey the impression, that their personal convictions, and only theirs, reflect the true teaching of Christ. A new revelation has been given them. Whatever the Church may have taught in the past, it could not be the *true* Church, or the church of *true* Christians, were it to tolerate war under any circumstances in the future." Ibid., 26–27.

59. "Rome Consultation," 694.

60. Ibid.

61. Final Text, 15.

62. All quotations in this paragraph from Final Text, 13.

63. Ibid.

64. Ibid., 13–14.

65. During their two day meeting in Chicago, the bishops were faced with considering 515 amendments to the third draft. The bishops accepted 174 amendments; many of the remaining 341 were withdrawn, and the rest were defeated. In one key vote, after almost no debate, they adopted by a substantial majority an amendment proposed by Archbishop Quinn of San Francisco registering their "opposition on moral grounds to any use of nuclear weapons." A few moments later, Bishop J. Francis Stafford of Memphis suggested that "we have a problem" with the whole stance of the pastoral letter in light of that amendment. Cardinal Bernardin, chairman of the drafting committee, agreed. On a reconsideration, the amendment received only a few scattered "ayes." Jim Lackey, "Bishops Approve War and Peace Pastoral," *The Catholic Standard and Times* (Philadelphia), 5 May 1983.

66. Final Text, 14.

67. Ibid., 16.

68. Ibid., 18.

69. Ibid., 26.

70. Ibid.

71. Ibid.

72. Ibid., 28.

73. Ibid. See also the letter from the late Terence Cardinal Cooke of New York, head of the U.S. Military Ordinariate, to Catholics in the military service regarding the bishops' pastoral on war and peace, June 7, 1983. Text in *The Catholic Standard and Times*, 16 June 1983.

Chapter 6

1. Final Text, 2.

2. Karl Jaspers, *The Future of Mankind*, trans. E. B. Ashton (Chicago: University of Chicago Press, 1958), p. 4.

3. Final Text, 9.

4. Ibid., 21.

5. *A Race to Nowhere: An Arms Race Primer for Catholics* (Chicago, Ill.: Pax Christi-USA, n.d.), esp. 71–72.

6. China, a poor sprawling country with a billion people, is a much less attractive target for Soviet occupation than, say, West Germany, yet it would never occur to Chinese leaders to give up military defense in favor of nonviolent resistance, though this form of resistance would be more familiar to them than to Western peoples. Sweden, Austria, Switzerland, India, and Yugoslavia all profess some kind of neutrality or nonalignment, but they are all prepared to defend themselves with armed force. No state able to make any provision for its own defense has ever traded that option for NVR. Christian pacifists who heroically renounce violence in their own defense are to be admired for their witness, but they vitiate their own case when they resort to far-fetched political arguments to justify it.

7. For the logically clever but politically unpersuasive arguments for unilateral disarmament and nonviolent resistance, see Erich Fromm, "The Case for Unilateral Disarmament," in Quincy Wright, *et al.*, eds., *Preventing World War III: Some Proposals* (New York: Simon and Schuster, 1962); Jerome D. Frank, "Human Nature and Nonviolent Resistance," ibid.; Mulford Q. Sibley, "Unilateral Disarmament," in Robert A. Goldwin, ed., *America Armed* (Chicago: Rand McNally, 1961); Jessie Wallace Hughan and Cecil Hinshaw, "Toward a Non-Violent National Defense," in Mulford Q. Sibley, ed., *The Quiet Battle* (New York: Anchor Books, 1963), pp. 316–56.

8. Quoted in Ernest Conine, "Bishops Depend on Miracles," *The Los Angeles Times*, 9 May 1983.

9. For a discussion of how pacifism and appeasement in Britain and France helped to create an international climate conducive to aggression, see Christopher Thorne, *The Approach of War 1938–9* (London: Macmillan, 1967), Chap. 1, esp. pp. 7–12. Thorne notes how easy it was for leaders to pursue a policy of appeasement which enjoyed a large measure of public support; the immediate pain had to be borne by others—the Austrians, the Czechs and finally the Poles. Appeasement, says Thorne, which usually involves a distortion of the truth to rationalize or justify the actions of the aggressor, became a noble mission in England, at least in the eyes of Chamberlain and his supporters. "Missions," he adds, "can corrupt as much as power." Ibid., 20.

10. Final Text, 14–17.

11. James Finn, "Nuclear Terror: Moral Paradox," *America* (19 February 1983), 127.

12. Michael Novak, "Moral Clarity in the Nuclear Age: A Letter from Catholic Clergy and Laity," *Catholicism in Crisis* 1 (March 1983): 15.

13. Germain Grisez, "The Moral Implications of a Nuclear Deterrent," *Center Journal* 2 (Winter 1982): 9–24.

14. Herbert C. Kelman, "International Relations: Psychological

Aspects," *International Encyclopedia of the Social Sciences* (New York: Macmillan, 1968); Werner Levi, "On the Causes of War and the Conditions of Peace," *Journal of Conflict Resolution* 4 (December 1960): 411–420; and Dougherty and Pfaltzgraff, *Contending Theories of International Relations*, Chapters 5, 7, and 8.

15. Albert Carnesale, Paul Doty, *et al.*, *Living with Nuclear Weapons* (New York: Bantam Books, 1983), p. 247.

16. James Finn, "Nuclear Terror: Moral Paradox."

17. Final Text, 18–19.

18. Ibid.

19. Ibid., 18 and note 84 on p. 32.

20. For fuller discussion of these strategic intricacies, see Roger D. Speed, *Strategic Deterrence in the 1980s* (Stanford, Calif.: Hoover Institution Press, 1979), pp. 74–80; Richard Burt, "Reassessing the Strategic Balance," *International Security* 5 (Summer 1980): 37–52; Warner R. Schilling, "U.S. Strategic Nuclear Concepts in the 1970s: The Search for Sufficiently Equivalent Countervailing Parity," *International Security* 6 (Fall 1981): esp. 70–72; Keith B. Payne, "Deterrence, Arms Control and U.S. Strategic Doctrine," *Orbis* 25 (Fall 1981): 747–69; Donald M. Snow, *Nuclear Strategy*, pp. 126–27 and 206–8; and Victor Utgoff, "In Defense of Counterforce," *International Security* 6 (Spring 1982): 44–60.

21. Schelling, *Arms and Influence*, p. 1.

22. See "Transcript of President Reagan's Address on Arms Reduction," *The New York Times*, 19 November 1981; Stephen Haseler, "The Euromissile Crisis," *Commentary* (May 1983): 28–32.

23. Final Text, 18.

24. Second Draft, in *Origins*, 317; Third Draft, 90. See also Kenneth A. Briggs, "Bishops' Letter on Nuclear Arms is Revised to 'More Flexible' View," *The New York Times*, 6 April 1983.

25. Roy Larson, "Prelates' unit urges N-arms 'halt,'" *The Boston Globe*, 29 April 1983; Kenneth A. Briggs, "Bishops to Finish Atom Arms Letter," *The New York Times*, 1 May 1983.

26. Footnote 85, Final Text, 32.

27. Kenneth A. Briggs, "Roman Catholic Bishops Toughen Stance Against Nuclear Weapons," *The New York Times*, 3 May 1983. Bishop John J. O'Connor of the Military Vicariate in New York feared that this would "politicize a pastoral letter by favoring a political formula for a nuclear freeze" but John Cardinal Krol of Philadelphia deemed "halt" a more accurate term, "more consistent with the entire presentation."

28. Former Defense Secretary Harold Brown opposed the freeze because "stopping the competition at its present level will not by itself reduce either the likelihood or the lethality of nuclear war: and because the freeze does not "address the stability of a strategic balance through the survivability and diversity of forces." "No. It's a Diversion From the Main Event," Debate in *The Washington Post*, 28 March 1982. The Harvard Study Group found the

more sweeping freeze proposals destabilizing, unverifiable, probably unnegotiable and possibly self-defeating. "The Realities of Arms Control," *Atlantic* 251 (June 1983): 45–46.

29. Matthew F. Murphy, "Nuclear Weapons and the Criterion of Proportionality," *Center Journal* 2 (Winter 1982): 25–36.

30. Andrei Sakharov, "The Danger of Thermonuclear War: An Open Letter to Dr. Sidney Drell," *Foreign Affairs* 61 (Summer 1983), 1001–16, at pp. 1009–11.

31. Excerpts from Report of the Commission on Strategic Forces, *The New York Times*, 12 April 1983; Charles W. Corddry, "'Build-down' concept may lead to compromise on nuclear arms," *Baltimore Sun*, 9 May 1983; Lou Cannon, "President Considering Revised Arms Proposal," *The Washington Post*, 11 May 1983; Lou Cannon and George C. Wilson, "President Backs Arms Build-Down," *The Washington Post*, 13 May 1983; Vernon A. Guidry, Jr., "3 senators say U.S. should seek 'double build-down' arms pact," *Baltimore Sun*, 12 September 1983.

32. Final Text, 15.

33. See James E. Dougherty, "The Study of the Global System," in James N. Rosenau *et al.*, *World Politics* (New York: The Free Press, 1976), pp. 618–23; and Dougherty and Pfaltzgraff, *Contending Theories of International Relations*, pp. 38–41 and note 132 on p. 53.

34. Albert Wohlstetter, "Bishops, Statesmen and Other Strategists," p. 17. For skeptical views on the possibility of limiting nuclear war, see Desmond Ball, *Can Nuclear War be Controlled?* Adelphi Papers, no. 161 (London: International Institute for Strategic Studies, 1981); Spurgeon M. Keeny, Jr. and Wolfgang K. H. Panofsky, "Mad Versus Nuts," *Foreign Affairs* 60 (Winter 1981/82): 287–304; and Michael Howard, "On Fighting a Nuclear War," *International Security* 5 (Spring 1981): 3–17.

35. Donald M. Snow, *Nuclear Strategy*, p. 7.

36. John Erickson, "The Soviet View of Deterrence," *Survival* 24 (November/December 1982).

37. Second Draft, *Origins*, 314.

38. Ibid., 314–15.

39. McGeorge Bundy, George F. Kennan, Robert S. McNamara and Gerard Smith, "Nuclear Weapons and the Atlantic Alliance," *Foreign Affairs* 60 (Spring 1982): 753–68.

40. Karl Kaiser, Georg Leber, Alois Mertes and Franz-Joseph Schulze, "Nuclear Weapons and the Preservation of Peace: A Response to an American Proposal for Renouncing the First Use of Nuclear Weapons," *Foreign Affairs* 60 (Summer 1982): 1157–70. Quoted on p. 1158.

41. Judy Freedman, "Centimeter of doubt for bishops on N-ban," *The Boston Globe*, 1 March 1983.

42. Final Text, 15.

43. Ibid., 21.

44. These summary figures are drawn from the articles by Robin

Ranger on "Defense" in the *Encyclopaedia Britannica Books of the Year* for 1981, 1982 and 1983; and the *Annual Report to Congress of the Secretary of Defense for FY 1984* (Washington: USGPO., February 1, 1983), p. 4.

45. *World Military Expenditures and Arms Transfers 1969–1978* (Washington: United States Arms Control and Disarmament Agency, 1980) and the I.I.S.S. *Military Balance* for the years from 1979–80 to 1982–83. (See entries under specific countries.)

46. Chart in *World Military Expenditures*, p. 5. U.S. defense spending as a percentage of the total federal budget was 51 percent in 1955, 23 percent in 1980 and is projected at 28 percent for 1984. *Annual Report to Congress, FY 1984*, p. 4.

47. *Budget of the United States Government: Fiscal Year 1983*, pp. 3–34, cited in Michael Novak, "Moral Clarity in the Nuclear Age: A Letter from Catholic Clergy and Laity," in *Catholicism in Crisis* 1 (March 1983): 11, 22.

48. Ibid., 11.

49. Ibid., 10.

50. Weigley, *The American Way of War*, pp. 400–3; Robert E. Osgood, *NATO: The Entangling Alliance* (Chicago: University of Chicago Press, 1962), Chap. 5 and 6.

51. Timothy Stanley, *NATO in Transition* (New York: Praeger, 1965), Chap. 5; Alvin J. Cottrell and James E. Dougherty, *The Politics of the Atlantic Alliance* (New York: Praeger, 1965), Chap. 3.

52. For a cogent account of the failure of the Kennedy administration, and especially Defense Secretary McNamara, to persuade NATO Europe to eschew a nuclear in favor of a conventional strategy, consult Bernard Brodie, *War and Politics* (New York: Macmillan, 1973), pp. 396–405.

53. See, for example, in addition to the articles listed in Notes 39 and 40, Senator Sam Nunn, "Deterring War in Europe," *NATO Review* 25 (February 1977): 4–7; Robert Komer, "NATO at Thirty: Looking Ahead," *International Security* 4 (Summer 1979): 108–16; *Strengthening Conventional Deterrence in Europe*, Report of the European Security Study, April 1983. One of the few conservative strategists to question the first use option was Fred Charles Iklé, in "NATO's First Nuclear Use: A Deepening Trap?" *Strategic Review* 8 (Winter 1980): 18–23. Iklé, who feared that such an option could rip the alliance apart in time of crisis, became the No. 3 man in the Pentagon in the Reagan administration.

54. Laurence Martin, "The Role of Military Force in the Nuclear Age," in the book he edited, *Strategic Thought in the Nuclear Age* (Baltimore: The Johns Hopkins University Press, 1979), p. 16.

55. See Anthony H. Cordesman, *Deterrence in the 1980s: Part I—Strategic Forces and Extended Deterrence*, Adelphi Papers no. 175 (London: I.I.S.S., Summer 1982). The German bishops make this point quite effectively in their pastoral letter of April 1983. See p. 000 below.

56. See Michael Getler, "Atom Arms Debates Overlook Key Fact: They're Cheap," *The Washington Post*, 29 October 1982; Bradley Graham,

"U.S. Stressing Conventional Arms for NATO," *The Washington Post,* 2 November 1982; Charles W. Corddry, "Non-Atom Arms Asked for NATO," *The Baltimore Sun,* 17 May 1983; Robert C. Toth, "NATO Develops New Weapons," *The Los Angeles Times,* 31 May 1983; John Tagliabue, "Bonn Balks at Weinberger's Arms Plans," *The New York Times,* 1 June 1983; Elizabeth Pond, "Can NATO lessen its nuclear tilt?" *The Christian Science Monitor,* October 14, 1983.

57. Irving Kristol, "'No First Use' Requires a Conventional Build-up," *The Wall Street Journal,* 12 March 1982.

58. Wolfram von Raven, "A Grim Perspective for the Bundeswehr," *German Comments: Review of Politics and Culture,* 1 (April 1983): 25–31. For 1983, says the author, the manpower pool (born in 1964) was 360,000. In 1994, it will be 177,000.

59. This principle was enunciated by Victoria in *Relectio de potestate civili,* 13 and by Suarez in *De bello,* iv. See Midgley, *The National Law Tradition and the Theory of International Relations,* 65.

60. General Bernard W. Rogers, Supreme Allied Commander, Europe (SACEUR), strongly favors strengthening NATO's conventional forces to provide a "reasonable prospect" of frustrating a Soviet nonnuclear attack by nonnuclear means, but he is also opposed to a "no first use" policy for the reasons already cited and because it would be perceived as a weakening of the American commitment and decoupling of Western Europe's defense from the U.S. strategic nuclear umbrella. "Greater Flexibility for NATO's Flexible Response," *Strategic Review* 11 (Spring 1983): 13.

61. Press Statement of the Bishops Conference of England and Wales, November 27, 1980. Quoted and documented in Francis X. Winters, S.J., "Nuclear Deterrence Morality," 432. The Scottish hierarchy, in contrast, issued a statement on March 16, 1982, condemning all uses of nuclear weapons as morally unacceptable because of the danger of escalation. Ibid., p. 435. See also Peter Hebblethwaite, "Bishops of Europe 'supportive but distant,'" *National Catholic Reporter,* 13 May 1983.

62. Ibid., 432–33.

63. Peter Hebblethwaite, "Nuclear Morality debated in Europe: Bishop to bishop, nation to nation, little consensus," *National Catholic Reporter* 28 January 1983; "European Bishops Concerned Over Pastoral, *National Catholic Register* 6 February 1983.

64. Msgr. R. P. Bar, "Views of Church Groups in the Netherlands on War and Peace," NATO Review 30 (February 1982): 23–27. Hebblethwaite, "Nuclear morality debated . . ."; *Catholic Trends,* National Catholic News Service, 13 (July 2, 1983): 1.

65. "French Bishops Face Up to Nuclear Peril," Excerpts from "Win the Peace," *The Wall Street Journal,* November 25, 1983. See also John Vinocur, "French Bishops Explain A-Arms Vote," *The New York Times,* 12 November 1983. For official attiudes of the French government, see Michael Dobbs, "French 5-Year Military Plan Shifts Priorities from Conventional Forces to Nuclear Arms," *The Washington Post,* 21 April 1983.

66. James M. Markham, "Atom Debate Stirs Catholics in Germany," *The New York Times*, 9 January 1983; Gert Schmidinger, "The New Pacifism," *Swiss Review of World Affairs* 32 (October 1982): Gerhard Wettig, "The New Peace Movement in Germany," *Aussenpolitik*, English edition 33 (Fall 1982).

67. The posing of a considerable risk to a potential aggressor "is essentially what the policy of deterrence is all about. It aims at making it clear to an adversary that the trouble and expense of launching an attack or an attempt at coercion are out of proportion to the benefit to be derived from such an action and are therefore not advisable. The French term for this concept is *dissuasion*. More effectively than the German word *Abschreckung*, or the English equivalent "deterrence," it places the issue at stake into the proper political context. Under the given circumstances, then, nuclear weapons too are a means of preventing war and thus maintaining peace. Without a quid pro quo and reasonable chance of making peace secure in other ways, it is impossible to dispense with them. Statement adopted by the Plenary Assembly of the Central Committee of German Catholics (ZDK), November 14, 1981, "On the Current Peace Discussion," 13–15.

68. "Justice Creates Peace," Pastoral Letter of the West German Bishops, translated from excerpts in *Frankfurter Allgemeine Zeitung*, 28 April 1983. The full text was published in English as *Out of Justice, Peace* (Dublin: Irish Messenger Publications, 1983).

69. Cardinal Hoeffner pointed out that the eighty-five page German pastoral differed from the American one. "We do not touch on the use of nuclear weapons. We deal with the promotion of peace, the reduction of force and the avoidance of war, in the hope that this stopgap arrangement never fails." John Tagliabue, "German Bishops Uphold a Case for A-Arms," *The New York Times*, 28 April 1983.

70. "Justice Creates Peace," *Franfurter Allgemeine Zeitung*, 28 April 1983.

71. James M. Markham, "Bonn Aide Reproaches U.S. Bishops for Nuclear Arms Stand," *The New York Times*, 23 November 1982.

72. "Should Church Oppose Nuclear Arms? Yes," Interview with Bishop Thomas Gumbleton, *U.S. News and World Report*, 20 December 1982, p. 47.

73. For a spectrum of views concerning the different U.S. and Soviet approaches to deterrence and arms control—the former emphasizing retaliation and the latter a preemptive strike, with corresponding contrasts en attitude toward refraining from deploying weapons posing a first strike threat—see Stanley Sienkiewics, "SALT and Soviet Nuclear Doctrine," *International Security* 2 (Spring 1978): 84–100; Fritz W. Ermarth, "Contrasts in American and Soviet Strategic Thought," *International Security* 3 (Fall 1978): 138-55; James E. Dougherty, "A National Arms Control Policy for the 1980s," *Annals of the American Academy of Political and Social Science* 457 (September 1981): 174–81; Raymond L. Garthoff, "Mutual Deterrence and Strategic Arms Limitation in Soviet Policy," *Strategic Review* 10 (Fall 1982): 36–51; and Richard Pipes, "Soviet Strategic Doctrine: Another View," *Strategic Review* 10 (Fall 1982): 52–63.

74. Transcript of President's News Conference, *The New York Times*, 5 May 1983.

75. Gerald P. Fogarty, S.J., "Why the pastoral is shocking," *Commonweal* (3 June 1983).

76. Editorial, "Bishops and the Bomb," *The New York Times*, 6 May 1983.

77. "Impact of Bishops Call for Nuclear Freeze," *U.S. News and World Report*, 16 May 1983.

78. Editorial, "Bishops and the Bomb," *The New York Times*, 6 May 1983.

79. Gerald P. Fogarty, "Why the pastoral is shocking."

80. Bill Prochnau, "Catholics' Quandry Unresolved," *The Washington Post*, 8 May 1983; Douglas C. McGill, "Builders of Nuclear Weapons Ponder Bishop's Peace Letter," *The New York Times*, 9 May 1983; "Bishops' Nuclear Arms Letter Divides Catholic Lay Panel at Forum," *The New York Times*, 12 May 1983; Cardinal Cooke's letter to Catholics in the armed forces, June 7, 1983; Susan Chira, "Catholic Church Consciousness-Raising About Nuclear Arms," *The New York Times*, December 16, 1983.

81. John Garvey, "The Ambiguous Pastoral: Church Authority and State Power," *Commonweal* (6 May 1983), pp. 264–65.

82. "Arms Stand of Bishops Praised," *The New York Times*, 14 May 1983; John C. Bennett, "The Bishops Pastoral: A Response," *Christianity and Crisis*, 30 May 1983.

BIBLIOGRAPHY

Books

Abbott, Walter M., ed. *Documents of Vatican II*. New York: American Press, 1966.

Annual Report to Congress of the Secretary of Defense for FY 1984. Washington: USGPO, February 1, 1983.

Arms Control and Disarmament Agreements: Texts and Histories of Negotiations. Washington, D.C.: U.S. Arms Control and Disarmament Agency, 1982.

Bainton, Roland H. *Christian Attitudes Toward War and Peace: A Historical Survey and Critical Re-Evaluation*. Nashville: Abingdon Press, 1960.

Ball, Desmond. *Can Nuclear War be Controlled?* Adelphi Papers no. 161. London: International Institute for Strategic Studies, 1981.

Bennett, John C., ed. *Nuclear Weapons and the Conflict of Conscience*. New York: Charles Scribner's Sons, 1962.

Bigongiari, Dino, ed. *The Political Ideas of St. Thomas Aquinas*. New York: Hafner, 1957.

Brock, Peter. *Pacifism in Europe to 1914*. Princeton, N.J.: Princeton University Press, 1972.

Brodie, Bernard. *Strategy in the Missile Age*. Princeton, N.J.: Princeton University Press, 1959.

———. *War and Politics*. New York: Macmillan, 1973.

Cadoux, Cecil John. *The Early Church and the World*. Edinburgh: T. & T. Clark, 1925.

Carnesale, Albert, Paul Doty, *et al.*, *Living with Nuclear Weapons*. New York: Bantam Books, 1983.

Challenge of Peace: God's Promise and Our Response. Pastoral Letter of the

U.S. Catholic Bishops on War and Peace. Origins, Washington, D.C.: National Catholic Documentary Service. 13 (May 19, 1983).

Clark, Ian. *Limited Nuclear War* (Princeton, N.J.: Princeton University Press. 1982).

Cordesman, Anthony H. *Deterrence in the 1980s: Part I—American Strategic Forces and Extended Deterrence.* Adelphi Papers, no. 175. London: IISS, Summer 1982.

Douglass, James W. *The Non-Violent Cross: A Theology of Revolution and Peace.* New York: Macmillan, 1968.

Ellis, John Tracy. *American Catholics and Peace: An Historical Sketch,* Pamphlet. (Washington, D.C.: Division of World Justice and Peace, United States Catholic Conference, 1970.

Finn, James, Ed. *A Conflict of Loyalties: The Case for Selective Conscientious Objection.* New York: Pegasus, 1968.

Fiorenza, Francis P. "Political Theology and Liberation Theology: An Enquiry into Their Fundamental Meaning." In *Liberation, Revolution and Freedom: Theological Perspectives,* edited by Thomas M. McFadden. New York: Seabury Press, 1975.

Frye, Daniel. *Risks of Unintentional Nuclear War* (Geneva: United Nations Institute for Disarmament Research, 1982).

George, Alexander L. and Richard Smoke. *Deterrence in American Foreign Policy: Theory and Practice.* New York: Columbia University Press, 1974.

Guèrry, Émile. *The Popes and World Government.* Translated by Gregory Roettiger, O.S.B. Baltimore, Md.: Helicon Press, 1964.

Hughan, Jessie Wallace, and Cecil Hinshaw. "Toward a Non-Violent National Defense." In *The Quiet Battle,* edited by Mulford Q. Sibley. New York: Anchor Books, 1963.

Jaspers, Karl. *The Future of Mankind.* Trans. E. B. Ashton. Chicago: University of Chicago Press, 1958.

Johnson, James Turner. *Just War Tradition and the Restraint of War: A Moral and Historical Inquiry.* Princeton, N.J.: Princeton University Press, 1981.

Kahan, Jerome H. *Security in the Nuclear Age.* Washington: Brookings Institution, 1975.

Lawler, Philip F., ed. *Justice and War in the Nuclear Age,* for the American Catholic Committee. Lanham, Md.: University Press of American, 1983.

Lockwood, Jonathan S. *The Soviet View of U.S. Strategic Doctrine* New Brunswick, N.J.: Transaction Books, 1983.

McBrien, Richard P. *Catholicism*, Study Edition. Minneapolis, Minn.: Winston Press, 1981.

Martin, Laurence, ed. *Strategic Thought in the Nuclear Age.* Baltimore, Md.: The Johns Hopkins University Press, 1979.

Merton, Thomas, ed. *Breakthrough to Peace*. New York: New Direction Books, 1962.

Midgley, E. B. F. *The Natural Law Tradition and the Theory of International Relations.* New York: Barnes and Noble, 1975.

Morgan, Patrick M. *Deterrence: A Conceptual Analysis.* Beverly Hills, Calif.: Sage, 1977.

Murray, John Courtney. "Theology & Modern War." In *Morality and Modern Warfare*, ed. by William J. Nagle. Baltimore, Md.: Helicon, 1960).

Murray, John Courtney. "War and Conscience," Commencement Address, Western Maryland College, June 1967. In *A Conflict of Loyalties: The Case for Selective Conscientious Objection*, edited by James Finn. New York: Pegasus, 1968.

Nagle, William J., ed. *Morality and Modern Warfare: The State of the Question.* Baltimore, Md.: Helicon Press, 1960.

Niebuhr, Reinhold. *Christianity and Power Politics.* New York: Charles Scribner's Sons, 1940.

————. *Moral Man and Immoral Society.* New York: Scribner's, 1947.

O'Brien, William V. *The Conduct of Just and Limited War.* New York: Praeger, 1981.

O'Connor, John J. *In Defense of Life.* Boston: St. Paul Editions, 1981.

Osterle, William H., and John Donaghy, eds. *Peace Theology and the Arms Race.* College Theology Society Sourcebook Series. vol 1 (mimeographed) 1980.

Out of Justice, Peace: The Church in the Service of Peace, Joint Pastoral Letter of the West German Bishops, April 1983. English translation pub. by *The Irish Messenger.* Dublin, 1983.

Peace and Disarmament: Documents of the World Council of Churches and the Roman Catholic Church. Geneva and Rome, 1982.

Potter, Ralph B. *War and Moral Discourse.* Richmond, Va.: John Knox Press, 1969.

Preston, Richard A. and Sydney F. Wise. *Men in Arms: A History of Warfare and Its Interrelationships with Western Society.* 4th ed. New

York: Holt, Rinehart and Winston, 1979.

Quade, Quentin L. ed. *The Pope and Revolution: John Paul II Confronts Liberation Theology.* Washington, D.C.: Ethics and Public Policy Center, 1982.

Quester, George. *Deterrence Before Hiroshima.* New York: Wiley, 1966.

Ramsey, Paul. *War and the Christian Conscience: How Shall Modern War Be Conducted Justly?* Durham, N.C.: Duke University Press, 1961.

————. *The Just War: Force and Political Responsibility.* New York: Charles Scribner's Sons, 1968.

Rommen, Heinrich A. *The State in Catholic Thought.* St. Louis: B. Herder, 1947.

Russell, Frederick. *The Just War in the Middle Ages.* Cambridge: Cambridge University Press, 1975.

Ryle, Edward R., ed. *The Social Mission of the Church.* Washington, D.C.: Catholic University of America Press, 1972.

Schilling, Warner R. "U.S. Strategic Nuclear Concepts in the 1970s: The Search for Sufficiently Equivalent Countervailing Parity." In *Strategic Deterrence in the 1980s,* edited by Roger D. Speed. Stanford, Calif.: Hoover Institution Press, 1979.

Shannon, Thomas, ed. *War or Peace: The Search for New Answers.* New York: Orbis, 1980.

Sharp, Gene. *The Politics of Non-Violent Action.* Boston: Sargent, 1973.

Sibley, Mulford Q. "Unilateral Disarmament." In *America Armed,* edited by Robert A. Goldwin. Chicago: Rand McNally, 1961.

Snow, Donald M. *Nuclear Strategy in a Dynamic World.* University, Ala.: University of Alabama Press, 1981.

Stein, Walter, ed. *Nuclear Weapons: A Catholic Response.* New York: Sheed and Ward, 1962.

Stratmann, Franziskus. *War and Christianity Today.* Translated by John Doebele. Westminster, Md.: Newman Press, 1956.

Strengthening Conventional Deterrence in Europe. Report of the European Security Study, April 1983.

Tooke, Joan D. *The Just War in Aquinas and Grotius.* London: SPCK, 1965.

Thompson, Charles S., ed. *Morals and Missiles: Catholic Essays on the Problem of War Today.* London: James Clarke, 1959.

Tucker, Robert W. *The Just War: A Study in Contemporary American Doctrine.* Baltimore: The Johns Hopkins University Press, 1960.

————. *Just War and Vatican II: A Critique.* New York: Council on Religion and International Affairs, 1967.

World Military Expenditures and Arms Transfers 1969-1978. Washington: United States Arms Control and Disarmament Agency, 1980.

Zahn, Gordon C. *War, Conscience and Dissent.* New York: Hawthorn Books, 1967.

Articles

Berryman, Philip E. "Latin American Liberation Theology." *Theological Studies* 34 (December 1973).

Blechman, Barry. "Is There a Conventional Defense Option?" *The Washington Quarterly* (Summer 1982).

Bundy, McGeorge, George F. Kennan, Robert S. McNamara, and Gerard Smith. "Nuclear Weapons and the Atlantic Alliance." *Foreign Affairs* 60 (Spring 1982).

Burt, Richard. "Reassessing the Strategic Balance." *International Security* 5 (Summer 1980).

Childress, James R. "Just War Theories." *Theological Studies* 39 (September 1978)

Corbishley, Thomas, S.J. "Can War be Just in a Nuclear Age?" *New Blackfriars* (September 1965).

Dewart, Leslie. "War and the Christian Tradition." *The Commonweal.* 2 November 1962.

Dougherty, James E. "The Catholic Church, War and Nuclear Weapons." *Orbis* 9 (Winter 1966).

———. "Just War, Nuclear Weapons and Noncombatant Immunity." Review Essay in *Orbis* 25 (Fall 1982).

Draper, G. I. A. D. "The Origins of the Just War Tradition." *New Blackfriars* (November 1964).

Eppstein, John. "The Ethics of War I: The Principles." *Christian Order* 24 (January 1983).

Erickson, John. "The Soviet View of Deterrence," *Survival* 24 (November/December 1982).

Ermarth, Fritz W. "Contrast in American and Soviet Strategic Thought." *International Security* 3 (Fall 1978).

Finn, James. "Nuclear Terror: Moral Paradox." *America* (19 February 1983).

Ford, John C., S.J. "The Morality of Obliteration Bombing." *Theologi-*

cal Studies 6 (September 1944).

Frye, Alton. "Strategic Build-Down: A Context for Restraint," *Foreign Affairs* 62 (Winter 1983/1984).

Garthoff, Raymond L. "Mutual Deterrence and Strategic Arms Limitations in Soviet Policy." *Strategic Review* 10 (Fall 1982).

Grisez, Germain, "The Moral Implications of a Nuclear Deterrent." *Center Journal.* 2 (Winter 1982).

Gutierrez, Gustavo. "Liberation and Development." 21 *Cross Currents* (1971).

Hebblethwaite, Peter. "The Popes and Politics: Shifting Patterns in 'Catholic Social Doctrine'." *Daedalus* 3 (Winter 1982).

Haseler, Stephen. "The Euromissile Crisis." *Commentary* (May 1983).

Hollenbach, David S.J. "Nuclear Weapons and Nuclear War: The Shape of the Catholic Debate." *Theological Studies* 43 (December 1982).

Howard, Michael. "On Fighting a Nuclear War," *International Security* 5 (Spring 1981).

Keeny, Spurgeon M. and Wolfgang K. H. Panofsky. "Mad Versus Nuts." *Foreign Affairs* 60 (Winter 1981/82).

Langan, John, S.J. "The American Hierarchy and Nuclear Weapons." *Theological Studies* 43 (September 1982).

Murphy, Matthew F. "Nuclear Weapons and the Criterion of Proportionality." *Center Journal* 2 (Winter 1982).

Novak, Michael. "Arms and the Church." *Commentary* (March 1982).

_____. "Moral Clarity in the Nuclear Age: A Letter from Catholic Clergy and Laity." *Catholicism in Crisis* 1 (March 1983).

O'Brien, William V. "The Peace Debate and American Catholics." *The Washington Quarterly* (Spring 1982).

Payne, Keith B. "Deterrence, Arms Control and U.S. Strategic Doctrine." *Orbis* 25 (Fall 1981).

Quade, Quentin L. "A Question of Competence." *Thought* 57 (September 1982).

Riga, Peter J. "Selective Conscientious Objection." *The Catholic World* (July 1970).

Rizzo, Robert F. "Nuclear War: the Moral Dilemma," *Cross Currents* 32 (Spring 1982).

"Rome Consultation on Peace and Disarmament: A Vatican Synthesis." *Origins* 12 (7 April 1983).

Ruyter, Knut Willem. "Pacifism and Military Service in the Early Church." *Cross Currents* 32 (Spring 1982).

Ryan, Edward A., S.J. "The Rejection of Military Service by the Early Christians." *Theological Studies* 13 (March 1952).

Schmidinger, Gert. "The New Pacifism." *Swiss Review of World Affairs* 32 (October 1982).

Sienkiewicz, Stanley. "SALT and Soviet Nuclear Doctrine." *International Security* 2 (Spring 1978).

Slocombe, Walter. "The Countervailing Strategy." *International Security* (Spring 1981).

Snyder, Jack L. "Rationality at the Brink: The Role of Cognitive Processes in Failures of Deterrence." *World Politics* 30 (April 1978).

Steinbruner, John D. "Beyond Rational Deterrence: The Struggle for New Conceptions." *World Politics* 28 (January 1976).

Utgoff, Victor. "In Defense of Counterforce." *International Security* 6 (Spring 1982).

van Voorst, L. Bruce. "The Churches and Nuclear Deterrence." *Foreign Affairs* 61 (Spring 1983).

Winters, Francis X., S.J. "Nuclear Deterrence Morality: Atlantic Community Bishops in Tension." *Theological Studies* 43 (September 1982).

———. "The Bow or the Cloud? American Bishops Challenge the Arms Race." *America* (25 July 1981).

Wohlstetter, Albert. "Bishops, Statesmen, and Other Strategists on the Bombing of Innocents." *Commentary* (June 1983).

INDEX